Daughters
of the
Sun

Theresa Vivanco

DEDICATION

To Momma Bebe, without whose influence, I would have never even considered writing this book.

Cover Photography
by
Morfi Jiménez Mercado

Book Cover Design
by
Michael Overhauser

TABLE

OF

CONTENTS

ACKNOWLEDGMENTS

My wonderful sons insisted I continue to research and write this book when I wanted to give up and cheered me on through the years-long and often harrowing process. When I grow up, I want to be just like them.

In addition, I would have not been able to finish this project without the creative atmosphere and fidelity provided by the love of my life, Michael Overhauser.

Thank You and a Request from the Author

Dear Historical Novel Reader,

With so many entertaining book options, I would like to take this opportunity to thank you for purchasing Daughters of the Sun and, assuming that you enjoy your read, I would also ask you to take a few moments to write a (hopefully positive) Amazon review.

I thank you in advance for your time and energy.

Creatively yours,

Theresa Vivanco

CHAPTER ONE

1522 A.D.
Keulap Fortress
Chachapoyas, Northern Peru

Knots of vipers slither over cobblestone paths leading to the town square, thick with clouds and surrounded by circular stone homes with cone-shaped thatched roofs. Bleating and spitting in frenzied protest, a herd of wild-eyed llamas clop out of harm's way.

"I beseech Urcaguey symbol of chaos and force of darkness," Sorcerer Macavilca prays, "our Supreme Serpent God, to bestow a safe and successful journey upon us so that we may all prosper."

Chanting in the click and hiss-filled Language of the Serpent, Cloud Warrior men eye the serpent horde unflinchingly as a full moon casts an eerie glow over the town located 10,000 feet above sea level in the eyebrow of the Great Jungle and secured by a broad western sixty foot wall.

Tall and muscular with unruly blond hair curling out from his knit cap, Catequil regards his son, Pillihuaman who scoops up two deadly vipers, one in each hand, and raises them overhead; a stiff breeze whips the teenager's fiery red hair across his freckled face. After praying softly then blowing over the writhing creatures, making them limp as rope, the sorcerer claps, signaling the end of the group chant. Pillihuaman releases the reptiles, who with thousands of others wriggle down the steep eastern slopes toward the confluence of the Marañón and Utcubamba River. Cloud Warriors follow a safe distance behind them, leading llamas laden with sacks of corn, potatoes, root vegetables and knitted and woven goods. Many tribes covet this trade route, gladly exchanging pottery, jewelry, boats or animals for prized Cloud

Warrior textiles.

A beady-eyed Inca bureaucrat watches from the safety of the high fortress overlooking Keulap. Through a series of uneasy truces, the Incas appointed Qullqi to keep the savage Cloud Warriors in line after a crushing defeat by the empire over a decade ago. Though Mayor Qullqi is little more than a pesky tax collector, Catequil feels something amiss. Normally playful and relaxed, in the last few weeks, the swarthy mayor has become withdrawn, avoiding eye contact with Catequil whom he interacted with often. For several months, alarming though unverifiable reports reached the ears of many Keulap inhabitants. Knowing how mountain dwellers tend to exaggerate, Catequil attempted to banish these nightmarish rumors from his mind, though his stomach feels possessed by the spirit of an evil wind.

"We must go now," Sorcerer Macavilca says, tugging on the reins of two large pack llamas, "if we want to be back before nightfall." He scrutinizes Catequil's face, abnormally pale and lined with worry. "What is troubling you, my son?"

Catequil points at Mayor Qullqi observing them from the tower.

"Look at that worm," he says with a frown, "he's never up this early."

"Oh, don't worry about Qullqi, my son," Macavilca says giving his son a reassuring pat on the back, "We'll be back soon enough."

Since provisions are running low and this merchant trip can no longer be delayed, Catequil leads his llamas down the jungle path but stops and turns; he catches a final look at the shifty-eyed mayor, who quickly averts his eyes then steps away from the tower window.

Qullqi waves a bright yellow Sun God banner from the top window of the Keulap fortress tower. Within seconds, hundreds of tattooed warriors creep in from the eastern jungle, bypassing Keulap's protective western wall; their quivers are full, axes and daggers sharpened, battering rams ready.

Holding up a sword, Inca Captain Paucar Usna surveys his troops then, with all eyes on him, brings his weapon down, signaling the start of the raid. Consumed with loathing for the snake worshiping savages, warriors fill the air with blood curdling battle cries, ramming open thick wooden doors, dragging occupants screaming and crying from their warm beds.

"We'll give you Cloud Warrior savages less than one minute," Captain Paucar Usna barks, "to stand at attention outside of your homes."

After smoothing his army issue scarlet and white checked tunic, he adjusts his bronze helmet embedded with blue and yellow feathers forming an ear-to-ear fan.

Throngs of defenseless old men, women and children scramble to obey, as Inca soldiers loom over them, weapons drawn; residents who attempt to pull on woolen capes against the cold mountain air are thwarted by the sharp end of Inca swords.

Carrying a bronze bowl of burning incense, thin lips twitching under a crescent-shaped nose ring pressed into his nasal columella, making him look more like a demon from *ukhu pacha*—the underworld than a man, Inca high priest, Villac Umu eyes each family. He knows just what he's looking for.

After handing his sniveling assistant the incense bowl, Villac stops to inspect a sobbing red-haired toddler, holds her face in his long thin hand then pulls off her tunic; she hisses then kicks the priest's shins as her mother looks on helplessly. After adjusting his gaudy disc-shaped earrings hanging from over-stretched earlobes, Villac dusts off his tunic, spins the girl about and locates a large misshapen mole on her upper back.

"Go back to your mother," he snarls.

The child jumps into her mother's waiting arms; they quickly scurry back to their family hut.

Villac Umu ambles toward a young mother holding her sleeping newborn, swathed in several layers of simple woven cloth. Face twisted into a scowl, he knows that she knows what she should do now. The frightened woman unwraps the infant, who awakes with a high-pitched cry. After scrutinizing the child's body, the priest finds an abdominal birth mark and waves her away.

"Leave me!" he yells.

Head bowed, the mother presses her infant to her bosom and races home.

Glowering at the priest, a tall red-haired beauty, Sangama stands between her shivering daughters; Solsol is eight years old, her sister, Pispis, seven. The girls inherited piercing emerald eyes from their mother and wavy blond hair from their father, Catequil.

Cocking his head and flashing a toothy grin, Villac catches sight of the sisters. He knows regardless of any physical imperfections that would make them ineligible for *capacocha*— human child sacrifice, these beauties would be perfect for the emperor.

"Seize these two," the priest orders.

"Only cowards," Sangama hisses, her chest heaving, "invade a village devoid of able-bodied men. The Inca Empire will soon pay for their transgressions against my people." She lunges at the priest but a warrior smashes the flat of his palm wood sword against her left temple and she sinks to the ground.

After tossing the sisters over their shoulders like sacks of maize, warriors laugh at their futile attempts to escape; Cloud Warriors teach their children to wriggle, kick, bite, scratch, punch, flail and fight to the death rather than be taken prisoner, especially by the Incas.

"Mamáy!" the sisters screech.

The warriors lug the sisters to a litter built with a wooden cage on top. Broad sloping shoulders and thick calf muscles bulging, a Lucanas man opens the cage door and guides the young captives inside then motions them to sit.

The kind man speaks haltingly to the terrified girls having learned their language when he himself was captured and imprisoned by a Cloud Warrior tribe long ago.

"You must calm yourself, my doves," he says, "and remember your power. Yes?"

Emerald eyes aglow, Pispis and Solsol regard their battered mother then chant in the language of the serpent gods. Soon reptiles approach Keulap by the hundreds, as their sorcerer grandfather, Macavilca summoned them just a few hours ago. After dozens of the cold-blooded creatures form a protective circle around Sangama, she regains consciousness, sits up, touches her bruised temple and joins her daughters' incantations as do the rest of the infuriated Keulap residents; their voices rise into a spine-tingling howl.

Qullqi rushes out of the confines of the Keulap tower toward the priest, his voice and hands trembling.

"No. Don't take these girls. Their grandfather is a sorcerer, their father a celebrated Cloud Warrior." the mayor says, thick black eyebrows twitching over dark blood shot eyes. "I assure you, they will be nothing but trouble." He points east. "Look."

Broad heads and pointed snouts swaying side to side, vipers fill the cobblestone streets as villagers chant unabated. Inca warriors attempt to fend off the reptilian invasion, thumping them with swords and battleaxes. One soldier triumphantly cuts a serpent in two but success is short-lived. To his dismay the creature transforms into two snakes, which coil around his feet, calves, thighs, waist and upper torso. When the creatures reach his shoulder, they sink their fangs into the tender flesh of his neck. The man collapses, choking and convulsing; blood seeps from his nose and mouth. Fellow warriors gaze wide-eyed at the gory scene, at the high priest then at their captain as hordes of snakes wind toward them.

Beads of sweat forming on his furrowed brow and underneath his fine white and gold tunic, Villac Umu forces a grin in a feeble attempt to disguise his fear of the Cloud Warriors' infamous powers of serpent sorcery. Escaping through the eastern jungle is not an option now as the forest floor is thick with vipers heeding the chants of the Cloud Warrior snake worshipers.

The priest gazes at the captured sisters, snaps his finger then scurries toward a narrow western exit at the foot of an endless sixty-foot-wall leading to a series of descending steps; the priest and his immediate entourage wriggle through the egress as chants, hisses and the moans of poisoned warriors fill the mountain air.

* * *

Catequil shoves Mayor Qullqi through the curving corridors of the gargantuan two story Keulap fortress, the quick slap of their sandals echo off its stone walls.

"I'm just a simple farmer, like yourself, Catequil," the mayor protests, though his extravagant golden earrings, wrist cuffs and necklaces would suggest otherwise; he shuffles toward an open door. "I . . . have a family, just like you," he pleads, though if true, Catequil's never seen any evidence of such; it would be hard to believe any decent woman would want anything to do with a vulgar worm like Qullqi.

"We had a treaty," Catequil spits, "which has been violated time and time again. But now you and your people have gone too far."

"I had nothing to do with this," Qullqi lies.

Inside the circular room, Sorcerer Macavilca and thirteen-year old grandson, Pillihuaman sit upon plump woven mats placed on the stone floor, a fire crackling in a small fireplace opposite them. The sorcerer's luminescent green eyes could slice a man in half. Pillihuaman flashes his dark blue eyes, which sparkle like polished opal in the firelight.

Mayor Qullqi is one of thousands of bureaucrats who live to collect taxes for the vast Inca Empire in whatever form they can get their greedy hands on: corn, coca, livestock and, especially, woven and knitted goods. To the Incas, nothing is more valuable than fine textiles to adorn and warm the bodies of royalty, alive or mummified and nothing more gratifying than exploiting the talents of their vanquished arch enemy, the Cloud Warriors—the most talented knitters and weavers in the empire. Their depictions of colorful coiling serpents, condors, pumas and tropical birds are rumored to be the product of powerful serpent gods.

"Let me explain," the Inca mayor mumbles, "Cloud Warrior maidens are the most beautiful in the empire. Daughters of the Sun bring great honor to their families and ancestors. Your girls might even become the emperor's concubines, the envy of many women in the empire."

Catequil smacks the mayor on the back of his head; he falls and whacks his nose on the cold stone floor; blood drips from his wide flaring nostrils and onto his tunic trimmed with wide bands of crimson and black

"My daughters are little girls," Catequil roars, green eyes ablaze.

"Well, the truth is," the mayor says, wiping his bloody nose with his sleeve, "the emperor likes the young ones . . . there are worse fates."

Catequil bends over then squeezes Qullqi's stout neck with vise-like hands, lifting him off the floor. Attempting to pry Catequil's fingers away, the Inca lackey pants and gasps, legs flailing, pinched face crimson.

Macavilca hops up and opens a window shuttered with cotton and wool insulated wooden planks to keep out the cold. Pillihuaman clasps Qullqi's left shoulder then helps his father lower the mayor through the window. Enormous earrings jingling, Qullqi faces the rocky slope below, grunting and squealing like the tapir he resembles.

"Where did the Incas take my daughters?" Catequil growls.

"How should I know?" the mayor says with a strangled sob, "I'm just a lowly bureaucrat." Catequil and his son lower him farther, dangling him by his heels over the vast canyon. As the mayor struggles, a gold cuff loosens and falls into the canyon. The men shake him and Qullqi loses an earring, also but he's too terrified to notice. "All right, all right. They probably took them to Cuzco because that's where the emperor is staying right now."

"How do you know this?" Catequil asks.

"It's what the *chasquis*, the Inca messengers told me," Qullqi admits. "I swear it on the life of our blessed Shepherd of the Sun, our Lord and Emperor Huayna Capac."

"How many other Cloud Warrior children have been kidnapped?" Macavilca demands, "Answer truthfully, and we'll pull you back inside."

"Though the emperor already has over 3,000 concubines," Qullqi confesses, "his thirst for Cloud Warrior females appears to be unquenchable, so he's told his generals to disregard all treaties . . . I don't know any more than that."

"I see," Macavilca says. He gazes at his son and grandson. "Bring him back in."

After Catequil and Pillihuaman pull the sweat-covered man inside, he smooths his tunic, inspects his wrist and notices that a gold cuff is missing. Eyes squinted in irritation, he checks his ears and discovers an earring is lost, too.

"The emperor will be very angry when he discovers," Qullqi says, pointing a finger at Catequil, "I've lost jewelry because of you."

"Well, then," Catequil says with a sardonic smile, "you'll need to go fetch them, won't you?"

He pitches the mayor through the window; his high-pitched squeals echo throughout the region until he bounces and cartwheels over the unforgiving canyon walls below.

CHAPTER TWO

1522 A.D.
Palace Throne Room
Cuzco

Though the Twelve Year War is finally over, Emperor Huayna Capac still limps, suffering from the effects of an early battle with the rebellious Carangui tribe of northern Peru. In the midst of a wild melee, the royal litter had been tossed about until it came crashing down, spilling the emperor to the ground. Some of his more resolute Inca warriors came to the rescue, barely able to drag the ruler out from under enemy lances; his right leg was nearly severed in the attack, the limb saved by the prodigious skill of several Inca surgeons who prayed, sweated and staunched the life-threatening hemorrhage with judicious applications of tourniquets, cauterizations and medicinal herbs. The life-saving battlefield surgery lasted well over ten hours.

Despite chronic pain, the Inca warlord variously known as Inca Sapa, Shepherd of the Sun and Supreme Holy Emperor of the Inca Empire, often spends much of his day throwing spears, practicing archery and wielding battle-axes, for this is a man who enjoys confronting the enemy and grows bored and restless when not at war. But now, he sits contentedly on a low wooden stool, carved on either side with two roaring black jaguars, embedded with slanted eyes of blood-red rubies, highlighted with gold leaf. His fine *vicuña* wool tunic is scarlet and bright blue and woven with Inti the Sun God motifs of spun gold and silver; it will only be worn once then burned in the Qorincancha—the Temple of the Sun, keeping over a dozen Daughters of the Sun engaged full time with the emperor's lavish wardrobe demands.

High priest and second in command, the slit-eyed Villac Umu

stands alongside a host of armed guards, dressed in simple red and white checked army tunics. Esteemed military commanders, most of whom are related to the emperor in some fashion, stand at attention wearing military uniforms adorned with rare feathers and shells.

The court goes silent when twelve year old Princess Cura sweeps into the elegant throne room, a silky indigo and crimson gown gracing her svelte frame, midnight black hair cascading over her shoulders and down her back. She flutters her velvety eye lashes, bows, stopping within arm's length of her emperor father; this is the first time she can ever recall meeting him so she's unsure of how to proceed.

Shortly after Princess Cura Occlo's birth in Cuzco, Huayna Capac returned to Quito to engage in battle with the stubborn Chachapoyas tribe of northern Peru, the Cloud Warriors. Tales of the People of the Cloud had always fascinated the princess; she'd been practically fixated on the subject. She hoped to meet one some day. Her mother told her that many of these savages had bright emerald eyes that glow in the dark, giving them a distinct advantage in battle and long flowing locks, as golden as the rays of the sun. But they had one big flaw; they stubbornly resisted the rule of the Inca Empire and were willing to fight to the death for their freedom.

"Welcome, my beautiful dove," The Inca Sapa says beckoning his daughter closer. She steps forward, her attention fixed on her royal father's dark brown eyes. Huayna pats her rosy cheeks, holds her chin, their faces only inches apart, "It has been too long, daughter."

"Yes, Tatáy" the princess says, flashing her sparkling light brown almond-shaped eyes, "much too long."

A white-haired half blind *mamacona*—an Inca high priestess, one of several who work in the Temple of the Sun, tugs on the white tunic sleeves of two young girls.

"My Shepherd," the old woman rasps, "the Cloud Warrior sisters, as requested." She squints in the direction of the emperor and realizes she might be intruding, "Forgive me. We can come back later."

The emperor licks his lips and rubs his hands together salaciously.

"Nonsense," he says, "Bring them closer. They are quite lovely."

"Yes, my Shepherd," the *mamacona* answers with a deep bow, pushing the girls forward, emerald eyes glaring with contempt.

Despite being kidnapped and trapped inside the confines of the gold plated walls of the Qorincancha, the sisters still have rebellion and fierce determination written all over their faces.

"Is it true," the emperor asks, "that Cloud Warriors teach their offspring to disobey and rebel against authority?"

Solsol spits out a string of words in her native tongue.

"What did she say?" asks the Emperor.

"Forgive me, my Shepherd," says the *mamacona*, face flushed with embarrassment, "She put a curse on you."

"I see," the emperor says with a tilt of his head.

"The truth is that we *mamaconas* have tried our best to instruct these savages with the tenets of the Inca religion," the old priestess says with a sigh, "but, more often than not, they reject our Lord

Inti, the Sun God, claiming their serpent gods are more powerful. These snake worshipers continually run away and when caught, hiss, curse, bite, kick, scratch, scream then worst of all, summon their evil reptilian gods."

High priest, Villac Umu dressed in a simple white tunic without his usual adornments, so as not to compete with the emperor, turns his brown and yellow slanted eyes upon the girls. He remembers kidnapping them not so long ago and the chaos their serpent gods foisted upon his troops; he cringes at the thought as his heart beats wildly out of his chest. He faces the *mamacona*.

"Tell these Cloud Warrior barbarians," Villac says with a deferential bow, "that their serpent gods have no power here in Cuzco."

"Don't tell that to the people," the old woman croaks, "who have been killed by the unholy reptiles they summoned." An eerie green glow emanates from the sisters' eyes; they chant with the rattle and hiss of a snake, which reverberate off the high stone walls of the throne room. The *mamacona* shoots Villac a dirty look, "Now look what you've done. Challenging the powers of their gods, is akin to trying to stem the waves of the ocean." She takes a deep breath, eyelids hooded over her dark eyes.

The girls fixate on a gaudy golden skull chalice propped near Huayna Capac's low throne.

"What are they saying now?" the emperor asks.

The high priestess sweeps back her wispy white locks.

"Forgive me, my shepherd," the *mamacona* says, "They're saying your late father, the Emperor Topa Inca Yupanqui murdered Xanturupaya, High General of the Cloud Warriors," she continues, shaking a thin crooked forefinger at the gruesome gold encrusted skull "after a treaty had already been signed guaranteeing his safety."

"Is that true, Tatay?" Cura Occlo asks. Over the years, she had heard upsetting rumors about the empire's treachery in dealing with the Cloud Warriors and other subjugated tribes. She wanted to believe they weren't true but now . . .

Pispis twists and writhes; her older sister directs her deep emerald eyes at Cura Occlo.

"The Cloud Warriors will have their vengeance," she states din the royal language of *Incasimi,* proving the sisters are able to learn those things which serve their purposes. "the days of the Inca Empire are numbered."

"Take them away," the emperor orders, a chill running up and down his spine.

"Yes, my shepherd," the *mamacona* says.

"Tatáy I would like permission," the princess asks demurely, "to accompany these girls to the Qorincancha."

Forehead furrowed, the Inca witnesses the frail *mamacona* desperately trying to pull the Cloud Warrior sisters out of the throne room back to the Temple of the Sun. *Perhaps my daughter can find a way to calm these savages,* he muses.

"Permission granted," the Inca says, "but you must return in time for tonight's feast celebrating the end of the Carangui War. We have much catching up to do."

"Thank you, Tatay." the princess says with a dimpled smile. She squeezes in between the siblings, gently edging the elderly *mamacona* aside, removes a gold ring from her left hand and slides it onto Solsol's ring finger; it fits perfectly and the sisters admire the gift, mouths agape, thick lashes fluttering, eyes gleaming in astonishment. "Do you like it?" Cura asks in *Runasimi,* the language most citizens of the empire have at least a working knowledge of.

The girls' lips curl into a grin. The princess detaches a fine silver and gold bracelet from her wrist and affixes it onto Pispis's slender arm. "Friends?" the princess asks. The bewildered sisters steer their attention from their new acquisitions to each other, tacitly acknowledging that Cloud Warriors, as an egalitarian society, wear very little if any jewelry except for the occasional crude wooden ear plugs; to do otherwise is considered an attempt to elevate yourself above members of your tribe.

"I think we can become very good friends, don't you?" Cura asks. The siblings remain mute; Incas are their tribe's arch enemy, never to be trusted much less communicated with. But when the princess grabs their hands, the sisters accept her friendly gesture girls then stroll out of the throne room with their new friend sneaking glances at their newly acquired adornments along the way. Jaw dropped in astonishment, the old *mamacona's* never seen the Cloud Warrior savages so cooperative.

When earthquakes recently rocked the royal palaces in both Quito and Cuzco, comets lit up the sky and two fiery red rings encircled the full moon, Villac Umu asserted that these were signs of Timpu Pisti, a huge reversal of fortune, an apocalypse where the Inca Empire would soon be annihilated. At the time, the Emperor scoffed at what he considered to be the priest's paranoid delusion; surely the Sun God was pleased with the thousands of sacrifices, human and otherwise and would not eradicate his vast hard-won empire.

But now, the aging warlord, who had been fervently engaged in vicious battles against rebellious provinces most of his life regards his daughter's diplomacy with a sworn enemy uneasily. He picks up the gaudy goblet of the vanquished enemy and inspects it closely; the cursed thing appears to be smiling, something he never noticed before. It is widely believed that Cloud Warriors are more powerful dead than alive. Overwhelmed by the urge to purge the palace of all Cloud Warrior relics, he shudders then smashes the cup onto the polished stone floor; it shatters into shards of bone and gold but the smiling jawbone remains intact, as if taunting him.

CHAPTER THREE

1522 A.D.
Village of Sonqo
50 miles northeast from Cuzco

The sun is sharp and dancing in the late afternoon sky; I help my father plow a new irrigation canal in our *puna*, a high mountain grass field. *Pachamama,* our sacred Mother Earth is fat and warm; she nurses the potatoes lying on her breast and the potatoes nourish us. The rains have stopped, making it easier to break through the soil and dig proper irrigation ditches. Melted snow from surrounding mountains must be diverted to our prized *abaguña*, purple potatoes, thirsty vegetation which can easily drown if over-watered or quickly shrivel up in drought years.

As I push my wooden spade into the black soil, an *enqa*, a small stone figure pops up from the ground between my feet. When I bend over to pick it up, an energetic *salqa* wind surrounds me, pure and wild. It blows past me, through me and around me in a whirlwind. Now I'm somewhere else but curiously, also in the exact same place; it's cold and dark, the sky lit only by a full blue moon. The bird stone grows shiny black feathers, soars until it's a tiny black dot in the perfect sky, returns like lightning to my hand then turns back into stone. I'm reminded of my dear departed pet parrot, Yana and I wonder—*could it be that she's returned to me in another form now? Just like my mother said she would?* The thought makes me hopeful; I press the *enqa* close to my heart then hold it up to my lips.

"Yana?" I whisper, "Is that you? Can you give me a sign?"

I twirl around to tell Tatáy but he's disappeared. Instead, the *Machukuna,* the Old Ones, the giant Children of the Moon loom over me, broad smiles showing off perfect square, shiny teeth as they press their feet against their own gargantuan foot plows, their world—and now mine, too at least temporarily—lit by a full moon, the only light that does not burn their delicate translucent skin.

"T'ica," declares one of the giants, moonlight reflecting off his cold blue eyes, his deep voice warm but firm, "it is essential to journey to Mistress Mountain, *Apu Salkantay* soon."

When the giants speak, it's like a dream and I am paralyzed, unable to respond verbally, though they seem to glean my thoughts.

You already know what Tatáy will say, I think, as my heart twists in agony, my mental lament piercing the ether like a fine spear into the giants' minds, *I have already asked many times. It's not possible.*

"You must find a way to convince him this time," says another kind giant. He digs an irrigation canal in his fourth dimension *puna*, creating a trench as deep as the ocean, "You must do this soon, for yourself and your family's sake. We will be there to ease your burden."

I need a specific reason to convince my father. I beg. *Please, give me a reason.*

But the *Machukuna* shake their heads then fade away, just like they always do.

Another *salqa* wind blows and now I stand, my head spinning, my face glowing like a flower, next to Tatáy as he curses his foot plow.

"*Aargh!*" he shouts, when a large stone refuses to budge. Evidently, the *Machukuna* have pushed a large rock into my father's path, a thing they often do when they crave a mountain farmer's attention.

"Tatáy" I shout excitedly, holding out the small perfect stone condor in my palm, "Look!"

"A gift from *Pachamama,* Mother Earth," my father says, dropping his plow, examining the now lifeless *enqa,* "It's for good luck."

"No, Tatáy" I say, breathing heavily, "It's from the *Machukuna.*"

He stares a hole through me with his coal black eyes.

"Stay away from the *Machukuna*," my father says, picking up his foot plow again. "They are jealous of us."

"But they say it's urgent for me to go to *Apu Salkantay.*" I insist.

His dark wind-blistered face grows darker still.

"No, daughter," Tatáy declares, head down, furiously stomping on his foot plow, the formerly black earth now filled with large, unyielding stones and boulders. "We will not argue about this again."

"But Tatáy . . . "

"Why must I repeat myself?" Tatáy says, beating the ground with his foot plow like a mad man; stones seem to crop up from nowhere, refusing to move or break down. "There are pumas, thieves, rapists, murderers and demons like the *Amaru,* the giant serpent from the underworld and son of Mistress Mountain. Only men must do the traveling, particularly to sacred places like *Apu*

Salkantay. The goddess of this glacier mountain makes the rain fall, the sun rise and earth quake. But when Mistress Mountain is unhappy, she becomes the Mountain that Eats People, for many have made this pilgrimage and never returned."

I bite my lower lip and squeeze my eyes shut.

"I know, Tatáy, I know," I say, "I've heard all the stories more than once but . . ."

"Yes, you *say*, you know," says my father, panting from exertion as he shoves his foot onto his plow only to encounter even larger stones, making little progress on our much needed irrigation canal. "But you do not *comprehend.* There are certain things that you should never experience, Lord Inti willing. Do I have to tell you again what happened to my own brother, your uncle and his wife, your sweet mother's own flesh and blood?"

"No, Tatáy," I say, shaking my head, as I strike my foot against the plow. The rocky earth doesn't budge an inch, despite my efforts. "You don't have to tell me again; you've already told me so many . . ."

"Shortly after you were born, your Uncle Tupakusi ventured to Mistress Mountain with his wife, your Aunt Asiri. A beautiful woman who everybody wanted, but your handsome uncle, my dear brother won her heart." my father continues despite my loud sighs, and eye-rolling. The formerly loose, fertile soil now seems to be composed of solid rock; he stops wrestling with the foot plow and gives me the heartbroken, sad-eyed look he always does when he tells me this oft-repeated tale of familial woe. "Your uncle was a joyful soul, my best friend." He holds up a forefinger, shakes his head, a warm smile of recollection lights up his handsome face. "I warned him that bringing a woman would court the jealously of Mistress Mountain but he refused to listen. As soon as they arrived at the foot of the mountain, a giant boulder rolled down, crushing them both instantly."

I cringe every time Tatáy recounts my uncle and aunt's horrible fate.

"Oh, Tatáy," I whisper. "I know but . . ."

"Your Uncle Tupakusi was a musician, like myself. He could play anything. Oh, and what a wonderful voice he had!" Tatáy says interrupting me like he usually does. He chokes back tears, presses his lips together, strikes the foot plow in another useless attempt to dig through rock. "Yes, but they were lucky! Runaway boulders and landslides injure or kill many. Some, driven by madness caused by a bad case of high altitude sickness fall or jump off the mountainside; many do not die instantly, wandering the mountains, half-dead, half-alive, like the *kukuchi*. Is that what you want?"

"Though I respect the mountain spirits, I do not fear them because I am their daughter." I declare. After setting down my foot plow, I pull off the flat plaited rope sling from around my forehead, pick up a stone, load it into my simple weapon and whir it overhead. "As for thieves, rapists, murderers and hungry pumas . . ." I release the projectile; it hits a white stone used for target practice far off in the distance.

Tatáy nods and smiles.

"You've been practicing, my daughter," he says, leaning on his plow. "You are *munay warmikuna*—a women of substance. All women should know how to defend themselves. Have you also been practicing your Rumi Maki?"

I bend over, pick up my wooden foot plow, thrust it into the air, catch it behind my back and spin it rapidly. In Rumi Maki—Stone

Hand—we learn, among other things, that anything can be used as a weapon. I assume a fighter's stance, beckoning my father closer with my left hand.

"I'm ready to be promoted to Stone Hand level five, Tatáy" I say. "Come on. I'll show you."

But he waves me off.

"I'm in no mood to fight today," he says, "Maybe some other time." He eyes my long lean body, white skin, hair as pale as spring corn and sky blue eyes sadly.

Now that I'm old enough to ask questions about the stark difference in my appearance from the rest of my family, Tatáy avoids eye contact with a shrug and Mamáy claims that my complexion greatly resembles that of a great great aunt whose name she can't remember.

Prone to nightmares, a couple of times a month, Tatáy sobs and calls out unfamiliar names in a voice strangled with grief.

"Shhh," Mamáy whispers tenderly, "I'm here, dove of my heart. I'm here." She lies on her side and rubs his neck and back until he is calm again.

The next morning, when I ask, "What happened last night? And whose names was Tatáy calling?" I receive nothing more than sidelong glances; Tatay's face grows solemn; Mamáy is quick to distract me with a delicious breakfast.

"T'ica, you are like a *ch'aska* unable to find her place in the sky," he says warmly, a hint of a smile playing on his full lips. When Tatáy calls me a bright star—a *ch'aska* as he often does, I know he loves me more than any other father in this worldly realm of *kay pacha* has ever loved his daughter.

"The *Machukuna* will protect me on my journey." I say evenly. "They tell me I must do this for the sake of my family, my village, and all my loved ones."

After a few moments, Tatáy sighs, his broad bronze face made even broader by his toothy smile.

"The *Machukuna* do not love you like I do, daughter." he says warmly. "But I will talk to your mother tonight. Then we will ask the leaf diviner to consult the gods for their wisdom. But I will remind him that you are only eleven years and my one and only daughter. I can not lose you. I will not sacrifice you to the whims of the Children of the Moon. The gods are sensible. I'm sure they'll see things my way. After consulting the shaman, there will be no more arguments; the gods' words will be final. Agreed?"

I nod tentatively, knowing not to show too much enthusiasm for it is important for *runakuna*—simple villagers to maintain a certain amount of dignity in these matters. I tuck my *enqa*—my precious bird stone in a small pouch hung around my neck then set it directly against my fluttering heart. I don't know why but I have a good feeling about what the gods will say.

I dig into the rocky black soil with renewed vigor. Tatáy shoves the foot plow deep into the ground with the strength of a dozen Machukuna. The stones and rocks crumble then give way to rich loamy soil; he quickly plows a long irrigation canal.

"Look!" he yells, sweat-covered face beaming, proudly pointing at the now-finished canal running along the north side of our potato plants. He races to the top of the terrace, then runs to the far south side, plowing another canal like a man possessed, "Surely *Pachamama* blesses our family with her bounty this season!"

Triumphantly holding their enormous foot plows overhead the

Children of the Moon flash their shiny teeth; I smile and wave at them for helping us break up our rocky soil. It's well known that the giants live in an alternate dimension, often helping industrious high altitude farmers, the common man—the *runakuna* care for their families, plow their fields and dig canals. Tatáy is too busy admiring his perfect ditches to notice them.

"Tatáy, look!" I point at the *Machukuna* but they've already faded away into the sunset.

"Yes, my dove, the sun is setting. Time to go home."

I sigh in frustration. *How can Tatáy be so blind?* I think testily.

He lays down his foot plow, claps the black soil off his calloused hands and motions me to do the same. After peering at our rich plots of soil then at the mountains, Tatáy holds out his arms as if to embrace Pachamama. He reaches into his coca pouch hanging from a braided rope slung across his left shoulder that ends at his waist, pulls out a few of the dull green leaves, places them shiny side up in his open palm, crumbles then blows the leaves onto the Earth Goddess's breasts.

"*Pachamama, Tirakuna*—bringers of all good things and doves of my heart," he says making a proper coca *phukay*—a prayer and offering with great sincerity and concentration to Mother Earth and the sacred places, "please make our walk home pleasant and uneventful . . . and thank you for your help with our irrigation ditches."

Satisfied with his libation, he reaches back into his pouch, pulls out a wad of six coca leaves along with a chunk of *llipt'a,* presses the combination into his cheek and chews slowly, a synthesis which imparts warm energy making the trek back home easier on his weary bones.

I caress the pouch containing my bird stone, my filthy fingers warming to its touch. Envisioning the promised encounter with the coca leaf diviner, I stroll beside my father, determined to suppress the overwhelming urge to contradict him by telling him it was the Machukuna, not Pachamama who made swift work of our plowing chores today. However, contradicting your elders can lead to a painful beating of the bottom of your feet, so I've learned to keep my mouth shut. Well, sometimes.

CHAPTER FOUR

Catequil hunkers down beside his wife, Sangama lying in her low bed; she tries to smile as she holds a large loosely woven bandage over her right temple, swollen from the Inca warrior's blow. Her father-in-law, Malcavilca and her son, Pillihuaman stand by, a look of grave concern on their faces.

"We will travel south," Catequil says as he tenderly strokes his wife's face, "to find our Pispis and Solsol. The Inca kidnappers can't have gone that far."

"I will go with you," Sangama says. She releases the bandage, props herself up on her elbows then, wincing, quickly lies back down.

"Well then, wife," Catequil teases, "you must do better than that."

Sangama nods with determination, and with a groan, strains to sit up again. Her husband and son gingerly pull her to her feet. Immediately, she busies herself searching along the far wall of the large circular family hut, selects a colorful cap embroidered with snakes and reptiles from a pile of knitted goods, pulls it on, drapes herself in several layers of thick woolen clothing then stuffs a large sack with assorted provisions

"I will go with you as far as the weapons cache. We'll do some much needed hunting, as our food supplies are running low. Then I'll return to Keulap. Alone." Macavilca announces. "The Incas will undoubtedly seek retribution for Mayor Qullqi's execution. We should know more when our messengers return."

"I will stay behind with grandfather," Pillihuaman says bravely, "to defend our homeland."

"No," Catequil says, "I need you to come with me."

"Your father's right," Malcavilca says, "I will be ordering evacuations of all women and children soon anyway."

"But I'm no longer a child!" the teenager sulks.

"I've already lost two daughters," Catequil says. He fixes onto his son's deep blue eyes.

"But grandfather needs my help!" Pillihuaman insists.

"Are you so anxious to journey to the heavenly realm of *hanan pacha* this soon?" Malcavilca asks. Pillihuaman lowers his eyes then shakes his head slowly. "Our race is systematically being killed off by the empire. I am old and dispensible; I will journey to the upper world soon, regardless of what happens with the Incas. But you, like other Cloud Warriors your age must thrive in this earthly realm of *kay pacha* before extinction claims us."

Before the steep mountain path connects to the paved stone road at the mountain's base where the jungle river roars, Catequil stops and surveys his surroundings warily. Since the peace treaty was signed, the Incas have forbidden Cloud Warriors to carry or own weapons of any kind, even for hunting. Leery of Cloud Warrior rebellions, the Inca's punishment for disobedience is death. When certain that all is clear, the Cloud Warrior family pushes left onto a narrow trail, overgrown with weeds and saplings and walk two hundred yards.

"There it is," Macavilca says, pointing at an unassuming mass of large gray rocks and boulders.

Catequil and Pillihuaman shove a boulder aside, uncovering a secret weapons cache hidden in a cave.

"Beautiful women of substance get first pick," Catequil says politely to his wife.

Sangama scrutinizes the assortment of meticulously crafted arrows—some with sharp obsidian tips, some tipped with bronze—and fills her empty quiver. Catequil lifts a hefty black palm wood sword and hands his son another while Macavilca counts weapons, tying one knot for every set of ten similar weapons on a *quipu*, a web of long multi-colored strings invented by the Cloud Warrior tribe for record keeping.

Wavy red hair blowing in the breeze, Pillihuaman parries with his father feigning left then right; Catequil's too distracted by his daughters' kidnapping to properly counter attack. He shakes his head.

"Come on!" the teen goads, "You're letting me win!"

"You're getting stronger," says Catequil, grunting as he fends off his son's bold strokes, "You may become even a better warrior than me one day," he states with a groan and a chuckle. The Cloud Warrior thrusts his sword, smacking his son's sword out of his hand.

Pilli quickly retrieves his weapon, feigns left, spins right then kicks the broad side of his father's sword. The weapon spins high in the sky; the teenager catches it before it hits the ground.

"You lose!" the young man trills.

"Oh ho!" yells his father, his hands up in mock surrender midst his son's laughter and Sangama's proud smile.

"Look," Macavilca says with satisfaction. He holds two red

quipus whose strings are tied into voluminous knots. "And that's just swords." The sorcerer counts out ten battle axes then ties one knot on a long braided yellow string. After handing Pillihuaman a *quipu* strung with light brown strings, the old sorcerer points to an assortment of flat braided slings.

"Count them," the old man tells his grandson, "You do know how to count. Don't you?"

"Of course he does," says Catequil proudly, "I taught him myself."

Macavilca holds up a jumble of purple *quipu* strings.

"Good," says Macavilca, "Then you can count, too. One knot for every ten of these maces . . . "

"I know how to do it, Tatáy" Catequil says as he gathers a pile of the stone star-shaped weapons.

"We are in good shape," Macavilca says with a smack of his lips, "When I get back to town, I'll organize a group of men to come back and retrieve more weapons. We're going to need all we can get."

A tree packed full of chattering parrots suddenly falls silent. In a nearby clearing, a doe steps in and begins to forage. Pillihuaman places an arrow in his bowstring.

"No," Macavilca says lowering his grandson's arrow, "Never hurt the female. She may be pregnant, she may have little ones."

The doe sprints away.

"Another thing about females," Catequil teases, "Always let them think they're the boss."

"If you want to be happy," Macavilca chimes in.

"Or if you want to stay alive," Sangama jests, brandishing her bow.

Catequil places a forefinger to his lips as amazingly, a three point buck steps into the same clearing. Pillihuaman takes aim. Voices in the distance makes the buck's ears twitch and the spooked animal leaps away. The voices grow louder and transform into high pitched wails. Litter carriers carry a bamboo cage full of a half a dozen Cloud Warriors girls, their fair faces and light-colored eyes red and swollen from sobbing. A stocky Inca captain struts beside the litter wearing golden earrings the size of small plates.

"If you don't shut up," he growls, "You'll never see your families again."

"We know what the Incas will do to us," a teenage Cloud Warrior, named Yuraq spits, cradling her newborn. "And we already know we'll never see our families again."

"Maybe the Daughters of the Sun are hungry?" an Inca soldier with a big mouth asks. He waves a piece of llama jerky at the girls. The girls shake their heads, too traumatized to think about eating. He shoves the meat between over-sized teeth and tears off a chunk. "You don't know what you're missing," he says smacking his lips loudly.

"So the rumors were true," Macavilca murmurs, "May the gods help us all."

"Do you see my sisters on the litter?" Pillihuaman asks as he squints through the foliage.

Light red hair tumbling over her shoulders, Sangama's emerald eyes fill with tears of disappointment.

"No," she says, "this is another group altogether."

Catequil aims an arrow through the dense brush.

"Four soldiers and four litter carriers." he whispers, "But leave the litter carriers alone, they're only slaves. And make sure not to hit any of the girls." He turns to look at his son. "Pilli, run into the forest and wait for my signal."

The boy takes a few hesitant steps then races off as a wild-eyed Inca bangs his sword on the bamboo cage.

"If you don't shut up, we'll be forced to return to your village," Wild Eye shouts as the terrified girls cringe, "and torture and kill your families. Is that what you want?"

Yuraq embraces the children as they scramble to her side, causing the litter to tilt; carriers strain under the unbalanced load.

"Now look what you've done," a warrior with a large square head shouts at Wild Eye, pointing at the lopsided cage, "You're making things worse!"

"Straighten that thing out," the Inca captain orders. The litter carriers strain to re-balance their load. "Do it now!" He whacks a sad-eyed carrier on the shins with the flat of his sword; the man remains stoic, apparently used to being beaten without mercy for no reason.

"Please," Sad Eye asks the captured girls haltingly, "spread out or litter fall. No want to hurt girls."

Before the girls can rectify the litter's imbalance, Catequil zings an arrow through Wild Eye's left iris; the warrior screams then collapses onto his back. Dead. Dark brown eyes darting about for the source of the attack, the litter carriers set down the conveyance then dart into the jungle. The captive girls crouch in a tight corner of their bamboo prison, trembling in fear. Still chomping on a chunk of jerky, Big Mouth wields his sword, squinting and turning his head from side to side. Macavilca raises his bow and shoots an arrow into his right shoulder. He spits out his jerky, falls backward then with a loud groan, pulls the arrow out of his flesh. Catequil shoots him again, this time in the heart. As Square Head turns and dashes for cover, Sangama loads her sling, whirs it overhead, releases the projectile which instantly crushes the warrior's skull.

Materializing behind the unsuspecting Macavilca, a scar-faced warrior lifts a mace overhead but before he can bring it down, an arrow pierces his left shoulder blade. He gasps then turns to see Pillihuaman who spins and kicks the mace out of the Inca's hand. The weapon soars into the sky. In one smooth move, Pulli catches, swings and cracks the mace onto Scar Face's skull. He crumbles to the ground, spewing a fountain of blood.

Pillihuaman surveys what he's done, trembles then vomits into the brush; it's his first human kill.

Yuraq, a mass of long blond hair spilling over her chest, unlatches the narrow gate of their litter; six girls tumble out, like guinea pigs out of a wooden box.

"I want to go home," a green-eyed, tow-headed toddler lisps, "I miss my Mamáy and Tatáy."

"We can't take you home right now," explains Catequil, "We have to find a place to hide first, then, when it's safe, we'll take you back to your families."

At first, the little girls stare at him in shocked silence trying to absorb the meaning of his cruel words. Within seconds, they bleat like sacrificial llamas, eyes and noses flowing like waterfalls.

"But we want to go home now!" another child cries.

"Maybe," Catequil says to Sangama after placing his hands over his ears, "we should give them back to the Incas." She glares at her husband. "Just kidding, wife."

Sangama waves her husband off, picks up a crying toddler with strawberry blond hair much like her own.

"We will take you to your home," she says as she strokes the little girl's head, "but we must find a place to rest first."

The little girls wipes her face, rubs her runny nose, sucks her thumb then cuddles against Sangama's ample bosom.

"That's right," says Yuraq, wiping tears from her own gray eyes. She embraces as many children as her arms can reach, dabbing away tears and leaky noses with a corner of her cloak, "We'll go home soon. I promise."

Pillihuaman searches the Incas' lifeless bodies for valuables; he finds several sacks stuffed with jerky, doles out generous strips to the famished girls, who sit cross-legged on the ground munching on the delicious dried meat. Their tears gone for now, the shaken children start to chat and smile, though their faces hidden in a mass of blond and red curls.

Catequil shoves the wooden litter into a tangle of jungle foliage but stops at the sound of leaves rustling; a litter carrier steps out, hands up. Macavilca, Pillihuaman and Sangama instantly pluck arrows from their quills, place them in bowstrings and take aim. Sad Eye crouches then covers his head with his massive arms.

"What are you doing here?" asks Catequil, "Go home. You are free."

"No home," says Sad Eye in broken *Runasimi*—the common language of the Empire but not his native tongue. "Lucanas tribe, only slaves," he says, pointing to his large sandaled feet, "Feet of Incas."

The Cloud Warriors lower their weapons.

"Do you know how to fight?" Catequil asks.

Sad Eye stares and shrugs, uncertain of what Catequil is getting at. The Cloud Warrior hands him the hilt of a dead Inca's sword; the muscular slope-shouldered man brandishes the hefty weapon with ease.

"Fight," Sad Eye says, smiling shyly, "Fight Incas."

The litter carrier beaten on his shins by the Inca captain limps into the clearing, hands up, followed by two more Lucanas.

"You can put your hands down," Sangama says, "You are safe here."

Four toddlers surround the kind Lucanas men then scramble into their huge arms; the gentle Feet of the Incas carefully put the children onto their muscular backs.

"Very light, like feather, " Sad Eyes says with a wide grin, " . . . of dove."

The other Lucanas men nod in agreement, their kind dark eyes glistening. Golden-haired twin sisters hold Macavilca's hands.

"We will go with you, grandfather," one of the twins says.

Yuraq straps her baby onto her back. The children giggle and chatter like little monkeys as they continue to gnaw on llama jerky.

Sangama turns slowly, her emerald eyes glowing as she surveys the area, aware of the possibly that more Inca troops could be in the vicinity. She must encourage the girls to be quiet without upsetting them further so, she gazes into her son's blue eyes. He nods, apparently able to read his mother's thoughts.

"Have you ever been hunting?" Sangama asks the girls.

The toddlers regard each other then shake their heads, wisps of light blond or red hair falling into their fair faces.

"Tatáy" the strawberry blond says, her emerald eyes surrounded by thick brown lashes "says that little children can't go hunting because they're too loud."

"Your father was right. Everyone has to be really quiet," Pillihuaman whispers, "or you'll scare the animals."

Catequil puts a finger to his lips then points to a trail. After setting several children on their backs, the four Lucanas men follow the Cloud Warriors softly into the dense green foliage.

CHAPTER FIVE

Mamáy's hands and feet are rough and gnarled like tree bark from working in the rugged high mountain climate; she sprinkles *chicha* —sweet corn beer over her new, larger stove of stone and mud over which a huge ceramic pot hangs, filled with a rainbow assortment of boiled potatoes seasoned with hot peppers.

"Purest little nurturer, you will care for us and cook well. You will help us feed our honored guest," Mamáy sings to her stove. The stove sizzles and sparks as if responding to her libation.

I finish setting a low table in honor of our esteemed village *pago,* a religious specialist. He's also a *hampiq,* knowledgeable about medicinal herbs. Some in our village say he's a *layqa,* a sorcerer; if he is, I'm not sure if that's a good or bad thing.

"T'ica, my dove," Tatáy says, "did you know that our village *pago* is an *altumisayuq*—a diviner of the highest order?"

Mouth open in surprise, I'm unaware that we had such a highly skilled holy man in our midst. Before I can reply, someone raps lightly on our humble wooden door.

"Here I come, little Mamáy! I'm coming to visit!" the ancient *pago* rasps.

"Come in!" Mamáy chirps, always happy to have visitors, but especially now that she and Tatáy have finished building the new stove.

The *pago* enters, tapping the ground with his rough-hewn walking stick, left eye cloudy, right eye black as coal. Though blind for as long as anyone can remember, the old man somehow manages to get around the village with little or no assistance. He's *runakuna,* a simple person, just like the rest of us living in the highlands. *Runakuna* know every hill, plain, ridge, rock, outcrop, lake and stream. Each location possesses a name and a personality; they are our friends, our guides and our nurturers.

"Thank you, my dove, my own heart. May the gods repay you!" the old man croaks, poking his walking stick through the door then shuffling into our modest home.

I guide him by the elbow to the seat of honor at the head of our low rectangular wooden table. The old man hunkers down cross-legged on the freshly swept and scrubbed wooden floor. Tatáy sets a large mug of *chicha* in front of him. We must wait for the holy man's libation before eating. He dips two fingers into his goblet, sprinkles the sweet purple brew over each corner of the table, pours some *chicha* onto the ground for Pachamama and flicks some in the air for Tirakuna—the sacred places.

"*Ukyakunsunchis*," the old man says, lifting his wooden cup, "Let us drink together."

Though thin and frail-looking, the old man gulps down an entire goblet of *chicha* then shovels my mother's tasty morsels into his toothless mouth like he hasn't eaten in a year. After devouring enough food for an Inca battalion, he's not shy about heaping his plate and bowl for a huge second, then third serving of potatoes, grilled llama, vegetables and fruit. He nods enthusiastically, occasionally tittering in delight, smacking his lips and burping appreciatively. Tatáy remains stoic but Mamáy and I shoot each other sidelong glances, trying desperately to suppress our giggles as vast quantities of food magically disappear into the scrawny leaf diviner's stomach.

"Where does he put it all?" I whisper into Mamáy's ear.

Mamáy shrugs, bites her lower lip then moves closer to me.

"We better eat before all the food is gone," she murmurs with a chuckle.

We serve ourselves and eat until our stomachs hurt. Delicious as usual.

My father sets a large clay *quero* of *chicha* in the middle of the table, so everyone can serve themselves and properly wash down the delicious meal. Instead, the shaman lifts the jug, presses it to his lips and gulps down its entire contents then wipes his mouth with his tunic sleeve, burping loudly. Suddenly, as nimble as a man half his age, the ancient man springs up from the table a big grin on his dark wrinkled face.

"Thank you, my dove, my own heart, may the gods repay you," he sings in a high falsetto voice.

To my horror, the leaf diviner of the highest order grabs his walking stick then totters toward the door. I stare wide-eyed at my bewildered father, who simply shrugs.

"Do something, Tatáy!" I hiss. He responds with a curt nod.

"Honored *altumisayuq*—won't you share the wisdom of Father Coca?" Tatáy finally asks. He stands, retrieves a pouch of freshly harvested coca leaves from under his tunic and hands it to the old *pago* who fumbles with it for a moment, opens the pouch and inhales its essence.

"*Pachamama's* fragrance," the ancient man pronounces, tapping his walking stick on the floor; our hut fills with the pungent green scent. He tucks my father's generous gift into his tunic. I stand, retrieve another jug of *chicha* then set it on the other side of the table, as far away from the old man's greedy lips as possible.

The leaf diviner dodders to the far side of our hut, sniffs, turns, nods, lays down his walking stick then folds his stick thin legs cross-legged on the floor. After digging into the neck of his tunic, he brings out a finely woven cloth—an *unkhuña* in which his own stash of fresh coca is wrapped; he opens it and spreads it flat on the floor.

While he sets up for a leaf divination of the highest order, my baby brother stirs from his cradle in the corner. Like a dutiful sister, I pick him up, kiss his chubby red cheeks and adjust his bright knitted cap. He coos and smiles as I nuzzle him then becomes restless again.

"Are you hungry, little Wawa?" I ask. Wawa isn't really his name; it's just a name given to all highland children, male and female, until they turn two when the biggest risk of infant mortality is past. He starts to wail in earnest. I immediately hand him to Mamáy; she opens her tunic, tucks him under an alpaca blanket. He latches on and settles down immediately.

"I call on *Pachamama,* Father Coca and on all the sacred places." the shaman prays, in a eerie high-pitched voice, which thankfully doesn't disturb my baby brother, who apparently has fallen to sleep after getting a belly full of breast milk, "We will obey your commands and trust you to accurately determine the nature of events in space and time. Your abundance is our abundance; your beauty is our beauty. We walk the earth only by the power of your grace. We are simple *runakuna,* springing out of the ground like toads when the sun was created and the blessed giant Children of the Moon took refuge in their eternally moonlit world."

He pulls a shiny golden coin from his tunic pocket and places it in the center of the cloth, stares at me with sightless eyes then points.

"Do you know what this is, T'ica?" he asks.

"A golden coin?" I answer, knowing that's probably not the right answer.

"This, in actual fact, is the sweat of the sun, my dove, containing magical properties. It's a *ñawin*. A third eye." he says with a grin. His face contorts, his eyes bulge, looking as though they could explode out their sockets any second. His right glass eye pops into the palm of his thin wrinkled hand. "Two eyes are better than one and certainly better than none!" He laughs as if an eyeball popping out of its socket is the most normal thing in the world.

My parents are mute but I observe the scene with a mixture of awe and confusion; Wawa awakes and emits a laugh which sounds magical, like a little bell. Mamáy adjusts her tunic then pulls the blanket away from the baby's face.

"Yes, Wawa," the ancient holy man coos, "You understand because you have just come down from *hanan pacha*—the glorious upper world and still remember how things really are. Don't you?"

Wawa sighs, smiles, kicks his tiny feet, nuzzles against Mamáy's full breasts then falls back to sleep.

The old shaman places the eye neatly on top of the golden *ñawin*; the eyeball spins slowly, seemingly taking in everything.

"Tell me clearly, sacred coca! Lord Coca always knows! The *Machukuna* insist our golden-haired daughter, T'ica make a dangerous pilgrimage to a sacred place. the mountain of *Apu*

Salkantay. The gods who live in this glacier mountain make the rain fall, the sun rise and earth quake. Tell me clearly, sacred coca! I implore you, Earth Goddess!" the leaf diviner exclaims.

His cloudy left eye rolls back in his head until only white with a labyrinth of fine red capillaries appears; he chants in a tongue unknown to me, pours the coca leaves through his fingers onto the magical coin, his empty eye socket shut tight. He lifts his hands and the coca leaves stir, almost imperceptibly at first then take on a life of their own—leafy gray-green whirlwinds blow frantically around the hut. The coca leaves rises shapelessly to the ceiling then slowly transform into a full breasted woman; Pachamama gazes lovingly at my mother and infant brother.

"Your milk is rich and nourishing; your baby will grow to adulthood," Goddess Earth says her voice soothing and dreamlike t "and will live to be big and brave and help his older sister."

Tears of joy and gratitude flow down Mamáy's cheeks; she pulls the sleeping Wawa closer and kisses him on his fat cheek.

"Thank you, Pachamama. Thank you," Mamáy whispers.

Still in a deep trance, our pago chants so softly now as to be barely audible.

"And what of my daughter's mission, Goddess of the Earth? Tatáy asks. "She's only eleven and . . . "

Pachamama's form fades as the gray green leaves settle down on the *unkhuña,* shiny side up, forming a neat pile in front of the leaf diviner, except for one leaf which lands dull side up.

"Thank you, Pachamama, thank you, my dove, my heart," the village pago chants in his strange high falsetto. He picks up his glass eye, covered with debris. Mamáy quickly pours fresh *chicha* into a clean *quero* and hands it to him. He plops the dirty eyeball into the *quero*, washes it carefully, pulls it out, shakes off any excess liquid then pops the orb back into his quivering eye socket.

Thunder claps overhead; *rayu*—lightning strikes our hut. Mamáy and I scream but the baby laughs. The *pago* smiles serenely.

"Don't be afraid," the ancient diviner says calmly. "for divination of the highest order, we need the help of Father Lightning."

Another deafening thunderclap and a blinding bolt of lightning passes through our thatched roof and sears the coca. The pungent smell of toasted leaves permeates the room.

"One more bolt of lightning," Tatáy calmly whispers, "then our *pago* will have all he needs."

Thunder rumbles then roars overhead; lightning strikes the third time, this time burning the delicate coca leaves to a crisp. Wawa coos, titters and claps his chubby brown hands in delight.

The *pago* kneels on all fours to sniff the blackened leaves from all angles, occasionally nodding and mumbling unintelligibly. When done, he sits cross-legged, picks up another *quero* of *chicha*, gulps down every last drop and belches loudly. After gathering up the burnt coca in his *unkhuña* and stowing the cloth away under his tunic, he stares sightlessly at my father who patiently awaits the old *pago's* divination; however, the holy man is expecting my father's offer of reciprocity. In our small village, we are family, if not by blood, by heart, therefore we assiduously avoid conversations on the topic of payment. After what seems like hours but in reality is just a few minutes of silent staring, Tatáy smiles, pulls out a large gold nugget from his waist pouch and places it into the pago's hands. The ancient man lifts the golden "sweat of the sun" as if offering it to the gods; it gleams in the firelight. Then he gnaws on it. With a gummy grin, he daintily places the gift into his pouch then arises with the help of his walking stick.

"Your daughter's journey to Mistress Mountain will be a productive. Lord Coca told me she must walk all day until nightfall. She must reach the summit as quickly as possible." he says. "Hungry pumas on lower mountain paths often seek tired and sick hikers therefore, she must move with the speed and cunning of Goddess Jaguar. *Pisti Timpu*—world reversal—is nigh and her mission critical."

Lips pressed together tightly, Mamáy glares at my father then collapses into sobs.

"I'm reduced to a piece of *ch'uño!*" she squeaks, a popular thing for grief-stricken villagers to say; *ch'uño* is freeze-dried potatoes, a staple which sustains *runakuna* in the cold season.

I collect my baby brother from Mamáy's arms and hug him tightly, suddenly afraid. I scrutinize Tatáy; he's sipping *chicha,* looking into the distance and drifting into his own universe again.

CHAPTER SIX

1511 A.D.
Piajajalca Fortress
Chachapoyas

Pounding on a drum created from the skin, bones and limbs of a vanquished foe, the drummer uses the poor devil's own arms to beat on its own stomach. Dressed in bearskin, claws, a fierce bear skull strapped to his head, an Inca bear dancer—an apoya—*leaps and twists to the rhythm in hopes of eliciting the favor of the mighty* Machukuna, *the giant ancestors who live in a parallel universe under eternal moonlight.*

Exhausted and thirsty from their long, rocky trek to the wilds of the northern empire, Inca warriors watch the apoya *dance and suck on flasks of* chicha, *retrieved from under their red and white checked army-issue tunics.*

A hunch-backed Inca sorcerer, in a plain white tunic, raises the holy offering overhead—a cloth filled with coal-black seeds of the canihua *plant, coca seeds, black llama wool, incense, several gold nuggets, shells and a starfish. Eyelids heavy, his eyes roll back in a drugged euphoria.*

"Inti Tatáy", the sorcerer intones, "Give us victory over the savage Cloud Warriors of the Piajajaca Fortress."

He sets the offering on a small pile of dried twigs and a similarly dressed, young assistant lights it with a torch. It ignites instantly, hot seeds sizzling then bursting red hot into the air. The sorcerer chants and the drum beat rumbles like thunder. The giant ancestors roar and a cloud of smoke twists into the moonlit dawn.

CHAPTER SEVEN

Through the window of his Quito palace, Inca Emperor Huayna Capac studies the smoke billowing from Inca fortresses built at the foot of the dormant Pambamarca volcano. Dark brown eyes blood shot, he hasn't slept in days, his mind filled with gory images of the war twenty years ago also waged against the same fierce Caranqui-Cayambe-Pasto Confederation. *So many lives lost then as will be now*, he ponders feeling every bit of his age of sixty.

"I grow weary of these rebels," Huayna Capac says to his son, Atahualpa, whose mother was a Quito princess. Though only eighteen years old, Prince Atahualpa is tall, muscular, mature and handsome with exceptional military skills. "You, my son, will organize a powerful army and put a quick end to this."

"Yes, father," Atahualpa states with a nod. "I will send word to General Rumiñawi to discuss an appropriate military strategy."

Fresh troops from neighboring province wait for the sacrifices to begin. Scores of black llamas in makeshift corrals are burned alive, their squeals keening into the heavens. High priestesses hand newborns to Villac Umu, who lifts each tightly swathed infant while praying to the Sun God then thrusts them into freshly excavated graves. Grim grave diggers work their spades to fill in the burial sites. Older Daughters of the Sun have been preparing to participate in *capacocha*—child sacrifice for many years; priests lead them to the summit of sacred mountains where the sacrificial ritual can take place closer to the gods. Girls too young to make the trek are drugged, their eyelids drooping; local priests quickly dispatch them to *hanan pacha*—the heavenly realm by bashing their tender skulls with heavy, gilded clubs; they sink to the ground without so much as a sigh for they have learned that it is important to die well. Spectators, many of whom are warriors who will soon see their last days in this physical realm of *kay pacha,* too, reward the Daughters of the Sun's sacrifices with frenzied whoops and wild cheers.

The requisite ceremonial two day fast and sacrifices over, excessive feasting commences. Warriors break their fast by eating and drinking their fill of every sumptuous food and drink available in the empire. Some eat and drink so much that they vomit then eat and drink even more late into the evening.

"No fighting is permitted on the new moon," the unctuous high priest, Villac Umu warns Prince Atahualpa, who sits at a table with his father, the emperor. Villac squints at the lunar sliver hanging in the sky. "Bad luck."

"We have wasted enough time already, priest," Atahualpa snarls, scarcely able to eat, weighed down with the responsibility of leading thousands of warriors. "We will start our campaign tomorrow, as planned."

"As you wish, your highness," Villac says with a low bow.

The high priest shuffles backward, head lowered; the prince wipes his face, guzzles the remainder of his *chicha,* stands then with a bow to the emperor, takes his leave.

In an incredible show of discipline, Atahualpa gazes at the sea of 75, 000 foot soldiers, in red and white checked tunics, silently gathered before dawn on the border of Inca territory and that of the Caranqui-Cayambe-Pasto Confederation. In the distance, Inca fortresses hastily constructed of local wood, field-stone and mortar, are still smoldering instead of the imperial style of massive indestructible interlocked earthquake-proof stones. Out of twenty Inca fortresses built near the Pambamarca volcano, rebels have demolished eighteen, using salvaged stones to reinforce their sprawling impregnable fortress called Quitoloma.

Atahualpa sits in his gilded canopied litter and passively notes the curls of smoke wafting into the sky.

Quito general, Rumiñawi waits on foot nearby; Rumiñawi means Stone Face, an apt sobriquet since his prominent nose and cheekbones appear to have been chiseled from granite, his mouth set in a perpetual frown.

"Start the maneuvers now," Atahualpa orders.

"As you wish, my prince," Rumiñawi replies.

Upon his signal, musicians thump gargantuan drums—*wancaras,* mimicking the heartbeat of the Inca gods. Percussion players shake *chajchas*—large rattles made from llama hooves and the teeth and bones of vanquished enemies; the spectral sound pierces the sky and grates on the ear. Men blow into giant conch shells—*pututus,* emitting a distorted, disorienting sound which appears to come from several directions at once. Flutists play a variety of native instruments: *mosheño, quena, pinkillo, tarka* and ocarina. Singers join in with songs honoring Emperor Huayna Capac's innumerable conquests. Acrobats and dancers leap and swoop in the cool mountain air. Warriors whip stone-loaded slings overhead, creating a hypnotic whirring that engulfs the region then switch hands, a display of ambidexterity demonstrating the ability to continue fighting despite losing a hand or an arm in battle—an all-too-common occurrence. Archers march in place, muscular arms gleaming in the morning sun, lifting and lowering bows in perfect synchronization. Javelin throwers thrust spears overhead then to the fore, grunting with each movement. Warriors wielding maces, clubs and battle axes twirl their weapons, toss them overhead, then catch them without a miss as guidons—bright triangular pennants depicting Inti the Sun God ripple in the faint glimmer of the morning sun. It is an awe-inspiring military parade intended to demoralize the rebels.

After the Inca's long military display, the Caranqui-Cayambe-Pasto Confederation is neither impressed nor demoralized. From the safety of the Quitoloma high fortress, the rebels respond with their own contingent of highly trained warriors, musicians, dancers and acrobats who perform on the stronghold's vast terraced platforms. Thousands of rebels shout and cheer as their energetic leader, Chimbo Sancto paces back and forth upon the platform built upon the highest recesses of the fortress, overlooking the sacred high altitude Lake Yahuarcocha—Blood Lake along whose shores a fierce battle was waged almost twenty years ago; a battle so gruesome, it turned the water of the lake blood red. At that time, the young emperor Huayna Capac, tired of fighting, successfully negotiated a peace treaty whose stipulations have been largely ignored since then, fomenting animosity with taxes in the form of forced labor and military service taking its toll. Even more onerous: the conqueror's custom of kidnapping and sacrificing the Confederation's precious children to greedy Inca gods. Chimbo holds up his hands to quiet his enthusiastic followers so all can hear him speak.

"Citizens!" the rebel leader says, his voice resonating from the acoustically engineered platform, "I congratulate you on our fortress, Quitoloma, the crown defensive jewel of our confederation!"

Arms open wide, he proudly displays the immense, all but

impregnable Quitoloma, built upon the southernmost part of Pambamarca at an elevation of over 12,000 feet. Constructed of volcanic material called *cangahua,* the fortress consists of more than a hundred buildings, which serve as living quarters, storehouses and administrative buildings, surrounded by three concentric walls, only accessible through gates defended by towers, bulwarks and moats. "Although many of us may speak different languages and worship different gods, we fight with one heart for our freedom against the perfidy of the Inca!"

Erupting in cheers, rebels clang bronze and stone weapons upon padded shields. Men and women dressed in lavishly feathered costumes sing songs disparaging Inca Emperor Huayna Capac and his "bastard" son and traitor, Atahualpa. The singers voices rain down upon the Inca enemy below.

Prince Atahualpa rolls his eyes and yawns, accustomed to attacks upon his character. His long-deceased mother was Princess of Quito who married Emperor Huayna Capac as part of the original peace treaty some twenty years ago with the Caranqui-Cayambe-Pasto Confederation, something which most natives never forgave her for, particularly since the Incas were and are still infamous for breaking treaties throughout the empire.

"Forward!" General Rumiñawi bellows.

Inca archers and spear man commence peppering enemy lines; the rebels respond with a volley stones, fracturing skulls, pummeling arms and legs and arrows; their spears pierce Inca shields, leaving warriors writhing and screaming in agony as life drains from their battered bodies. Atahualpa scans the battlefield pensively; the Incas have bungled their attempt to soften up the well-protected rebels, his men succumbing in ever increasing numbers.

Wielding maces, clubs and battle-axes, wave after wave of Inca troops run full throttle toward Quitoloma; entrenched rebel forces mow them down. Inca javelin throwers join in; the giant foot of the rebel confederation, safe inside their fortress, flatten them.

A third of Inca troops attack the fortress in a pincer-like movement but are massacred within minutes. Rebels cheer their leader, Chimbo Sancto who hid warriors and a vast cache of weapons behind every fortress wall.

"We will lay a full frontal siege on the rebel fortress," Atahualpa shouts from his litter, "and will bombard it continuously until victorious."

"We will vanquish the enemies of our emperor, Son of the Sun God, the Shepherd of the Sun, Emperor Huayna Capac!" General Rumiñawi yells, his voice echoing over the vast army, "And we will not stop until every last rebel is dead!"

With an unearthly roar, another battalion of Inca warriors pound their shields and race toward Quitoloma. The rebel arrows, stones and lances darken the sky; the Incas tumble to the ground like tin soldiers. Another wave sprints fearlessly behind them with the same result. Then another. And another.

With at least half of his warriors dead or dying, Atahualpa peers at General Rumiñawi.

"We have made the fatal mistake of underestimating our enemy." Atahualpa says. "And with our own fortresses burned to the ground . . . "

" . . . we are at a distinct disadvantage, my prince," Rumiñawi replies, his stone face betraying no emotion, "that is correct."

An arrow hits a litter carrier through the heart; he slumps to the ground. The remaining carriers strain to keep the now lopsided litter from dumping the prince onto the battlefield.

"Down!" Atahualpa orders.

Maintaining his composure, he steps off the litter, relieving the carriers of their burden then stands eye to eye with General Rumiñawi.

"The gods have spoken." the young royal asserts, "Give the order to retreat."

The general nods. A *chasqui*—a young feathered Inca messenger stands nearby.

"Send a message to the emperor," Rumiñawi says, "that we underestimated our enemy's tactical advantage and must retreat."

The *chasqui* knots the message into his *quipu* then sprints north toward Quito. Secretly happy to be running out of harm's way, a smile spreads across his face though the moans of dying men ring in his ears as rebels continue to pulverize vulnerable Inca troops, open targets without the protection of fortresses.

Pututu trumpeters blow in unison. Despite the din of fighting and screaming and thundering of war drums, Inca warriors recognize the unmistakable sound for retreat, turn north and sprint for their lives, dodging arrows, stones and spears mercilessly rained down upon them from the heights of the rebel fortress. Withdrawal is chaotic; rebel arrows fly, ripping through necks, backs and shoulders, shattering ribs and puncturing lungs, leaving men gasping for their last breaths. Stones split open skulls, propelling warriors with a thud to their knees. Javelins skewer men like peccaries.

Chimbo Sancto waves his arms frantically from the fortress's highest platform.

"No mercy!" the charismatic leader yells, "Kill them all! Don't let them escape!"

After rushing down Quitoloma's endless stone and mortar steps, unlatching and swinging open heavy wooden gates through a triad of concentric walls, rebels scale four bulwarks, lower a wide timber platform over a moat then cross the watery barrier to dry land. Out of the confines of their fortress now, they stumble over mounds of dead and dying Incas, slowing their offensive. Atahualpa's retreating troops are too far ahead to be caught but the men give chase anyway, determined to obey Chimbo Sancto's orders to annihilate the despised Inca invaders—a fatal mistake.

CHAPTER EIGHT

Before I open my eyes, I perceive at least six Children of the Moon looming over me.

"Wake up, T'ica," one of the giants says, his voice soothing like the low roar of the ocean. "It is time. They are coming."

I'm cold and groggy since I tossed and turned most of the night. When I did finally fall asleep, my dreams were fraught with odd images of children's toys: three knitted dolls (one orange, another blue, another red), three tiny silver llama bells and three brightly painted pieces of pottery the significance of which I can't ascertain.

I groan, roll over and drag my thick blankets over my head.

"There's not much time," another Machukuna insists, "They're coming."

"Who? Who's coming?" I ask. Instead of an answer, I get a vague notion that slips away elusive as a bad dream you can't recall no matter how you try. My good luck charm, my *enqa* stirs in its pouch, its presence a comfort to me. I kiss the bird stone and hold it close then with a groan, arise from my warm bed to the smell of Mamáy's cooking.

My father squats, holding fresh coca leaves in his right palm, shiny side out and blows softly; the gods of the surrounding snow-covered mountain peaks smile down upon our modest *phukay* offering, of this I'm sure.

"Goddess of the Earth, Sacred Places, Mistress Mountain," he prays. "I beseech you to grant my daughter, my only daughter, the dove of my own heart, a safe pilgrimage."

He places a neat sheaf of coca leaves in Mamáy's palm then another into my palm, pulls out a chunk of black *llipt'a,* to activate the coca, breaks it into thirds and distributes a piece to each of us. I place the coca and the *llipt'a* in the back of my mouth and chew; I feel my body grow strong, warm, energetic and brave, all doubt and fear dissipate, like white smoke rising from our new stove and vanishing through the thatched roof into the heavens.

My father chews the coca leaves, eyes closed in intense concentration; his dark brown face and cheeks turn rosy and warm. In contrast, my mother chews her coca listlessly, murmuring, shrugging and sighing loudly. *Runakuna* should chew coca with bravery, with thankfulness, not resentment as Mamáy appears to be doing. Properly chewed, coca leaves will absorb grief and pain; it will comfort the chewer like a mother.

Tatáy smiles, face glowing; he stands then pulls Mamáy and me onto our feet.

"You are my only daughter. You are everything to me." Tatáy hugs me close, choking back his tears. "Do you understand?"

I inhale the essence of his powerful body. I want to tell him that I love him but I can't without bursting into tears. Unwilling to appear weak, I simply hug him as hard as I can. I take a deep breath, release myself from his embrace and turn to face Mamáy.

"My dove," Mamáy whispers, tears streaming down her high cheekbones, "my beautiful sweet white dove." My tiny dark-skinned mother, physically so different from me, raises her arms and tiptoes to reach my neck; I bend over to accommodate her. She hums and nuzzles my neck, the way she's done since I was a baby, the way a llama cuddles her newborn *cria.*

My baby brother is sound asleep. I sidle over to his crib, touch him lightly on the cheek; he purses and works his lips as if nursing.

"Good-bye, little Wawa." I whisper. "I'll be back soon." His lush black eyelashes flutter for a moment; he sighs but doesn't awaken.

When I step out of the warm comfort of our tiny hut, I contemplate the vast high mountain wilderness with confidence, chewing a mouthful of fresh coca leaves and rubbing my distended belly—overfeeding before a long journey is a common *runakuna* tradition. Mamáy insisted I eat her huge breakfast of potatoes, skewers of grilled vegetables, guinea pig and endless quantities of fruit until I can barely move. I place a colorful, heavily laden *k'eperina*—a sizable folded tightly woven fabric on my back then knot it below my neckline so that it drapes over my shoulders; it's filled with so much food and provisions, my knees almost buckle under its weight.

"We are *runakuna*—people of the highlands able to orient ourselves in the present and future; we are people of substance. We are in communion with the Sacred Places and our deities. Father Coca knows your trip will be a safe one," Tatáy intones, while gazing at the distant snow-covered mountains and lifting his hands in prayer. "My daughter must go to the ice, Blessed Old Ones, sanctify her with your essence."

Tatáy hands me a long obsidian knife in a leather sheath and a small bag hanging from a sash, bursting at the seams with fresh coca leaves though where he collects coca from is a well-kept secret. My guess is that he's found it somewhere in the Great Jungle but, he'll never tell me or anybody else in on this mystery.

"You will need these, daughter," he says with a wistful grin.

"Thank you, Tatáy."

I tie the sash around me waist, hook the knife sheath over it, let out a long sigh then commence the long hike over the dusty trail to the sacred Salkantay Mountain. When I turn to wave, I see my father dabbing his moist eyes with a small handkerchief. When he's done, he hands the cloth to Mamáy who also wipes away her tears. My parents stand beside the door of our hut and wave for a long time. As I hike they become tiny dots slowly disappearing in the distance.

CHAPTER NINE

1522 A.D.
The Great Jungle
Northern Peru, Chachapoyas

A light drizzle starts, stops then starts and stops again, typical weather for beginning of the rainy season. Macavilca and Pillihuaman shoulder a massive six point buck as they follow Catequil, who lights the way with a torch. Two rescued girls carry small bundles of kindling; four sleeping toddlers are draped over the backs and arms of the Lucanas litter carriers, their loping gate as smooth and soothing as a mother's caress.

"This is it," says Catequil, torchlight illuminating a solid rock face.

Yuraq shivers, her baby strapped to her back; her thick blond hair in tangles, lips purple, gray eyes drooping.

Catequil touches the rock face in a crisscross pattern; the wall splits into two tall doors which slowly rotate revealing an enormous cave. Macavilca and Pilli enter then lower the buck onto the stone floor. They discover several torches on a far wall then light them with a flint. When all are safely inside, Catequil touches the doors again; they rotate until any semblance of an entrance has completely vanished.

"We'll be safe here," Pilli says, a confident smile spreading across his freckled face, "at least for a while."

Sangama places blankets on the cave floor; the Lucanas men gently lay the snoozing toddlers upon them.

"What is this?" Sad Eyes asks, gazing in wonder at ancient

drawings on the cave walls.

"Our ancestors discovered this cave," Sangama says, stroking the crude paintings of large wooden sailing ships, "I pray their spirits will protect us."

Macavilca places firewood onto an earthen and stone stove. Catequil guts the deer; Pillihuaman, Macavilca and the litter carriers help skin the carcass.

The men gnaw on the last remnants of roasted venison. Stove smoke curls up through a small hole in the ceiling. Yuraq carefully lays her infant on a blanket then adds wood to the smoldering fire. The children cuddle on blankets interwoven with bright green serpents whose scarlet eyes seem to glow in the firelight.

"Come! Come!" Sangama says, motioning all to scoot closer. The men sit cross-legged near the stove. Yuraq follows suit. Hair tumbling over her shoulders and glowing ruby red near the firelight, Sangama inhales then clears her throat.

"Our ancestors came from a faraway place where winters danced with snow and ice, a blessing from the gods after sweltering summer days. But war came; our people were forced to flee and sail across the endless blue water, until they reached a remote land of unrelenting humidity, sunny beaches and untamed forest. The gods had guided them to the Great River which, flowed west to east into the great blue water. But Pachamama saw her children were unhappy in the unbearable heat of the wild eastern shore; she lifted her skirt, causing great destruction and killing many. Afterward, the Great River flowed west so ships could sail effortlessly into the thick verdant forest. Exotic animals and natives greeted them along the banks as they navigated the rushing river. Many times, our ancestral fathers wanted to make land but wives and daughters longed for the coolness of their homeland. Finally, Mistress Mountain beckoned them and our people thrived in the coolness; they were safe and at home in the clouds."

An unfamiliar sound awakens Catequil. *Probably a rat*, he thinks then unperturbed, falls back to sleep, dreaming about his kidnapped daughters and reaching into the night to wrap his arms around them; they float away, a disturbing expression on their fair faces. Solsol's mouth transforms into a harrowing aggregation of jagged yellow teeth, Pispis's hair becomes a mass of shaggy black fur.

Catequil startles awake. A bear and her cubs crawl out from the bowels of the cave, her roar deafening as it echoes off the cave walls. Lucanas and Cloud Warrior men spring to their feet. The bear scrambles to the closed entrance, her cubs on her heels.

The children awake, rub their eyes and stare slack-jawed at the beast.

"Don't scream," Catequil whispers, one hand up, the other brandishing his sword.

"Stay calm," Macavilca says, "She just wants to protect her babies."

The Lucanas stand ready to protect their charges with swords, axes and halberds pilfered from the dead Incas

"Don't get too close," Pillihuaman says, arrow inserted into his bow string.

"Nice bear, nice bear," Catequil murmurs, "Good bear."

The bear stands on her hind legs, lifts massive front paws studded with long curved claws, open her white muzzle and a thundering roar splits the night air; the girls shiver and huddle, whimpering softly.

"Here," says Pilli, tossing chunks of leftover venison the bear's way, "Some nice deer meat."

The bear bends over, claws the meat and stuffs it in her mouth; her cubs stand on hind legs, squealing for their share.

"Give her some more," Catequil says.

Pillihuaman tosses the animal more meat but instead of taking it, Mother Bear drops onto her massive paws then sprints toward the terrified girls, sniffing the air with a mixture of curiosity and hunger.

"We've got to do something," whispers Pillihuaman as the beast's curious sniffing transforms into a low growl.

The Lucanas men stealthily approach the animal, chests heaving, weapons ready.

"Forgive us, Goddess Bear," says Sad Eye.

"On the count of three," says Catequil, sweat pouring from his brow. "One, two…"

"No," Sangama whispers, pointing to the bear cubs, "Don't hurt her."

Arising slowly, long elegant arms stretching a woven serpent blanket above her flaming locks, her emerald eyes glimmer in the firelight.

"Goddess Bear, these are my children" she hisses. She is

Goddess Snake, staring into the bear's chestnut eyes, "You cannot have them." The sow snarls and takes a hesitant step forward; Sangama can smell the animal's suffocating, sour breath. "We will not hurt your cubs," she whispers. With a flick of her wrist Sangama signals her son to toss the bear another chunk of meat, "And we will share more of our venison with your family."

Pillihuaman hurls a meaty hindquarter into the middle of the room.

"Open the doors," Macavilca whispers to Catequil.

When Catequil approaches the entrance, Goddess Bear screeches; he's getting too close to her cubs. He steps back and tries to shoo the bear cubs toward their mother.

"Go to your mother," Catequil whispers. "Go!"

Instead of getting closer to their mother, the bewildered cubs nimbly climb up the craggy cave walls, landing on an expanse of irregularly shaped rock jutting overhead; they curl into furry black and white balls, screeching and sobbing, sounding eerily like human babies crying for their mother.

Sangama stares down Goddess Bear, who continues to sniff the air near the frightened girls, their long tresses tangled, faces ashen, eyes red from sobbing. The sow's nostrils flare; she snuffles in the direction of the venison, as if unable to determine which would be tastier: the girls or the deer meat.

Mother Bear adequately distracted and cubs perched above, Catequil creeps to the cave doors again, touches them in a crisscross pattern; the stones pivot then creak open slowly. Mother Bear stands on her hind legs, lifts her snout, opens her mouth and growls. Sangama stands her ground knowing that backing down would lead to, not only her own demise, but what was left of her family, rescued children and the kind-hearted Lucanas men. The staring cannot go on forever so Sangama stands tiptoe and stretches the blanket to the ceiling.

"Go!" she roars in a deep other-worldly voice that echoes throughout the cave.

The bear blinks, crouches on all fours and scampers to the deer haunch, scooping it into her massive jaw; she rises onto her hind legs again and glowers at the terrified humans, who stare back at her, knees shaking, weapons primed. The beast growls long and low, shakes her massive head then lunges through the mouth of the cave into the wilderness. The cubs squeal, scamper down the cave wall, roll onto the floor then race through the exit after their mother.

Sweat pouring from his forehead, Macavilca steps out of the cave and takes a long slow breath; he pricks his ears as if listening to a sound faraway; Sangama, Catequil, Pillihuaman and the Lucanas men join him. They hear something, too.

CHAPTER TEN

The fleet-footed *chasqui* arrives at Huayna Capac's palace in record time then sprints down the corridor to the throne room. He stumbles through the entrance, chest heaving, unable to speak without catching his breath between words. The emperor sits next to his high priest, Villac Umu, who is whispering in his ear.

"My supreme shepherd," the *chasqui* interrupts, "forgive me but . . . Atahualpa's troops . . . have been forced . . . to retreat."

"Retreat?" the emperor exclaims, his forehead furrowed, "What is this madness of which you speak?"

"We've underestimated the rebels." the *chasqui* states, "They have burned eighteen of our fortresses surrounding Pambamarca, making it impossible to take cover. In contrast, the Quitoloma fortress is virtually impenetrable."

"Our losses?" the emperor asks.

"At least 50% of our troops have been massacred," the *chasqui* says, "with at least another 25% badly wounded."

The emperor glowers at the high priest.

"I you recall, I did advise Atahualpa to wait," Villac Umu explains, "until after the new moon."

"Enemy losses?" the emperor asks.

The messenger lowers his head and takes a deep breath.

"Negligible, my shepherd," the *chasqui* replies. *There is no point in attempting to diminish the horrible truth,* he muses. *My job is to convey the full truth of any given situation, no matter how unpalatable.*

"I will need your help to gather reinforcements." the emperor says.

"Of course, my shepherd," the *chasqui* replies with a deep bow. "I know what to do."

A sea of freshly conscripted men and women with hundreds more materializing every minute surrounds Emperor Huayna Capac's litter. Thanks to the Inca's efficient *chasqui* system of communication, citizens of nearby provinces have been alerted, culminating in the swift aggregation of over 100,000 trained soldiers. What's left of the overwhelmed Inca troops lumber behind General Rumiñawi and Atahualpa. The emperor notices with satisfaction that in the distance, the entirety of the rebel forces are giving chase.

"Father!" Atahualpa says breathlessly, "We must escape while there's still time."

"We have underestimated the enemy, my shepherd," Rumiñawi states, his stone face softened by exhaustion and fear.

Emperor Huayna Capac stands, grabs the neckline of his tunic, then rips the finely woven cloth down to his naval.

"Cowards! All of you!" he shouts, "Women are worth more than you!"

"But Father . . ." Atahualpa insists, pointing at the ragged and bloodied troops behind him. "Can you not see . . ."

"From what are you fleeing?" the emperor demands, "Are not the rebels men of flesh and blood? Are they endowed with special powers that Inca warriors do not possess? Or maybe you are running from the vicious Amaru—the omnipotent inter-species son of the mountain gods?"

"No, Father," Atahualpa replies, head bowed in shame, "No."

"You, Rumiñawi and I, along with reinforcements, will return to face the rebels together." Emperor Huayna Capac states. He turns to face the general. "All seriously injured men can report to the medics. All able-bodied men will fight."

"Yes, my shepherd," the general says with a nod. "As you wish."

Twenty thousand rebel warriors, in hot pursuit of Atahualpa's retreating troops, sprint toward Quito. In the distance, the rebel's General Quenti notes with alarm that Atahualpa's troops are no longer retreating; they are reversing course, accompanied by a swarm of reinforcements. The rebel general holds up his right hand to halt his troops as he grapples with the hopelessness of the situation: his confederation is outnumbered by fresh Inca troops at least two to one, no longer protected by the impenetrable walls of

Quitoloma, his rebel warriors are spent after running many miles without rest or hydration.

General Quenti attempts to mask the trembling in his voice when he turns to face his second in command, Lieutenant Unay.

"We must retreat." the general states.

"But why?" Unay asks in dismay. "We are winning. We are on the tails of the filthy Inca dogs."

"Behold!" Quenti says as he points into the distance.

Lieutenant Unay gazes at the expanse of advancing Inca troops. He smacks his forehead, mouth agape.
"

Trumpeters blow the sonorous signal for retreat; it permeates every corner of the battlefield. At first rebels leading the attack hesitate and ogle each other in bewilderment. After all, they had the wretched Incas on the run for the first time in history. Peering into the distance, they note the speedy progression of tens of thousands of imperial reinforcements, their blood curdling battle cries sending chills up their spines.

With the realization they've erred in abandoning the safety of their rebel fortress, leaving them defenseless against the retribution of a fresh, cruel and highly trained Inca regiment, the front rebel line turns to face their compatriots in arms and attempt to shout above the din of *pututus*.

"Retreat!"

Withdrawing south toward Lake Yahuarcocha and ultimately to the safety of their beloved Quitoloma fortress, the men stampede, unintentionally trampling fellow warriors, many of whom die underfoot without understanding why.

CHAPTER ELEVEN

As I hike, I don't ruminate on the purpose of my mysterious pilgrimage to Goddess Mountain Salkantay. Instead I put one foot in front of the other and think about my family, my father especially. After persistent questioning over the years, I know next to nothing about Tatáy's past. I'm not even sure where he was born. Mamáy is a different story; she was born and raised in our village of Sonqo. I also know that she was married to someone before Tatáy but I always get cold stares from both parents when I inquire further. I have a vague notion, that if I think long and hard enough, all the answers will come to me; but they never do. The fact is, *runakuna,* including myself, have little energy to spare after long draining days of farming, weaving, cooking and tending animals to ponder familial mysteries and generally fall asleep as soon as heads meet thick woolen blankets.

A cold all-encompassing fog covers my eyes and I can't even see my own sandals. A *salqa* wind whips my body like a cyclone, lifting me off my feet. Hills and ridges loom over me; when the mist lifts, I am completely lost. In a flash, Goddess Salkantay Mountain removes her coat of purple clouds revealing a brilliant pink and gold firmament. The day is still young; Inti, the Sun God dances in the perfect sky. I remove the stone condor *enqa* from my neck pouch then drop it on the ground. After it burrows into the earth, I extract coca from my pouch, crush then sprinkle the leaves on top of the little mound my stone bird makes.

"Continue to bless me on this journey, Pachamama," I pray. I gaze at Salkantay's snowy peak. "and Goddess Mountain allow me to return quickly and safely to my beloved family,."

The *enqa* shudders, kicks up dust, pushes its way out of the earth, transforms into an enormous black condor, which hops onto gigantic claws and throws off soil with a convulsive shudder. For a moment, the bird happily pecks at the coca, flutters its great wings, which stir up whirlwinds that fling my braids back, soars gracefully into the sky, circles lazily overhead, swoops into the distance, a dark fleck against the clear indigo sky. I don't know whether it will return or not but I don't feel sad: a condor catching the wind beneath its wings is good luck for hikers. The serene presence of Pachamama and the Machukuna pervades me; I am, content with the knowledge that I am not alone. After a deep breath, I continue my mission toward Goddess Mountain's snowy peak, start contemplating my family's history again, get a glimpse of the truth, which instantly melts away. I should be used to it by now, but even after many years, I'm stymied that my clan's history continues to elude me.

After a several hours, my feet ache and I get the frustrating feeling of not being any closer to Goddess Mountain's summit than I was before I started. My stomach growls; I am weak and famished. I retrieve a wad of coca from my pouch then blow over it, crumble and sprinkle it on the earth, a small libation to thank Goddess Mountain for allowing me to hike along her spine and blessing me with a perfect, cloudless day.

Inside my *k'eperina*, I spy a pouch of freshly roasted maize kernels my mother prepared for my journey. I loosen its string, take in the delicious aroma, plop down on a small trail-side boulder and pop each crunchy, salty kernel into my mouth. I could eat it all in one sitting but stop when I realize I have a long way to go and the salt is making me quite thirsty. I pull out my flask, uncork it and suck out every drop of water, confident I'll come upon a mountain water stream soon. After dust the crumbs off my tunic, I gather then knot the *k'eperina* around my shoulders—now a few ounces lighter—and hike energetically up the mountain trail, the sun warming my back. When I turn, Tatáy Inti grins at me; I say a short prayer of thanks.

Ascending ever higher, I inhale the bracing mountain air, determined to reach Salkantay peak in record time. Gradually, almost unnoticeably at first, my breathing becomes labored and shallow but I shrug it off. After a few more miles my legs feel as heavy as granite, lungs crushed. With each step, the mountain path gets steeper, narrower, rockier and muddier. Weak and dizzy, I slide and stumble, my head throbbing and my stomach churning, like waves roiling in a stormy sea.

What is the matter with me? I think in desperation.

"*Soroche,*" rumbles the voice of a giant Child of the Moon, who I imagine scrutinizing me sympathetically.

"*Soroche.*" I repeat, bleary-eyed with nausea. I hadn't thought about altitude sickness having never experienced it before.

I spew the contents of my stomach, as easily as water over a fall. I can hear Mamáy's voice in my head.

"*What a waste of good food!*" she would whine.

I heave, retch, gag over and over again. However, like a resilient *runakuna,* I continue to march up the steep mountainside though my body is no longer my own but merely a vessel emptied by the gods over again and again. Weak from dehydration, I shed my *k'eperina*, lie face down on the rocky trail, holding my pulsating head with both hands. I dig into my coca pouch, pull out a large wad of coca leaves and blow on them.

"Help me, Lord Coca." I pray between shuddering sobs, "I beseech you."

I stuff the leaves and a chunk of *llipt'a* into my mouth and chew, savoring the healing greenness seeping into my body. The babbling of a mountain stream a few feet from the trail attracts my attention. I stumble toward the sound, remove the coca wad from my mouth then thrust my face into the stream, slurping up water until I feel it sloshing inside my empty stomach. I slip the wad of coca and *llipt'a* back into my mouth and chew vigorously. The nausea subsides but my headache is unbearable, a pain I've never known. I creep over to the edge of a nearby cliff, stare into the rocky abyss below, stifling the uncanny urge to jump; how easy it would be to end my suffering here and now. But then I think about my family, who would mourn and blame themselves for the rest of their lives. I recall the horrific stories Tatáy told me about how Mistress Mountain becomes the Mountain That Eats People and for the first time, realize what he means.

So, this is how it happens. This is why people climb the mountain and never come back.

I banish thoughts of jumping by cramming more coca leaves and another chunk of *llipt'a* into the back of my jaw; I chew listlessly but it's the best I can do. I crawl back to the stream, and in desperation, stick my aching head into it, drenching my long blond braided tresses in the process. At first I feel instant relief then the head pain becomes more intense. Instead of a dull ache, it feels as though frozen needles are piercing my forehead, scalp and brain. Curiously, I witness my body from above writhing in agony, my hair wet and matted, my face covered in dirt. I look repulsive, like some sort of diseased mammal.

I remember I need to bring water, so I dig inside my *k'eperina*, retrieve my flask, uncork it, plunge it into the stream and let the water flow until it's fully distended. Exhausted by this simple but vital task, I groan, roll onto my back, take a sip, push the cork back in then close my eyes, shivering uncontrollably—soaking my hair was a big mistake but all I can do is hope it dries quickly.

I just need to rest now, I think. I

I vaguely recall the old coca leaf diviner's warning not to stop but though I try, I truly can't remember why.

"They're coming, T'ica," a *Machukuna* warns.

Though his voice is filled with a sense of urgency, I slip into a black pit of agonizing semi-consciousness too sick and exhausted to care.

CHAPTER TWELVE

1511 A.D.
Piajajalca Fortress
Chachapoyas

Exhausted, legs wobbling, head pounding from soroche, *Taquiri pulls out a flask of* chicha *from underneath his army tunic, a uniform he wears with shame, dribbles a few drops of the sweet brew on the ground as a libation to Pachamama—kind Mother Earth then takes several gulps. The alcohol warms and restores him while inducing obliviousness, so he can forget, at least temporarily why he's here.*

With a broad smile, large perfect teeth, expressive dark brown eyes and sculpted handsome face, Taquiri was born into a musical family on the outskirts of the southern province of Colla. At an early age, he and his brother built, played and traded exquisitely crafted drums and flutes, guided by their father, a master artisan and musician. Now Taquiri wields a different kind of instrument, an instrument of death: an ax. The thought sickens him. This is not who he wants to be.

"You are samiyug, *owner of liveliness and power," his father would say, acknowledging his young son's precociousness, "a genius, an ebullient spirit. Always remember that."*

"I will," the young Taquiri whispered, hugging his father's soft, warm neck, "I will never forget."

Almost as good with languages, as with music, after his capture, Taquiri was able to learn the Inca's expressive dialect, Runasimi in a few weeks, almost obliterating any memory of his own Colla native tongue. Like so many other soldiers, he tries to forget the past but nostalgia flows over him . . . until he drinks himself into a stupor.

CHAPTER THIRTEEN

"You have already given the order to take no prisoners, cut the throats of all males twelves years or older," the Emperor Huayna Capac confirms with Rumiñawi, "and dump their bodies in Lake Yahuarcocha?"

"Yes, my shepherd," the general says, his stone face void of emotion, as usual.

Emperor, prince and general are perched on remote hillside, overlooking Inca warriors massacring rebels down to the last man.

"Once again, in less than two decades," Atahualpa says, "Lake Yahuarcocha will earn its reputation as the Lake of Blood."

"And the rebel leader?" the general asks, "What should we do about him?"

"We must find this elusive man and make an example of him," Atahualpa says with scowl. "Perhaps skin him alive in the village square?"

"Have any of you seen this Chimbo Sancto?" the emperor asks.

"The rebels say he is a shape-shifter," Atahualpa says, "and impossible to capture."

"A rumor to discourage his enemies, no doubt." General Rumiñawi says, "I suggest a door to door search."

"Agreed. In the meantime, general, you muster the troops," the emperor says, "then assess casualties; we will meet you in Quito."

Leading a small herd of llamas laden with provisions, a band of guards and cooks follow Emperor Huayna Capac and Prince Atahualpa's immense litter. Upon entering a seemingly deserted village close to Lake Yahuarcocha, they notice a large community oven next to a stone hut against which an ancient woman attends her loom. Though her fingers are gnarled, she deftly weaves a colorful woolen blanket, taking little notice of the strangers.

"We are looking for Chimbo Sancto," Atahualpa says to the old crone, "The leader of the rebel confederation. Do you know where he is?"

The old woman looks up from her weaving and shrugs, infuriating the prince, who leaps off the litter and holds a sword to her neck.

"Show some respect, old woman!" Atahualpa says. "Now where is he?"

The woman's eyes seem devoid of life; her haggard face blank. She either doesn't understand what he's saying or doesn't care. The emperor addresses her in her dialect.

"How much for the fine blanket you are weaving?" Huayna Capac says diplomatically.

"It's not finished." the old woman responds tersely.

"How about a chalice of gold?" the emperor offers.

She winds bright blue yarn around a wooden spool.

"Can't eat gold," she murmurs.

A bevy of ten filthy children ranging from one to twelve and wearing rags, shyly peek out of the door of the old weaver's hut; they look thin, thirsty and famished.

"Who are they?" the emperor asks.

"My grandchildren."

"Where are their parents?" Atahualpa asks.

"Dead," the old woman says dispassionately.

The emperor surveys the desolate village.

"Where are your llamas?" the emperor asks.

"Gone." the old woman answers with a shrug, "Snatched by the rebel confederation to carry provisions then slaughtered for food."

Huayna nods at the royal cooks and servants who proceed to unburden their llamas then place the heavy sacks next to the community oven.

"Feed these people," the emperor orders. "And whoever else remains in this village."

"But," the head cook protests, "We only have enough for a handful of people. I doubt we can stretch what we have to feed this rebel village . . ."

"You are a royal cook, are you not?" the emperor interrupts, "You will pray to cook with the sacred hands of the gods; I will ensure we find the provisions you need."

"Yes, my Shepherd," the head cook says, eyes and head lowered, "of course."

Hundreds of famished villagers, mostly the elderly and mothers with their children gather for a feast that royal cooks have managed to conjure up with enough provisions fetched from nearby *tampus* to feed everyone.

After happily stuffing themselves, the emaciated villagers are encouraged to take enough food home to last for several days, which they do with gusto. Before taking their leave, each resident bows in appreciation to the Inca Sapa.

"Thank you, Shepherd of the Sun, Son of the Sun God," each recites in a high sing song voice, "Champion of the Poor, my heart, my dove."

The elderly weaver orders her grandchildren to help gather up bundles of food. Even the youngest aren't shy about heaping piles of food upon blankets then hauling them inside their hut. After all leftovers are stowed away, the grandmother works on her colorful blanket, takes if off the loom, ties the last knot and offers it to the emperor by thrusting it in his direction.

"A gift," she insists, "for you, my Shepherd."

Though he has no need of this item, the emperor accepts it, careful not insult the old crone's offer of reciprocity, so important to the dignity of the mountain people who will rarely accept a favor without offering something in return.

"Thank you, my dove," the emperor says, "I will treasure it always."

He hands the blanket to one of his guards, who folds it carefully and stuffs it into a sack tied across the back of a llama. The old lady nods in satisfaction, stands, then looks down a dusty village path; she points a gnarled finger at the last tiny stone house at the perimeter of the town.

"Chimbo Sancto," the old lady croaks, her formerly dull, lifeless dark eyes now gleaming.

When Atahualpa enters the hut, the only thing he finds is a mound of old blankets. The prince removes them one by one. At the bottom, he uncovers a sleepy-eyed dwarf.

"Who has uncovered me?" the little man fumes. "I wanted to sleep!"

"What is your name, dwarf?" Atahualpa asks.

The halfling rubs his light brown eyes petulantly.

"Chimbo Sancto," he says.

"Chimbo Sancto?" the prince asks incredulously, "Leader of the recently defeated Caranqui-Cayambe-Pasto Confederation?"

"Yes." Chimbo replies with a shrug. "What of it?"

The emperor limps in, rubbing his aching right leg, which is acting up again.

"Who is this?" Emperor Huayna Capac asks.

"This, Father," Atahualpa answers, his mouth pulled down into a frown, "is Chimbo Sancto."

"But," the emperor says with a bemused grin, as he limps forward for a closer look. "he's a dwarf."

Chimbo scrutinizes the emperor then grunting with effort, stands, removes his knit cap and combs his stubby fingers through a shock of thick black hair.

"Excellent powers of observation," Chimbo replies sardonically, as he dusts off his tunic, "for an old cripple."

"You will address my father," Atahualpa hisses, brandishing his sword, "as Inca Sapa, Lord Shepherd of the Inca Empire. Or you will pay for your lack of respect with your life."

"I suspect I will pay with my life regardless of what I do or say now," Chimbo says, drawing a squat forefinger across his neck. "like the rest of my compatriots whose throats you cut then threw in Lake Yahuarcocha. Might as well get it over with right now. Isn't that right Inca Sapa, Lord Shepherd of the Inca Empire?" he says with a deep bow. He steps closer to Atahualpa's sword, pulls down the collar of his filthy tunic, stretches out his stocky neck, puts his hands behind his back then closes his eyes tightly. "Go ahead. I'm ready."

"As you wish, dwarf," Atahualpa growls. The prince steadies himself, pulls his sword back aiming for a quick, clean beheading.

"Stop!" The emperor cries.

When the dwarf opens his eyes, he glares at the emperor then stomps his square feet.

"Don't tell me you're planning to torture me first?" Chimbo inquires with a frown, "Because if that's the case, I'll need some time to prepare myself."

The emperor sputters in consternation, chuckles, slaps his thigh then laughs maniacally at the impertinence of the squat little man and former leader of the rebel confederation.

Chimbo Sancto rides on the canopied multi-person litter, perched alongside Prince Atahualpa who attempts to sit as far away from the little man as possible; the litter carriers struggle with the conveyance's uneven distribution of weight. Chimbo notices this with glee. Though his hands are tied in front, he manages to pat the empty space beside him.

"Dwarfism is not contagious, Prince Atahualpa," Chimbo teases. "At least, I don't think it is."

"If this litter spills us," the emperor warns Atahualpa, "you will only have yourself to blame, my son."

An impatient scowl darkening his handsome face, the prince scoots closer to the center of the bench; the emperor sits on the opposite bench, facing his son and the dwarf. Ten litter carriers breathe collective sighs of relief as they shoulder the now level conveyance through the center of the little village. Curious villagers poke their heads out of crude huts to gaze upon the unusual sight, including children who titter with delight as they wave at their charismatic rebel leader. Chimbo lifts his tied hands and gives them a clumsy wave back. The entourage doesn't stop, instead heads directly toward the outskirts of the village then north to Quito.

"What will happen to them now?" Chimbo asks.

"What do you mean?" the emperor asks.

"Will surviving villagers be penalized for their treachery against the empire?" Chimbo asks. "Will you massacre them outright? Or will you simply salt their soil and slowly starve them to death as most Inca emperors are wont to do?"

"The villagers have been punished enough for right now," the emperor says. "that is why I fed them. But soon I will send envoys to . . . "

" . . . select candidates to become Daughters of the Sun?" Chimbo asks, trying unsuccessfully not to roll his eyes in disgust.

"*Capacocha* is one of our most sacred religious rituals, Lord Sancto," the emperor explains.

"We must placate the gods." Atahualpa asserts, "Lest they incur famine, floods, wars or even worse upon the empire."

Chimbo shrugs then surveys the passing scenery as do the prince and emperor. After a few minutes, the dwarf surreptitiously regards the emperor and the prince, resisting the urge to inform them how much resentment they stir up with their habit of kidnapping young children from provinces to indoctrinate them with the tenets of the Inca religion and ultimately sacrificing to them to their Inca gods. *What idiots they are to believe in such barbaric nonsense to begin with,* he muses. He decides the wisest course of action right now is to hold his tongue—an arduous task for the normally opinionated and loquacious dwarf. He doesn't know exactly what fate awaits him in Quito but he is cunning enough to know that, in the past, by using his wits alone, he was able to achieve what most men twice his stature could not dream of. He cringes at the fatal mistake of ordering his rebel warriors to give chase to the retreating Incas and daydreams about what life would be like if the confederation had stayed in the safety of their impenetrable fortress instead. Finally, he falls asleep, slack-jawed, snoring like a snarling puma as he leans against Atahualpa.

Not only is the prince greatly irritated by the presence of Chimbo Sancto on the royal litter (*a captured rebel leader should be shackled and walking behind us with soldiers kicking and punching him senseless,* Atahualpa ponders darkly) and his obnoxious snoring, he's also dismayed to notice that his father's brown eyes are gleaming adoringly in Chimbo's direction, as if he's just discovered a long lost son. For some inexplicable reason, the emperor has rapidly grown quite fond of the diminutive rebel leader; Atahualpa wonders what his father plans to do with the vile little creature once they reach Quito.

Chimbo Sancto is, after all, the former leader of the fierce though now thoroughly vanquished Caranqui-Cayambe-Pasto Confederation; Atahualpa thinks about the thousands of Inca warriors killed under the dwarf's leadership, his heart filled with loathing. He would take great pleasure in strangling the mouthy halfling in retribution here and now but has no desire to incur the emperor's wrath who expects unquestioning obedience, no matter the circumstance. The exhausted prince closes his drooping eyelids, and despite the dwarf's snores, is lulled to sleep by the pure high mountain air and gentle sway of the litter.

CHAPTER FOURTEEN

Eyes glowing like liquid gold in the late afternoon sun, a puma and her two young cubs pad down the Salkantay trail. Holding my breath, I step off the trail hoping they won't notice me. But the she-puma stops in her tracks, stares at me, bares her fangs and opens her mouth into a nerve-racking screech. I tremble uncontrollably; my feet feel as though planted in the soil, throat parched. Imagining the agony of the feline's drooling fangs ripping through my neck, before feeding on my internal organs, I decide to back away even farther from the trail, hoping she will realize I mean her and her kittens no harm. Slowly creeping toward me, head low, thigh muscles quivering, saliva oozing from her mouth in long wet strings, the puma is hungry and ready to pounce.

Though a deadly predator, I remind myself that the puma is a symbol of nature's all encompassing strength and power.

"Goddess Puma, you are a loving and patient teacher and caregiver to your young." I whisper in a low voice. I slowly slide the sling off my forehead, withdraw a stone from my tunic pocket, place it in the simple but deadly weapon and pray that the powerful feline will back down before I'm forced to defend myself. "I do not wish you or your cubs harm. I beseech you to let me be on my way."

The feline responds to my desperate plea with another high-pitched screech; my blood runs cold. I raise the sling overhead and twirl it, hoping the whirring will scare her off. Tears run down my cheeks thinking about her cubs' bleak future if I'm forced to kill their mother who is, after all, only following her instincts to protect and feed them. I stare directly into the brilliant eyes of Goddess Puma; I feel her courage and charisma. My heart is breaking at what the gods of nature are forcing me to do. I don't want to destroy the puma family, but I have my family, too.

Goddess Puma, just go, just run, I think, hoping she will pick up on my mental intention like the Machukuna often do.

Snarling and hissing, muscles tense, she pads another step in my direction.

"Pachamama," I murmur to the Earth Goddess, "I beseech your intervention now."

Goddess Puma snarls; my heart pounds out of my chest. I aim, intending to release the deadly projectile so that it hits the creature right between her glistening eyes . . . but the feline cocks her head as if perceiving a sound only she can hear, leaps gracefully into the sparse mountain brush, cubs scurrying close behind her. Within seconds, the clutter of pumas disappears into the thorny wilderness. I release the stone harmlessly into the perfect blue sky.

Overwhelmed by an enormous sense of relief and gratitude, I collapse onto my knees. The gods have seen fit to spare me—a simple *runakuna*; just as important, Goddess Puma and her cubs will live to hunt in the physical world of *kay pacha* another day.

"Thank you, Pachamama. Thank you, Sacred Places and Mistress Mountain." I pray. "Goddess Puma: may your power and courage keep you and your cubs from harm."

The *tampu,* a one room stone inn built and maintained by the Inca Empire, is nestled in a lush high mountain meadow perfect for grazing llamas and alpacas with a stream nearby. In addition, another smaller stone building sits adjacent to the little hut, probably filled with provisions: grains, jerky, clothes and perhaps weapons. The Inca Empire strictly forbids the use of *tampus* by anyone except royalty or warriors. I survey my surroundings for any sign of people or animals. With nothing in sight, I decide to pull the door open and peek inside; it's tidy with everything a weary traveler could want: a small earthen fireplace stove tucked in a corner and a straw bed covered by coarse wool blankets—a luxury for a simple *runakuna* like myself, accustomed to sleeping on blankets spread over cold unyielding floors.

Outside crisp branches and tree limbs lay scattered in small piles. I say a quick prayer of thanks to Pachamama and Goddess Mountain, bring bundles of crisp wood inside, arrange them in the fireplace, find a stone flint on a small shelf, strike it and light the fire on the third try. Outside the evening chill is taking hold so I sit cross-legged in front of the blaze, warming my hands and snacking absentmindedly on leftover roasted maize. After a few bites, I start to wonder why the Incas built this structure in such a remote area; *tampus* are generally built along main thoroughfares frequented by warriors to quell rebellions or used by *quipumayocs*—Inca tax collectors and bureaucrats who often meet with tribal leaders to negotiate trade agreements. The few people who live at this altitude are hidden away in tiny dwellings not yet discovered by the Inca Empire; most are poor subsistence herders or farmers, barely able to support their own families, much less pay tribute to the Incas.

I step outside to find that nighttime has arrived, bringing with it severe cold. Mama Quilla, Goddess of the Moon shines brightly in the cloudless sky. With a shiver, I go back inside to pay homage to her. After stoking the fire, I stare into the brilliant flame.

"Mama Quilla, blessed Goddess of the Moon," I pray, "I beseech your blessing for health, prosperity and a successful journey." I toss a few crumbled coca leaves into the fire and watch for Mama Quilla's answer. Flames pop and spark—an affirmative response. I smile, say a short silent prayer of thanks then nestle into the straw bed.

I'm getting closer to Goddess Mountain's glorious snowy peak, I muse before I fade into a deep slumber.

At dawn, I load my humble belongings into my *k'eperina* which I tie across my back and shoulders and knot below my neck. When I step outside, Father Sun smiles upon me as I catch the first rays of morning sun which hold the Moon Goddess's blessing for health and prosperity. I inhale deeply.

"Inti Tatáy" I pray, "Mama Quilla, I thank you for your blessings."

As the trail gets steeper and higher and zigzags through rocky terrain, Lord Wind blows in snow and icy cold temperatures that freeze my fingers, toes and nose. Despite this, I remain energetic and need little nourishment: just water and coca activated with a little *llipt'a.*

Soroche—high altitude sickness no longer has a hold on me, a change in circumstance for which I'm eternally grateful. After hiking endlessly up the steep switchback trails, I'm rewarded with the praying hands of Goddess Salkantay—gargantuan boulders that seem to reach to the sky to worship the creator god, Viracocha. Stumbling west over smooth rounded stones, I arrive at the shimmering turquoise Humantay Lagoon and gaze at the impossibly steep snow and glacier-covered Salkantay Mountain peak to my right. Surely the Machukuna didn't intend for me to ascend this perilous slope.

"Why am I here?" I yell across the lagoon, but the only

response is my own echo. "Mama Quilla, Machukuna! Please answer me!" I dig into my pouch and retrieve a few coca leaves from my dwindling supply nevertheless determined to make a libation to the gods. "Goddess Mountain, I have traveled far to this sacred place," I pray aloud, "and I hope that my journey has been pleasing to you. Children of the Moon, I beseech your wisdom. Why have you sent me on a mission so vital that its success could greatly affect my family and friends? Being a simple *runakuna,* I do not understand what I'm supposed to do now. I implore you to show me a sign—any sign—so that I may know the reason for my journey."

I blow over the coca leaves, then crumble them over the rocky ground; I will probably need the energy and warmth they provide to return safely to my village but brush off my concerns and trust the gods will somehow sustain me. Still I worry that I'll never see my parents and baby brother again. The thought of it crushes me as I survey the stunning but lonely high mountain landscape. I begin to believe that this quest was merely a trick played upon me by the Machukuna, remembering what my father said, *"Don't trust the Machukuna. They are jealous of us."* My chest heaving, my breathing shallow in the thin air, I'm appalled by my naivete.

Thick snowflakes float down from the heavens. I must seek shelter immediately until I can resolve my predicament. I peruse my surroundings and notice what looks like a cave set upon the top of a moderate incline. Though the climb may be difficult, ascension is far from impossible.

I place my right foot on the slope, then my left, struggling to keep my balance. I almost reach the apex but slip on the freshly fallen snow and slide to the bottom, scratching my chin on the way down. Knees shaking, legs rubbery, I rest for a moment, retrieve my flask, uncork it, squirt water into my mouth, stand and try again. I scrabble up the snowy, rocky surface and reach the top, gasping for breath in the thin air.

What I originally thought was a natural cave is a windowless man-made hut constructed of small to medium size rocks and boulders. I notice a narrow wooden door, pull it open, step inside then pull it closed behind me. The ceiling is so low, I'm forced to stoop but grateful that the farther I step into the hut, the warmer it becomes. I pick a cozy place farthest from the door, sit cross-legged, remove my *k'eperina,* spread it out and review its contents; there is more than ample food to keep me alive for several days. With my headache and queasiness gone, I realize just how famished I am. I gobble down the delicious food Mamáy cooked and wrapped in layers of corn husks: dried *cuy*—roasted guinea pig, tasty potato cakes, quinoa bread, dried sweet *uvilla* and *ayrampu* for dessert. As I chew, I lean onto the far wall, burp loudly and joyously, cover my knees with my tunic and wrap my *k'eperina* around my shoulders. Unlike the *tampu* I stayed in last night, there is no stove, no straw bed, no wood or kindling. But my stomach is full and I feel confident that I can survive here for at least one night. Upon hearing water trickling from a location deep inside the mountain, I inspect the hut and discover a flat piece of stone set against a wall. When I remove the stone, I find a hole which seems to descend into the bowels of Goddess Mountain. I stick my head in the opening, squinting into the shadows.

Maybe I will find a treasure, I think optimistically. *Perhaps some gold or silver?*

I have heard rumors of simple *runakuna* discovering fine gold or silver jewelry or artworks that they can trade for food, clothing, housing; some are so fortunate, they never have to work again, though I've never personally met these lucky people. I wriggle into the hole and find a tunnel big enough for an adult to crawl through;

it's long, winding and dark. After creeping fearlessly through the pitch-black, my efforts are quickly rewarded with what looks like a light at the end of the tunnel, so I keep moving. Finally, I bump into a wooden door then push it wide open.

A shaft of light pours through a hole in the ceiling illuminating a beautiful girl no more than fifteen years old; her legs are bent to her chest, her raven hair carefully fashioned into hundreds of thin braids, her tunic woven of fine vicuña wool—normally worn exclusively by royalty. A much younger boy and girl, perhaps five or six years old hold hands next to the older girl, dressed in colorful luxury textiles and strewn with now wilted flower petals— like royalty on their wedding day.

"Hello?" I say but they do not stir or respond.

I slide toward the older girl, hoping she's just sleeping. When I touch her cheek, I pull back my hand in horror; her skin is ice cold. After examining her lifeless body, I quickly discover that the back of her head is covered in dried blood.

I pant uncontrollably, everything goes white. I sit cross-legged, cover my face in an attempt to gather myself and force myself to breathe deeply and slowly, like Mamáy taught me. I miss my sweet mother so much now, my heart feels like it's breaking into a million pieces of crushed *ch'uño*—freeze-dried potatoes. I gather the courage to scrutinize the young girl and boy and realize they are younger than I originally surmised. Just toddlers, their skulls are bashed in, obviously murdered by the hands of a skilled executioner. I feel the blood drain out of my head; the Room of Death takes on an ominous glow and my ears fill with a loud buzzing.

I scrabble out of the room, into the tunnel and crawl as fast as I can. In my haste, I smack my head on the low ceiling and scratch my knees on the uneven stone floor. The tunnel now seems to have transformed into an endless maze until I reach the narrow hole that leads to the outer hut; I wriggle through, scramble to my feet then crack my head on the low ceiling, almost knocking myself senseless. Screaming in frustration, I grab my injured skull, stoop over like a bent and battered twig, limp to the door, bolt outside and retch until I cough up blood.

So, this abomination is what I was supposed to find? I think indignantly, hot tears streaming down my cheeks. *Children who have already been dead for weeks if not longer? Explain yourself, Machukuna. Why is this happening? Why did you send me here?*

Once again, the Children of the Moon remain mute. My stomach is sore and void from retching; I feel an emptiness I never felt before along with anger, sadness, loss, disgust, disappointment and so much more impossible to define. I find myself shivering from head to toe in the frigid mountain air, so I duck back into the stone hovel and slam the door shut. I consider my situation for a moment then decide I have no choice but to return to the dreaded Room of Death before I freeze to death. I have to buy some time to figure out what, if anything, this all this means.

I squeeze through the portal, crawl through the tunnel praying that what I saw was some kind of horrible hallucination. But when I push open the little door leading to the inner sacrificial sanctum, the children are still there, silent and lifeless. I gaze at a hole in the ceiling, the room's only source of light and ventilation. I stuff it with a thick blanket borrowed from the older dead girl. In a few minutes, the now pitch black Room of Death starts to warm. I lie as far away from the corpses as possible. Though exhausted, it takes a long while before I'm able to fall asleep; when I do, I dream about playing with my baby brother and though I know it's only a sweet illusion, I pray with all my heart to never wake.

CHAPTER FIFTEEN

2011 A.D.
Piajajalca Fortress
Chachapoyas

Taquiri pours chicha *from his leather flask down his unquenchable throat. Despite his drunken attempts to forget, he still thinks about his beautiful young wife, Kusi-quyllur, a joyful star brought to him from the heavens. He can see her long straight raven hair, parted in the middle and floating down her back like the finest threads of combed* vicuña *wool. Her exquisite full-lipped smile, pearly teeth, sultry voice and buttery soft dark skin instantly melted away his worst days.*

"Makiy kiwah," Kusi-quyllur would pray to the female weaver goddesses—the awaq machas—*as she offered coca leaves and sprinkled* chicha *on the ground. "Purest goddesses, let me weave with your hands." She had been famous in their little village for weaving some of the finest textiles ever created. She knew all the classic designs and took great pride in weaving breathtaking variations, incorporating golden butterflies, cobalt blue birds, snarling pumas and kohl black jaguars. She gathered insects, flowers, herbs and plants that would make the most colorful dyes. When she'd built her own adobe stove, she prayed again, to the house spirits, "Purest goddesses, let me cook with your hands."*

Then she'd given him his perfect son and named him Kusiñawai, an appropriate sobriquet because it meant "bright eyes."

No, I won't contemplate that day, *Taquiri muses, scooping up countless cups of* chicha *from the warriors communal jugs,* I will wash away the memory forever.

At first, chicha *does its job of dimming the memory of his beloved wife and child, until barely able to recall their images, as fragile as a reflection in a pool of water. But after his tenth cup, memories swoop over him like a tidal wave.*

A few years ago, when the Inca army assigned his regiment to the capital city of Cuzco, he thought he saw his wife and son walking down its cobbled streets. He managed to run past other soldiers and catch up with them. When the woman turned around and smiled, her teeth were missing and the little boy had fleas. His boy never had fleas; his wife regularly applied anti-flea concoctions she crafted after gathering herbs from mountainsides surrounding their small village.

"I'm sorry," he said, choking back tears, as the puzzled woman and her flea-bitten child eyed him warily. "My mistake. So sorry."

His family and his life were gone now. Everything was gone. An Inca raid swooped into his peaceful village, striking down everyone and everything in site. He'd told his wife and child to run, buying some time to escape by throwing a bale of burning straw at the attackers.

"May the souls of the Incas wander in ice and snow for all eternity," he yelled. His wife and son had vanished beyond the smoke but he could hear Kusi-quyllur's voice.

"Run, songó, my heart," *she called.* "I will love you always, my husband, sonqolláy, my own heart."

As Taquiri turned to escape, an Inca warrior struck him on the back of his head with the flat of a palm-wood halberd, knocking him unconscious. Days later or maybe it was just a few hours later, he didn't know, he awoke in a Cuzco prison, his head throbbing.

Sadistic Inca captains forced him into soldier training, punching, kicking, goading, and starving him until he could run, wield a sword and chop off the heads of sacrificial llamas or condemned men in one swoop.

He learned to devise star-shaped maces and fire-harden tips of palm wood swords. While other weapon-makers struggled to refine their craft, Taquiri fashioned his weapons as easily as he'd created his beloved musical instruments. He often thought about resisting his Inca captors but those who refused to cooperate were punished severely: guards hung reluctant soldiers by their ankles in the town square as passersby spit, beat, kicked and cursed them for being cowards. Soon, ravenous condors would swoop down, plucking out eyeballs, tearing out tongues and pecking away at rotting flesh until there was nothing left but bone.

There was a rumor that during the raid upon his hometown, the Incas beheaded the highly esteemed Colla leader, Chuchi Capac then burned his head at the Temple of the Sun. Though death by fire nullifies any chance of ascending to the heavenly realm of hanan pacha, *at least his death had been swift or so he hoped.*

Taquiri also heard that Inca soldiers had taken considerable delight in stripping the rest of the Colla leaders and throwing them into a samca hausi, *a dungeon filled with ravenous jaguars, deadly serpents and poisonous toads.*

He sharpens his ax blade with an adamantite stone and ponders the question sweeping over and over in his mind: Is it better to kill innocent men, women and children or is it better to be killed?

CHAPTER SIXTEEN

Tens of thousands of Quiteños greet the royal entourage with a victory celebration, reminiscent of so many festivities of the past with raucous music, singing, dancing, food and *chicha*. When the litter reaches Quito's center square, even more revelers, most of them drunk, join the fray; they stare at Chimbo Sancto with murder in their eyes. They heard the rebel leader was a dwarf—a *dwarf*—but few believed it until they saw the little prisoner for themselves riding astride the royal litter, hands bound.

A bold Quiteño digs out a gargantuan rotten tomato from a dirty burlap sack, takes aim and hits the little man square in the face, leaving a deep red splatter that covers him head to toe. Chimbo blinks, nods and, with whatever little dignity he has left, attempts to wipe the odious mess off his face, his hands still tied.

"This is just the beginning of your suffering, dwarf," Atahualpa says with an evil chuckle.

Before revelers have a chance to pummel the dwarf again, the emperor stands and raises his arms to quiet the increasingly unruly crowd.

"Citizens of the Inca Empire: hostilities between our people and the former Caranqui-Cayambe-Pasto Confederation are over. Therefore, I, emperor of the Inca Empire and Shepherd of the Sun, declare from this point forward, that this man," he says, indicating Chimbo with a dramatic sweep of his hands, "former leader of the rebel confederation be treated like my eldest son." the royal pronounces, "And because his warriors fought and died bravely, I pronounce Chimbo Sancto, an *Inca of the Heart.*"

The Quiteños mouths drop open; the shocked citizens murmur and gaze at each other in astonishment. Did they understand what the emperor just said correctly? Generally, residents, even little children, are given the honor of torturing rebel leaders for days and weeks on end in the town square, a source of gruesome amusement as well as an escape from the day-to-day rigors of their difficult lives.

With some effort, Chimbo Sancto stands on the litter's bench He takes his time to rotate his head and squint at the crowd, letting the late afternoon sun wash over his stubby rotten-tomato-juice-covered body. A grizzled old woman with furrows on her face deep enough to sow seed in, throws another tomato but this time, the little man ducks and it misses him altogether. His hands still tied, he does a back flip over Prince Atahualpa then takes a deep bow. At first the confused crowd applauds lightly then when he flips again, they erupt in loud cheers. The emperor looks on in amused satisfaction. Atahualpa scowls.

"Is it your intention, Father, to retain this hideous clown solely for our people's amusement?" the prince asks with a scowl.

The emperor smiles broadly.

"He is quite amusing, isn't he?" the older royal says.

The half man flashes an impish smile, large teeth gleaming in contrast with the tomato splatter, charming dimples digging deep into his cheeks. The crowd stares at him as if under a spell. Ogling the emperor who seems just as spellbound as the revelers, the dwarf cocks his head, lifts his tied hands, a questioning look on his large face. The emperor finishes off a gold and silver goblet of *chicha,* then catches a nearby guard's eye.

"Untie this man," he orders.

After a guard cuts his ropes, Chimbo rubs his chafed wrists for a moment until a servant hands him a large goblet of *chicha*. He gulps it down, grabs another cup, gulps it down, too. Thirst quenched for the time being, he does another back flip and the crowd roars.

"Let the festivities continue!" the little man croaks. waving his stubby arms.

Instantly, musicians take up their instruments, singers chant and dancers of all ages sway, twirl and gyrate.

His jaw set tight, Atahualpa glowers at the instantly popular dwarf; he dreams of flaying the half man alive, skewering him over an open fire and feasting on his roasted flesh but then decides that might not be such a good idea. What if consuming the flesh of dwarfs could cause his own offspring to be cursed with a similar affliction? No, he would just flay the little man alive then throw him into the Dungeon of Horrors.

Chimbo awakes naked under a cloud of vicuña blankets in the warmth of a royal bedroom but can't fully recall what happened the night before. He gingerly touches bandages wrapped tightly around his aching head and sniffs the strong scent of a medicinal ointment. When a vague memory of a humiliating tumble off the litter returns, he realizes that becoming impaired to the extent of losing control of his faculties was probably not in his best interests. He knows the Inca emperor is a fickle man and the novelty of having a dwarf for an "honorary eldest son" may very well wear off sooner than later. And who knows? The Inca may already regret having declared the former rebel leader an "Inca of the Heart." Chimbo also knows that if it was up to Prince Atahualpa, he would already be a dead man or worse, tied upside down in the square and exposed to days or even weeks of agonizing torture.

Sobriety is the only way to keep my wits about me for every moment living under Inca control is, in fact, a dangerous one, he muses.

He notices fresh clothes neatly folded on a low table, slides off his bed and trots barefoot across the stone floor. He scrutinizes the attire woven of silky bright blue fabric, probably vicuña generally reserved for royalty. Surprisingly, the new tunic and llama leather sandals fit him like a glove.

Probably originally made for a stocky royal child, he thinks with a chuckle.

He carefully removes the bandages wrapped around his head (*no sense reminding everybody of last night's drunken disaster,* he ponders as his face flushes with embarrassment), splashes water onto his wide face from a large silver basin and grooms his tangle of black hair with a pristine bristle brush, careful to avoid the area around his injured scalp. He smiles at his handsome reflection in a highly polished silver disc hanging on the wall above the basin, smooths his new tunic and walks out the door and into an immense stone corridor in what he presumes is located in the royal Quito palace. As he steps down the hall, his stomach growls; he wonders when and where meals are served and whether, depending on the Inca's mood, if he'll be allowed to eat breakfast at all, and if so, if it will end up being the last meal of his life.

CHAPTER SEVENTEEN

Upon awakening, the putrid scent of the dead children's bodies defrosting and decaying overwhelms me. I blindly reach toward the ceiling, find the thick blanket plugging the hole and pull it out. A beam of light instantly illuminates the room; I inhale deeply and the rush of fresh freezing cold air rouses my spirits.

"I will leave you now, my little doves," I say to the lifeless waifs, whose spirits I am certain are looking down upon me from the glory of *hanan pacha,* the heavenly realm. "but I will return soon."

After crawling through the long, winding tunnel, I wriggle through the opening into the stone hut, keep my head ducked down this time, open the door and step outside.

The entirety of the mountain landscape seems to have been sanctified by new snow; even the stone hut glimmers silvery in the afternoon sun. The warmth of Lord Inti shines down upon me.

"Thank you, Inti Tatáy," I say.

Clumps of gray clouds gather overhead and Lord Wind begins to blow; no surprise since mountain weather is often unpredictable. But then, I perceive something strange; I'm sure I hear the murmur of human voices. I survey my surroundings but see nothing. I tread on the silvery white carpet, taking special heed not to slip on the slick snow-covered stones. Upon reaching a large boulder overlooking the mountain trail, I peer around it. In the distance, I detect two adults and two children accompanied by a pair of heavily burdened llamas slowly trudging up the trail through the freshly fallen snow. They are too far away to discern who they might be but they are definitely there.

I listen to the men speak to each other in a language I don't understand. My tribe speaks *Runasimi*, the language of *runakuna*, but my father told me Inca royals speak a different language, *Incasimi*, though also versed in *Runasimi*. Educated often royals speak several tribal languages, especially the *quipumayocs*—Inca accountants who usually toil as tax collectors, forcing poor subjugated tribes to give up a large percentage of their home grown or handmade products for the good of the empire: fruits, vegetables, grains, salt, dried meat and fish, woven and leather goods and whatever else the greedy elites of the Inca government deem valuable. Tax resisters are punished severely: murdered, villages burned down to the ground and land salted to send a message to others.

As the little group draws near, Inti shines his golden light on the two children who stop to rest on a boulder; they're wearing colorful cloaks like royalty would wear. One man wears a bright blue and golden head band with brilliant yellow feathers in front. The other man doesn't wear as much jewelry and appears to be in charge of the llamas. I think of the three murdered children dressed like royals inside the Cave of Death and abruptly realize what I'm witnessing. My breath grows shallow and I begin to tremble as I recall the ominous words of the Machukuna which reverberate in my head.

They're coming. They're coming. They're coming.

So this is why I was sent to Mistress Mountain; it was not a wasted trip. I don't know how to feel now; a mixture of elation and fear grip me. I prepare my sling as the group continues to trudge up Goddess Mountain's spine and onto the stony outcrop looming next to the Humantay Lagoon. To steady my nerves, I pull out several coca leaves and a piece of *llipt'a* from my waist pouch, stuff them in my mouth and chew vigorously.

Warm me and give me courage, Father Coca. Bless your humble daughter with true aim.

The feathered priest shoves the children ahead; they traipse slowly toward the outcrop overlooking the lagoon.

Save the children, the low voice of a Machukuna whispers in my ear.

I pull a stone from my pocket, load it in my sling and wait for a clean shot.

One of the children turns, sprints past the priests over slippery, snow-covered rocks toward the downward trail.

Run, little one! Run! I scream inside my head; outwardly, I remain resolute and calm.

The man whom I assume is the lower priest who doubles as a llama herder curses and struggles to tie the llamas to a thin vertical rock. The feathered priest screams something at the lower priest, who pulls off his cloak, throws it on the ground, and stumbles over slick stones, nearly falling and cursing in *Incasimi*. In contrast, the young escapee leaps down the mountainside, soaring over rocks and snow with the grace of Goddess Puma, her cumbersome hooded cloak still draped over head and shoulders. When far enough ahead, she stops, turns and yells something, perhaps to the other child. It's a language that I don't understand and completely different from *Incasimi* and *Runasimi*. She finally pulls back her hood: her hair is tied in hundreds of long braids the color of summer corn, like mine.

So, there are others like me, I muse, my stomach fluttering in excitement.

While the lower priest continues to give chase, the other Inca priest and child arrive at the outcrop with one of the llamas in tow. Mumbling to himself, he digs into the beast's pack, removes a bulging flask, uncorks it, and, holding the child's head back, squirts a stream of purple liquid inside her gaping mouth. Her hood falls off revealing the same golden locks as her escaped companion. The girl chokes, shudders, shakes her head and sinks to her knees, swaying as if drunk, drugged, or perhaps both. The high priest extracts an ornate bronze and golden ax from a leather sheaf hung around his waist.

"*Apu Salkantay,* Goddess Mountain, the Inca Sapa offers you, the purest of beings, an untouched Daughter of the Sun!" he prays, eyes rolled back in his head, body quivering. The young girl pitches side to side, struggling to keep her body upright. My father once told me that Daughters of the Sun are indoctrinated to passively accept their fate but the addition of strong alcohol and drugs ensures their utter submissiveness.

"Thank you, Father Coca," I whisper, "for returning enough warmth to my body so that my aim may be true."

I whirl my sling overhead.

"*Apu* Salkantay,*"* the high priest continues, "I . . ."

He stops, distracted by my sling's whirring, lowers his ax, rotates his head, searching for the source of the unnerving sound then stares right at me; this will be a perfect shot. I let the projectile fly; it smacks him right between the eyes. He drops his ax, keels over then careens over the outcrop; I watch with elation as his body splashes into the lagoon. The little Daughter of the Sun drops to her side; I hope she's still alive. The lower priest witnesses what I've done then abandoning his attempt to recover the runaway, sprints toward me. Once again, I load my sling, whirl it overhead, then let it fly. He ducks; I miss his head by mere few inches.

"*Epunaman*, God of War," I pray, "Allow me to fight with your hands."

I load my weapon again, whir it overhead and correct my aim to compensate for the priest's evasive attempts. When I release my projectile, he ducks, as anticipated but the stone grazes his temple, not a perfect shot but not a total miss either. He seems dazed as he touches his bloodied head, licks the blood from his fingers, wields his ax then emits a blood-curdling scream which sends chills up and down my spine. He sprints uphill, his powerful thighs churning. Though close royal relatives are often chosen to be priest, many are selected because of their warrior skills; he must be one of them. When I dig into my tunic, my heart sinks; I have no more projectiles to load into my weapon; since the ground is covered in a blanket of snow, there is little chance I will find any.

"*Apu* Salkantay, Goddess Mountain," I pray, "I beseech you to . . ."

Before I can finish my desperate plea, dozens of translucent colored spheres float lazily in the clear blue sky. Goddess Mountain groans and the stony ground rolls under my feet. I'm startled by a deafening cracking sound; a snow-covered boulder the size of my family's hut dislodges from the mountain peak and plummets toward the priest. He dodges it easily. Mistress Mountain spits out yet another boulder, I dodge it, it tumbles then splashes into the lagoon. The priest leers at me but continues his vengeful ascent.

Humantay Lagoon churns as if boiling; a creature soars from its depths and flies into the heavens, shining like a morning star. The lower priest stops in his tracks and stares at the vision in disbelief.

"Amaru, Son of Goddess Mountain," I murmur. Though never a witness to any Amaru sightings himself, my father says that *runakuna* who make mountain pilgrimages often tell tales of frightening encounters with the powerful winged serpent with a llama head, fish tail and crystalline eyes. Most villagers ridicule those who claim to have seen Amaru, calling them drunk or crazy. But Tatáy says that there are too many stories from reliable sources to discount the legend altogether.

The creature opens his great red muzzle, covers the mountainside with a dense fog; rain falls from his feathered wings and giant balls of hail from his fish-like tail. The fog gives me a chance to run and hide. I take shelter inside the stone hut, crawl through the hole leading into the tunnel. As I creep, my frozen, bruised and bloodied feet, knees and hands, bash once again against the rough stone floor. I push open the Room of Death door, scrabble inside and search for anything that could be used as a projectile. Next to the dead children, I discover three small silver llama bells piled alongside other toys left behind with the murdered children: three colorful woven dolls and three colorful pieces of pottery—just like the ones I saw in my dreams. I shove the silver bells into my tunic, smash a piece of pottery on the floor, gather up its shards and shove them into my pocket.

I drag myself through the tunnel again, squirm through the opening into the hut then race outside. Through the fog, I see the man sprinting toward me; I load a llama bell into my slingshot and twirl it overhead with no time to say even a short prayer then fire it off; it dings as it smashes into the priest's right eye. He collapses backward, screeching and holding the bloody mess where there was once an eyeball.

A strange hiss emanates from the fog; Amaru's crystalline eyes appear in the gloom, gleaming and horrifying. The god-beast scoops up the man with its giant muzzle, soars into the sky, scales glittering in the sunlight. Amaru flips his fish tail, reverses course then heads toward the Humantay Lagoon. With a final roar and a whip of his tail, the god-creature dives into the lagoon and disappears; for a moment, all is eerily calm. Soon the lagoon bubbles then surges, the priest thrashes atop its whirlpool, gasping, spitting, screaming and flailing. The water recedes, dragging the man into a giant foaming vortex which drains into an abyss. What little water is left evaporates into a fog as Goddess Mountain yawns then shakes off a half dozen boulders from her rocky shoulders.

"Thank you, Lord Amaru," I mumble with a shudder never imagining I would ever witness something like this.

I climb down the slope toward the outcrop looming over the lagoon to tend to the unconscious child, who's either dead or sleeping. I say a short prayer for her well-being, bend over, check her neck and detect a pulse. The priests' llamas clomp about and bleat frenziedly, frightened, tired, hungry and cold. And though acclimated to frigid temperatures, even llamas can freeze to death if not protected from extreme conditions. I pat their long woolly necks.

"There, there," I coo. "Let's see what we can find for you."

I inspect the larger beast's sack. There's no llama food in it, but plenty of food for humans and some gold, silver and clay trinkets, knitted dolls and ornate clay pottery similar to what the dead children had in their stony tomb, intended to keep them amused on their way to the afterlife. I dig into the smaller brown beast's sack and find enough slightly fermented grain, grass and hay for a day or two. I pull out several handfuls for the famished beasts; they curl back their lips and whisk the food out of my hand with their thick tongues and long teeth.

The sated llamas trot over the stony outcrop, ascend the adjacent slope effortlessly and wait patiently at the hut's entrance. *It's as if they know exactly where to go.* I shudder at the thought that the beasts have probably carried victims of *capacocha* to their sepulcher in the depths of Goddess Mountain Salkantay.

I pick up the unconscious girl then toss her over my shoulder with a groan; though young, she's heavy and puts a strain on my lanky frame.

The Inca must have fed her well, I think.

I struggle to carry her up the slope strewn with loose snow-covered rocks that the llamas clopped up and over so easily. Weighed down, I struggle to breathe and move forward in the thin high mountain air. My ragged sandals slide as I search for crags, cracks and fissures to gain traction. I slip and fall onto my side, sliding half way down the slope. I pause for a moment to catch my breath, regain my composure and check on my human cargo; the little girl is unharmed. Shaken, I creep up the precipitous terrain again.

Upon reaching the top of the slope, I lug the girl to the entrance of the stone hut. Though spent, I manage to gently set the unconscious child onto her back. The llamas curl their lips back and bleat, sounding like infants crying for attention. I pat their necks.

"Good boys," I say. "Good boys."

After calming the llamas, I open the door, step in, drag the girl inside by her hood then set her next to the opening to the tunnel. Then I go back outside to retrieve the llamas, pull them inside and close the door.

At least they will be protected from the cold winds, I think.

I slither through the hole leading to the tunnel, gingerly slide the girl in after me then haul her through until we reach the Room of Death. After opening the tiny door and pulling her in, I cover her with my thick *k'eperina.* The room is freezing so I stuff the hole in the ceiling with the dead girl's blanket then search in the dark for my water flask.

The blanket falls out of the hole and lights up the room; the girl's lashes flutter and she looks at me with stunning emerald eyes, gasps at the sight of the dead children, glares at me, struggles unsuccessfully to get up then starts to sob.

"It's all right," I say, "No. No. I promise, I won't hurt you."

I dab her tears with my tunic then position my flask at her full pink lips; she gulps down the cool water, sighs, lies back down, touches her sunny braided hair then points at my tangle of blond hair.

"Chachapoyas," she whispers in her strange language.

"I don't understand," I say with a shrug.

She points at me, struggling to keep her eyelids open.

"Cloud Warrior," she mutters in *Runasimi* then falls into a deep drugged sleep.

CHAPTER EIGHTEEN

The dream spirits, machula aulanchis, *often invade Taquiri's sleep, bringing his beloved Kusi-quyllur to him, naked, her ample breasts overflowing with milk, as she meticulously weaves fluorescent green insects scattered among hundreds of burnished gold butterflies within her cloth. She nods and smiles sweetly and, after tying a final knot, flings it aside; the insects flap their giant wings and flutter lazily into the distance. Not only is Kusi a magnificent weaver, she is one of the most beloved performers in all of Colla. She dances over to him, singing a sad love song she'd sung a thousand times before about a young wife who suddenly takes ill ill and dies before her time, leaving her husband and children without a wife and mother.*

Then she giggles, lies down next to Taquiri; their bed is overflowing with soft warm alpaca blankets woven by her own hands. She slithers under him as softly and quietly as a feather. He caresses her, kisses her tender lips, strokes her perfect brown body; he nourishes himself with the sweet milk from her breasts then massages her groin, until she writhes and moans; he mounts, penetrates and fills her.

"Do you still love me?" he asks, panting, shivering, stroking her beautiful face. Before she can answer, he awakens, soaked by his own now-cold seed. He feels small, filthy and insignificant as a piece of ch'uño, *curls up on the dirt floor of the barracks of newly recruited Inca soldiers. A young boy soldier cries for his mother in the cold dark night. Taquiri asks the dream spirits to bring his son to him, but they remain mute and uncooperative.*

Now, despite his disdain for the Incas, he awaits his orders, like an obedient slave warrior. He looks around to see if he recognizes anybody from his native city of Colla. He heard that

Incas murdered most of the men there, but one hears many things, not always true. The Incas spared him; maybe other Colla natives were also spared. Perhaps the Incas saw him as a village simpleton, pliable and no threat to the empire; as an artisan he wasn't physically fit as most farmers, their arms and legs made sinewy by the hard work of tilling and plowing. His soft pudgy body had turned to rock from endless hours, hellish weeks and months of grueling warrior training where weak recruits were routinely knocked senseless by stronger more experienced men; Inca generals often brutally culled the weakest to ensure that all recruits put forth maximum effort.

He thinks of his sweet Kusi again . . .

His daydream is interrupted by the prince, the son of the Inca Emperor, who makes a grand entrance, accompanied by his entourage of priests and diviners.

CHAPTER NINETEEN

The hunch-backed servant can hear Chimbo Sancto snoring all the way down the breadth and depth of the long stone corridor. Knees creaking, she shuffles into his room with a pile of clothing.

"Lord Sancto," she says, "today is the day for *chacu.*"

The dwarf pulls his thick blankets overhead.

"Go away!" Chimbo growls, "I'm sleeping!"

"But Lord Sancto," the royal servant repeats, "Today is the day for *chacu.*"

The little man pulls the blankets off his head then props himself onto his elbows.

"What in the name of Inti," he asks, "is *chacu?*"

She places the clothing on a low table near his bed, including what seems to be heavier attire for outdoor use. Chimbo hasn't worn the same thing twice since he arrived, a custom normally reserved for Inca royalty . . . or those being prepared for the questionable honor of human sacrifice. The half man's blood runs cold at the thought.

"The Inca Sapa, our revered Shepherd of the Sun," says the servant, pulling a strand of silvery gray hair from her face, "will explain when he sees you at breakfast. Please, get up."

Chimbo yawns, stretches his stubby limbs and reluctantly rolls out of bed. He observes the mound of clothes with a grunt, stumbles over to them and tries them on. He starts with the heavy knit leggings; they fit well over his chunky legs. Next he pulls on a thin knitted tunic then a thicker woven one and covers himself with a warm cape which he secures with a long silver pin. Also included in the pristine ensemble is a colorful knitted cap with long ear flaps. He thinks about the feathered head-dresses worn by the chosen Daughters of the Sun, who are sent off to mountain peaks for the dreaded Inca sacrifice ritual of *capacocha;* he's relieved that this simple cap bears no similarity. Though the emperor and his royal entourage—except for Prince Atahualpa—have been more than courteous these past several months, he wakes up every morning with the nagging feeling that this day could be his last. Then he considers the emperor's stubborn insistence that Chimbo *eat, eat, eat* until he feels his stomach might explode; the same ritual that the *mamaconas*—Inca high priestesses insist upon at every meal for the Daughters of the Sun.

"Inca gods appreciate a well-fed sacrificial victim," he mutters underneath his breath. He pats his bulging belly, walks over to the large silver mirror and winces at his chubby cheeks and double chin, suddenly overcome by self-loathing. He's become a plump, lumpy sphere with appendages that resemble over-stuffed tamales.

Ugh! It is one thing to be born a dwarf, he ruminates, *but another thing to become a fat one. This will never do.*

He takes one last look at his reflection, sticks out his tongue, waddles out of the room then into the corridor.

Servants bring in tray after tray of sumptuously prepared breakfast foods; Chimbo sits in his usual place next to the emperor who seems especially affectionate this morning, complimenting the dwarf's fine clothing and advisory skills, maybe because Atahualpa isn't sitting at the breakfast table with them.

The prince is probably instructing the high priests on the fine art of properly sacrificing a dwarf, Chimbo ponders uneasily, his mind filled with visions of bejeweled axes crashing down upon his skull.

As he shovels down his meal, he imagines the scene, especially since Atahualpa knows first hand the dwarf's skills in combat and self defense; they have sparred dozens of times since Chimbo's capture:

"Chimbo is a slippery one," Atahualpa would say to the high priests, holding up his halberd, "He's stubby but fast. Don't let him fool you. The little man can jump, flip and disappear in a flash. Within seconds, he'll reappear from behind and you're done for."

But one thing that Atahualpa doesn't know is that the most vital of Chimbo's pugilistic tactics is his refusal to spar when the prince is sober; the dwarf always insists that copious amounts of *chicha* be consumed before each practice session. And he would always surreptitiously spike the prince's drink with a pinch of the hallucinogenic herb called the Spirit Vine, which not only made Atahualpa a lot friendlier but also decreased his weapon and martial arts acumen by at least half. Of course, also unbeknownst to the prince, Chimbo would take only a sip or two of untainted *chicha* from his own small goblet then throw the rest in the bushes. But he had to be careful, too much of the Spirit Vine herb could create the opposite effect, making the prince more aggressive and paranoid than usual. It was a balancing act, but so far had worked precisely as intended. He wonders if he'll be able to use the same tactic to slip out of the high priests' grasp, if the need arises.

"Are you familiar with the *vicuña*," the emperor asks, drawing the dwarf out of his mental machinations of saving himself from the horrors of Inca human sacrifice, "whose wool you have the honor of donning this very moment?"

Chimbo lightly touches his tunic then peers at the emperor with some irritation. He has no desire for small talk right now. He has to conjure up an escape plan, but he also has to be polite. *If small talk is what the emperor wants, then that's what he'll get,* Chimbo reminds himself. He pauses for a moment, summoning all he knows about the animal.

"*Vicuñas* are very shy animals . . ." Chimbo says between slurps of ripe mango, " . . . easily aroused by intruders, due to, among other things, their extraordinary hearing." He picks up then gnaws on a small pheasant leg; between nibbles, he wields the bone like a tiny club. "Like the guanacos, they frequently lick calcareous stones and rocks, which are rich in salt, and also drink salt water. Other than that, their diets consist mainly of low grasses which grow in clumps on the rocky ground. That's all I can think of for now."

Chimbo picks up a char-grilled guinea pig on a stick and takes a bite of its juicy flesh. The emperor shakes his head and dissolves into laughter.

"This," the emperor says, "is what I like about you!"

"What?" the dwarf asks suspiciously.

"You are intellectually curious, my son." Huayna Capac says. He pats the dwarf's back affectionately. "This is a great comfort to me in my old age. We can actually talk about things—so many things."

"If it pleases you, my Shepherd, " Chimbo says with a shrug. "I just enjoy talking."

Atahualpa steps into the dining area; he's in a sour mood as usual, a look of dark disdain on his face especially after witnessing

Chimbo socializing so easily with his father.

"It's time," the prince says ominously.

"Won't you join us for breakfast?" the emperor asks amiably.

"I ate earlier," Atahualpa says. "We need to get started now before it's too late."

"As usual," the emperor says amiably, "Atahualpa is right. It's time to go."

"Where, uh . . .where are we going," the dwarf asks nervously, ". . . if I might ask?"

"First I must address my people and then we will take you to a wonderful place," the emperor says sincerely, "you'll truly love it there, my son."

A wonderful place? Chimbo thinks. *That could mean anything. That could mean that today is the day I journey to the heavenly realm of* hanan pacha *via human sacrifice.*

Too overwrought to ask more questions, he searches his pockets for the phial of Spirit Vine; he's completely forgotten to bring it, absolutely essential if he has any chance of escape, since he knows the high priests enjoy a large chalice of *chicha* before lifting their axes upon sacrificial victims. If spiking the *chicha* proves to be impossible, it would be nice to drug himself so he doesn't screech and beg thereby dying with some measure of dignity. It's widely known that only the brave can journey successfully to *hanan pacha*—cowards strictly forbidden.

"I'll need to go to my room first," Chimbo says. "Please. I've forgotten something."

"No time for that," Atahualpa insists impatiently, "We are keeping too many waiting as it is."

"Correct again, Atahualpa," the emperor says, "After all, *chacu* only comes once every four years. The people are ready for us. "

When Huayna Capac, Atahualpa and Chimbo gather on the palace's top steps, thousands applaud, cheer, bang drums, dance and sing. Villac Umu ventures forth next equipped with a golden ax glimmering in the sun.

This is it, the dwarf thinks in panic. Paralyzed with fear, his face grows pale as chalk, blood rushes from his head.

Atahualpa and Huayna Capac wave to the citizens of Quito. The emperor leans down and whispers into Chimbo's ear.

"Wave," Huayna Capac says, "The people will love it."

Struggling to remain conscious, the dwarf lifts a chunky hand and tentatively flutters his fingers. The crowd's cheers intensify to the point that Chimbo thinks he might go deaf or insane, or both. The ear-shattering cacophony and overwhelming site of the frenzied crowd whirl around him. Lost in a daze of anxiety and panic, he rocks back on his heels and passes out cold.

After blacking out, guards dragged Chimbo inside the palace; a young Inca physicians rouses him by placing a strong smelling herbal concoction under his nose.

"Am I still alive?" the dwarf asks.

The handsome physician smiles kindly.

"You just fainted, Lord Sancto," he says. He puts a glass of medicinal *chicha* to the dwarf's lips, "Drink."

"No," the dwarf insists, "I must keep my wits about me. Especially today."

The bemused doctor tilts his head and raises his eyebrows.

"Today is a time for celebration." the physician says, "For today we join with the citizens of Quito for *chacu*—a very special event." The kindly doctor realizes from the look on Chimbo's ashen face, that he must have a misconception about *chacu*. "Do you know what *chacu* is, Inca of the Heart, honorary eldest son of the emperor?"

The dazed dwarf's face turns an even whiter shade of pale.

"I don't know and I don't think I want to know what *chacu* is," the dwarf mutters. He squeezes his eyes shut, bracing himself for the physician's explanation. "Tell me now. I'm ready."

"Today, thousands of Quiteños, royalty included, travel to the Cotopaxi volcano to make a communal effort to herd *vicuñas*. This is done only once every four years."

"*Chacu* is a vicuña hunting trip?" Chimbo asks, eyes springing open in relief.

"Well, we don't hunt the animals because their wool is too valuable a commodity." the physician explains. "They are simply corralled, shorn then released back into the wild. And since they are an elusive animal, who live at very high altitudes, 15,000 feet or more, it takes thousands of people to make a giant human chain to encircle them."

Chacu is just a vicuña *herding expedition,* he thinks, sighing in relief. *This changes everything.*

He reaches for the goblet, gulps down the medicinal *chicha*, stands, pounds his chest and strides outdoor unaided. The crowd roars when they see Chimbo rejoining the other royals. Atahualpa shoots the dwarf an embittered look, obviously jealous of the love Quiteños seem to have for the plump halfling. Villac Umu, the smarmy high priest raises his gilded ax to quiet the crowd.

"The *vicuña* is the reincarnation of a beautiful young maiden," he announces to the attentive crowd, his voice high and clear, "who received a coat of pure gold once she consented to the advances of an old, ugly king. Because of this, it is forbidden to kill the sacred *vicuña*. And no one, except for Inca royalty can wear its fleece."

Huayna Capac lifts his arms to the upper world. The hushed Quiteños wait, murmuring softly, for the emperor to speak.

"Let the expedition begin!" he declares.

Thousands of Quiteños bellow as musicians and singers provide musical accompaniment and like a swarm of ants, all head south to the semi-active Cotopaxi volcano, home of the elusive *vicuña* herds. Huayna Capac, Atahualpa and Chimbo descend to the bottom of the palace's seemingly endless staircase and, with the help of carriers, mount the royal litter awaiting them there.

"The view will be magnificent, Chimbo," the emperor says. He adjusts his plush *vicuña* seat cushions and takes a seat. "I'm sure you will enjoy this trip immensely."

"Of course, the goddess of the Cotopaxi volcano," Atahualpa adds, "must cooperate."

"Yes, the volcano can be very fickle," the emperor says with a nod. "But if the goddess of Cotopaxi is in high spirits, she will let us into her forests and the *chacu* will be successful."

"And if she's not?" the dwarf asks.

"Then she will burn us all to ashes in her countless inescapable rivers of lava," Atahualpa says stoically, "It has happened before."

Chimbo chuckles nervously.

"The prince is teasing me, is he not?" the dwarf asks.

The emperor adjusts his thick knitted cap then ties it securely under his chin. He adjusts Chimbo's cap, then pats him on the head but all but ignores his real son, Prince Atahualpa, who is similarly dressed for the frigid high mountain climate.

"Lead us to Goddess Cotopaxi," he says to the litter carriers. "We must make haste to get to the head of the procession."

CHAPTER TWENTY

I slide down the snowy slope leading to the outcrop overlooking the Humantay Lagoon.

"Hello!" I yell, "Is anybody out there?"

The stiff wind stinging my face like a swarm of angry bees, I pull my cloak over my head and hold it tight under my chin, open my waist pouch, pluck out a wad of coca leaves, stuff them along with a bit of *llipt'a* into my mouth and chew furiously. I feel Father Coca's gift of green warmth and energy and thank him for his help.

I set off over the large boulders leading to the mountain trail. I don't even know the runaway's name but I have to try to attract her attention somehow, so I keep on yelling, *hello, hello, hello.*

The only thing I hear in response is my own echo. I search for the cloak the girl threw off when she escaped from the priest to no avail. *Hopefully she came back and picked it up to keep warm while she was in hiding.* Trotting down the snowy trail, I call out and stop periodically to listen for a response. *Maybe she's injured,* I think, *or perhaps she's gone all the way back down to the* tampu. *She'd be all right for a night or two there since she surely knows how to make a fire.*

After searching for the girl for at least an hour, I think about making my way back to the hut to check on the young Cloud Warrior maiden sleeping there. She's probably starving by now and needs to be properly nourished since she's likely too weak to feed herself. But I also know she'll survive for another couple of hours without food since she seems to have been fed very well by the Incas. I need to find the escapee before nightfall or she will surely perish. I decide to call out one more time.

"Hello!" I yell, "Is anybody out there?"

Nothing—just my own echo again.

I turn to start ascending the steep trail.

"Help!" a voice calls out, though faintly. "Help!"

"Where are you?" I yell.

I cock my head to determine the source of the voice, not an easy task in the windy, reverb-prone mountains.

"Help!" the voice calls out again. "Help!"

It seems to be coming from the east side of the trail; I trudge through the snow until I reach the edge of a cliff then look down. The girl is lying on her side on a narrow escarpment twenty feet below, her breath rolling out in short frosty puffs, her blond hair gleaming in the golden rays of Inti, the Sun God; her lips are blue and she's shivering uncontrollably, clothed only in a crimson and cerulean long sleeve tunic, made of very thin *vicuña* wool. She gazes at me uncertainly; she doesn't know who I am or what I want.

"Both priests are dead." I shout down to her, pointing at the sling wrapped around my forehead. Although I did kill the high priest, technically, I didn't kill the lower priest; the Amaru did, although I relish the thought of making him suffer by blinding him first. But I can explain all that later. "Don't worry. I don't want to hurt you."

It starts snowing again, this time the snowflakes are larger and denser; the wind begins to gust. The girl curls up in a fetal position then tucks her head between her knees. I contemplate all rescue options. I can attempt to climb down to the escarpment and drag her back up the sheer face of the cliff. Not possible, I surmise, since I was barely able to carry her sister up the comparatively easy slope leading to the cave. I could hike back up to the stone hut and bring back ropes that were tied around the llamas' packs but even then, they might not be long enough to reach her; she might freeze to death by the time I get back.

"Can you climb?" I yell. She trembles, curls up again, head down, arms wrapped around her legs. "You have to try. I'll help you."

"I can't," she replies weakly.

"Let me see your sandals," I demand.

She squints, purses her lips, straightens her legs and pokes her feet out and up. Her sandals are almost new and quite sturdy; the kind of footwear that royalty and soldiers wear in battle and certainly good enough for climbing.

"You can do this." I say. I remove my coca pouch from my waist, tighten the strings that keep it closed and toss it down to her. "Stuff the coca and a piece of *llipt'a* in your mouth and chew vigorously. Then ask Father Coca to give you strength."

She opens the pouch and pulls out a few meager leaves.

"Use all the leaves," I tell her, knowing that we have enough coca left behind by the dead Inca priests.

She nods, pours out what's left into her palm, stuffs the coca and the last piece of *llipt'a* in her mouth; she chews tentatively at first, then more energetically. Almost immediately, I can see Father Coca's green nourishment flowing into her veins—her lips are less blue.

"Feel better?" I ask. Emerald eyes beaming, she nods. "All right. That's good." I say, trying to sound confident, "Now stand and find some cracks in the cliff wall that you can put your feet and hands into. And keep chewing."

She gets on her feet then searches for fissures in the stone; she finds one, puts her foot in it, finds another crack, puts her hand in it and pulls herself up.

"Father Coca knows!" she yells enthusiastically. She surveys the cliff wall, finds another crag, pulls herself higher.

"Good girl!" I yell, "Keep going, my dove!"

Heavy gray clouds roll over us; the wind howls and suddenly thick blankets of silvery white snowflakes cover the landscape; it's a white out and I can't see anything now.

"It's snowing and my hands are cold!" she screeches though I can't see her any more. "I can't hold on!"

"Follow the sound of my voice and keep moving," I yell. I lie on my stomach and reach out to her though I can only guess where she is. "Grab my hand!"

"I can't see!" she cries.

"The Moon Goddess is protecting us; we are her daughters. If we fight, she will ensure no harm will come to us." I yell into the howling blizzard. "Don't give up! Keep climbing!" I wait for a response, hear none but keep my hand outstretched. "Mama Quilla," I pray to the protector goddess of women, "Help your daughters."

My hands and feet are growing numb and stiff from the bitter cold, my limbs feel like icicles. I'm beginning to grasp the horrible truth: the poor girl's frozen hands and feet are making it impossible to move, much less climb; undoubtedly she's plunged soundlessly into the vast canyon below, her suffering over. I must accept what the gods have deemed and hike back to the hut, not only to save my own life, but to care for her sister waiting for me there.

"Are you there!?" I croak in one last desperate attempt, as snow accumulates quickly, "Answer if you can hear me!"

I wait a moment. No response. My breathing becomes shallow and labored; snow is accumulating on my back and I start to feel very sleepy.

I just need to close my eyes for a moment, I think as I drift off into blissful unconsciousness.

"Wake up," a Machukuna whispers, a look of grave concern in his clear blue eyes, "Wake up."

"I just need to sleep," I whisper, my mind a deep black fog, "just for a moment."

"Get up," he says, more insistently now, "Get up."

The Machukuna fades into the blinding whiteness.

My head feels as though weighed down by a boulder. It would be easier to just stay here and let myself go cold and numb forever. But I know what will happen if I do. I picture my baby brother growing up without me. Mamáy weeping for me and father trying to console her.

I lift my head, now covered in a layer of freshly fallen snow. In a stupor, I force myself to rise, fighting the urge to just lie down and fall painlessly asleep. But I think about my baby brother again and push myself onto my knees. I decide to enlist Father Coca's help so I reach for my waist pouch. To my horror, I realize I relinquished it to help the girl, to no avail. I weep; my nose runs and tears freeze on my cheeks. I strain to stand and groan from the stinging misery of blood flowing back into my toes as I clumsily hop away from the cliff's edge.

I tighten by hood under my chin against the thick fog, icy wind and stinging snow and stumble blindly on stiff feet in the direction I can only hope is the upward trail to the hut. An even denser cloak of fog and snow blankets the cruel Mountain Who Eats People. I have the alarming feeling that I'm wandering aimlessly as Lord Wind whips around me.

Before I left, I fed and took the llamas outside, where they are still waiting, covered in a thin layer of frost and snow, bleating pitifully. I follow their cries then struggle to climb up the slope leading to the hut; after a couple of stumbles and slides to the bottom, I finally make it. I limp over to the beasts, brush snow off their heads and stroke their woolly necks.

"Good boys," I coo, "I heard you. You saved me."

Their ears twitch as I pet them; the beasts shake the snow off of their broad backs. Inca royalty and priests seem to have endless resources to keep themselves and their animals fed and warm despite bad weather. Though these sturdy highland beasts are used to cold and snowy conditions and have the advantage of heavy blankets, they have their limits. I remind myself again that intense cold has been known to kill whole herds of llamas and alpacas, especially when inadequately fed to compensate for extreme conditions. I dig out great handfuls of hay and grass from inside the feed pack; the llamas pull back their lips and chomp on the food with elongated teeth.

Satisfied that the beasts are adequately nourished, I lead them back inside the hut and dig through some of the priests' provisions. My efforts are rewarded when I discover meticulously prepared, wrapped and preserved food of all kinds—fresh and dried fruits, dried llama and fish jerky, savory tamales wrapped in plantain leaves and so much more—more than enough to sustain several adults for a week, maybe more. The pack also contains another smaller package: several pouches of coca leaves and *llipt'a* as well as heavy woolen blankets. I tie the pack closed, cram it through the small opening into the tunnel, then drag it along as I crawl toward the Room of Death. When I arrive, I notice the room is warm and the girl's still sleeping deeply. I start laying provisions on the floor in front of me.

"Time to eat," I say cheerfully.

She blinks her emerald eyes open, yawns, smiles, lifts her head and props herself upon her elbows.

"Did you find my sister?" she asks.

I hand her a tamale; she unwraps it, takes a huge bite and smiles. As she chews, guilt overwhelms me.

How can I tell her that I wasn't able to save her beloved sibling?

Disappointment sours my appetite but force myself to eat or perish. Father used to say that sometimes the solution to life's problems can only be found in a full stomach. I pick up a tamale, peel away the corn husks and bite down.

CHAPTER TWENTY ONE

1511 A.D.
Piajajalca Fortress,
Chachapoyas

Heir apparent to the royal fringe, Prince Tito Husi Hualpa, whose name will be changed to Huayna Capac upon his coronation, is rumored to be even more tyrannical than his father, Emperor Tupac Inca Yupanqui. Aloft a resplendent feathered litter, the handsome youth dons a scarlet tunic, a thick cloak woven with gold and silver threads and embedded with gems. At the front of his golden helmet, two bright yellow feathers from the enigmatic Corenqueque bird sway in the breeze.

"Prince Tito," the high priest Mayta Yupanqui asks politely, "Are we ready to start?"

The prince tilts his head then raises his hand.

Taquiri and his fellow warriors watch intently as litter carriers gently lower the conveyance. Prince Tito adjusts his thick golden and silver wrist, arm and ankle cuffs and cumbersome over-sized earrings then steps off the litter.

Mayta spreads a small cloth, which contains coca leaves and a small gold coin—the all-seeing eye, the ñawin. Musicians, bear dancers and warriors await the divination.

"Coca always knows, Prince Tito," Mayta chants. He runs his fingers through the pile of leaves and lets them settle on the cloth in front of him. He examines the coca closely, counting each without touching. He knits his brow, counts the leaves again; dark eyes aglow, he raises his arms to the heavens. "Yes! The leaves tell us that it is a good time to strike the savage Cloud Warriors! Coca

always knows!"

The sorcerer leads the chant as Inca warriors chime in, "Coca always knows! Coca always knows!"

A servant hands the prince a gold-encrusted chalice, made from the skull of a vanquished enemy. Warriors eagerly dig under their bright red and white checkered tunics, extricating personal coca leaf pouches from around their waists. The prince raises the hideous skull chalice.

"Prayers, offerings and libations must be offered to Mother Earth, the Sacred Places and our Ancestors." the prince intones, "Their voracious appetites must be duly nourished to ensure our victory."

The high priest starts a long, poetic invocation as warriors blow softly over their coca then crumble a single leaf with calloused fingers over the ground, a gift to Mother Earth. Minor priests chant, meandering through the throng of soldiers, methodically strewing drops of chicha *from large clay jugs, then sprinkling drops into the air and onto restless llamas, weighed down with heavy packs containing food and medicinal supplies.*

"Hallpaykusunchis," Mayta says with an air of finality, "Let us chew coca together."

Warriors stuff coca into their mouths along with a bit of llipt'a *—ash to extract the coca's energizing essence, then concentrate on what they desire, their minds becoming clearer and stronger as the coca takes effect. Most pray for an honorable victory or escape from this world by a swift painless death. Coca endows some with courage disproportionate to their size and ability, stirring up visions of grandeur as they slaughter helpless villagers—hoping valor will earn them a prestigious post in the increasingly* *bureaucratic hierarchy of the Inca Empire. But valor normally wins a place in a shallow unmarked grave and food for the condor, especially in distant provinces. Other times, Mother Earth swallows dead soldiers during earthquakes or disintegrates them during rainy season. After routing the enemy, rebel tribes gleefully burn Inca corpses making it impossible for their souls to unite with their gods in the heavenly realm of* hanan pacha.

As Taquiri chews, the pungent leaves quickly absorb his sadness and pain, comforting him like a mother. The veil of grief lifted, he prays, too, but neither for victory nor death.

CHAPTER TWENTY TWO

Though the air at 15,000 feet is quite thin, it doesn't deter the hearty Quiteños who spend most of the day running down, encircling then funneling wild *vicuñas* into makeshift corrals constructed of tall wooden stakes and nets. After the animals are safely gathered, the emperor leads a brief religious ceremony.

"Pachamama and Cotopaxi Volcano Goddess," Huayna Capac intones, his arms raised in veneration to the gods, "we thank you for your cooperation in this divine *chacu*. We also thank the sacred *vicuñas* themselves, for providing their magical fibers, which keep Inca leaders warm even in the coldest of winters."

Sitting cross-legged in a circle of bright afternoon sunlight, a Daughter of the Sun, languidly chews a large wad of coca; well-fed, even a bit chubby and elegantly clothed, she's surrounded by knitted dolls, an assortment of tiny gold and silver puma and llama bells, figurines and brightly painted ceremonial pots.

Priests and their assistants ply the teenager with *chicha* with a particularly high alcohol content and spiked with a dose of the hallucinogenic Spirit Vine. She's not only docile but groggy and barely able to sit up. A *mamacona* sits next to her, occasionally straightening the maiden when she keels over or waking her when she dozes off. The emperor nods at the high priest, indicating that it is time for the first part of *capacocha* to begin.

Villac Umu begins a long religious song; throngs of lower priests join in then the priest chants solo. At the appropriate time, the lower priests join in again emitting a dissonant choral sound that makes the hair on the back of Chimbo's neck stand on end. The dwarf steps onto a large boulder next to the emperor so that he can whisper in his ear.

"If it is wrong to kill a *vicuña* because it had once been a beautiful young maiden," Chimbo whispers, "then why is it right to kill this beautiful young girl?"

"Chimbo," the emperor responds irritably, "why must you try my patience so?"

"You are the emperor," the dwarf insists, "and, as such, your citizens will obey any orders you give them, tradition or not. After all, you are the son of Inti the Sun God. You have the right to amend laws and religious rituals as you see fit, any time you wish."

Huayna rolls his eyes then shakes his head dismissively.

"Perhaps we can dispense with *capacocha*," he replies, "at the next *chacu*."

"The next *chacu* is four years from now. Correct?"

"Yes." the emperor answers.

"Who knows what can happen between now and then?" the dwarf states with a shrug.

The emperor gazes at the docile Daughter of the Sun, sighs loudly; his dark brown eyes meets Chimbo's light brown ones.

"Her name is Tanta Carhua." the emperor explains, pointing his chin in the sacrificial victim's direction. "Her father brought her to me while I was in Cuzco over four years ago. In subsequent years, she has become an expert weaver, chef and brewer of the finest *chicha* in the kingdom. As you know, only the most perfect children can be sacrificed."

"She is beautiful beyond exaggeration," Chimbo asserts.

"Due to her extraordinary beauty and talents, we honored her with extensive feasting and festivities while I was visiting my daughter, Princess Cura in Cuzco." the emperor says, "On our way back to Quito, we went through Tanta's high mountain village of Urcon. She told the villagers there, 'You can finish with me now because I was so highly honored and celebrated in Cuzco.' I appointed Tanta's father the *curaca* of his village with promises of further promotions in the near future, depending on his continued allegiance to the empire. He and his descendants will serve as a nexus between Urcon and the Cuzco. Tanta will be deified by the villagers after *capacocha* and the flourishing Urcon village will be forever subordinate to the empire. There is no way to change things now."

At least I have planted a seed, the dwarf thinks as he steps down from the boulder, *and that is all I dare do for right now.*

The chanting stops. The priests await the emperor's order to proceed. Huayna Capac nods; Tanta Carhua is lifted onto a small litter along with the old high priestess who holds the girl's feathered crown topped with an ear-to-ear white feathered fan. Litter carriers walk their human cargo toward the Cotopaxi volcanic peak. Once there, the *mamacona* will place the crown upon Tanta's head; priests will ply her with more drugs and alcohol, lower her into a shaft-tomb then wall her in as they pray to the mountain gods. She will perish in the freezing high altitude within hours.

CHAPTER TWENTY THREE

In between bites of tamale, Pispis tells me her sister's name is Solsol. Thankfully, she doesn't ask whether I'd found her sibling; I don't have the courage to volunteer the information that I'd found Solsol but couldn't save her. Pispis dozes off again after eating her fill.

It's starting to get very stuffy in the Room of Death and the dead children's decomposing bodies are starting to reek again. I unplug the ceiling hole; the room fills with fresh freezing air. I also hear Lord Wind howl, the llamas bleating from the connecting hut then a voice which sounds like somebody crying for help.

No, it couldn't be. I think.

But the crying persists.

I can't go back outside now. I'm tired, my feet are killing me and it's still snowing. If I go back, I will freeze to death.

Though the odds are that I'm simply hallucinating from exhaustion and the remnants of high altitude sickness, I decide to leave the sleeping Pispis behind. I crawl out of the Room of Death, creep through the tunnel and squeeze through the opening into the stone hut. The llamas are happy to see me; I give them more feed which they chomp down and swallow quickly though they've eaten less than an hour ago. Then I step outside.

It's stopped snowing; Lord Inti shines his golden light upon me and his warmth radiates throughout my body; I wriggle my toes and realize they don't hurt any more. I wait a moment and tune my ears to the environment. There it is again, the echo of someone crying for help. It can't be Solsol; she's fallen into the abyss and if that didn't kill her, she'd be dead from exposure by now. But I have to check anyway.

A condor swoops overhead, then lands heavily on my shoulder almost knocking me down.

"There you are," I say, so relieved to see my bird again; he squawks back in greeting.

I wait for him to hop down, burrow into the snow-covered ground, transform into a compact clay figure that hardens into stone, like he usually does. Instead he flutters off my shoulder, returns, glides away again then returns once more. It's as if he's signaling me to follow him.

He glides ahead; I slip and slide down the snow-covered mountain trail after him. My bird seems to be heading for the escarpment. As we draw nearer, I notice a kettle of condors circling overhead. My stomach turns when I realize these massive birds have spotted something to scavenge.

"No!" I shout. "Go away!"

Amazingly, the giant scavengers fly away instantly.

I race down the snowy trail, my condor hovering overhead. When we finally reach the cliff above the escarpment, I look down and see Solsol lying in a fetal position, motionless, a layer of frost shimmering like diamonds over her body.

"Solsol!" I yell, "Can you hear me?"

Silence. My heart sinks.

I will not let the condors scavenge your body, Solsol. I promise.

Out of the corner of my eye, I notice the big tan and white llama trotting happily down the trail toward me. He must have pushed the door open and made his way outside.

"What are you doing here?" I coo. I pet his woolly neck and strong broad back still covered by his thick woolen blanket. He pulls back his lips in a toothy grin, happy to be outside.

The condor lands on the llama's back; the bird squawks, goading him on. The llama snorts, stretches his neck then clops toward a group of boulders. My bird cranes his neck then squawks in my direction; I stumble after him. When I reach the boulder formation, the llama trots down a steep narrow path leading to the escarpment which was hidden from view until now. The beast lithely hops off the path onto the embankment, turns his head toward Lord Inti, soaking up the brilliant, almost blinding sunlight as it reflects off the silvery snow-covered mountainside; he bleats as if commanding me to follow him. I gingerly step down the impossibly narrow path, hugging the cliff-side; small rocks and stones loosened by my footsteps roll down into the seemingly bottomless abyss below. I leap off the path then tread toward Solsol's frozen body, hunker down and touch her white, icy cheek. Her eyes are open and unseeing without a flicker of life in them. I check her head and torso for signs of blows and breaks. It seems as though she made the fall without sustaining major external injuries. However, when I check her fingers and toes, I notice they're scraped and bloodied; it seems as if she tried to hold on as she slid down the cliff wall, until she crumbled onto the escarpment, too weak and frightened to answer me when I called out during the white out.

I touch her neck and wrist for a pulse. Nothing. I press my ear to her chest but the llama starts bleating so loudly, I can't hear a thing.

"Shh!" I hiss.

The llama snorts, takes a step back then falls silent; I slow my breathing and listen carefully. Ten seconds go by, then twenty, thirty, forty . . .

Thump.

I sit up in disbelief, then bend over and listen again. Ten, twenty, thirty seconds pass . . .

Thump.

Her pulse is weak and irregular, but it's there, I think in amazement. I try to remain calm and evaluate the situation—being brought back to life may not be a good thing. People revived after freezing often become warped, half dead and half alive, speaking nonsensically, wandering off in the middle of the night, unable to care for themselves much less weave, cook, farm or care for animals like normal *runakuna;* an inconvenience for men but a tragedy for *munay warmikuna,* a woman of substance. I behold the sky; though a few minutes ago it was sunny, gray and black clouds roll back in. Goddess Mountain is fickle; she's telling us to hurry.

I groan as I lift the girl's body onto the llama's waiting back; the beast grunts as I wrap frayed ropes from the llama's blanket and leash around her body. I lead him to the narrow path, then smack his hindquarters lightly.

"Ha!" I shout.

The beast nimbly trots up the narrow path; his human cargo slips inch by inch out of the loosely tied ropes, the abyss looming below. I close my eyes and hold my breath. *Oh no.* At the top of the path, her body slides off the llama's back, landing precariously near the cliff edge. I clumsily trip up the steep path, my lungs screaming for air. When I reach the top, I rest for a moment then use my last ounce of strength to pull myself up by holding onto the llama's sturdy legs. I pat its rump then nuzzle its long majestic neck.

"Good boy," I say. "Good job."

I lift Solsol back onto the beast's back but this time, I take the time to properly re-position and secure her with the increasingly frayed ropes. Satisfied with my knots for now, I pull the llama by his woolly mane; we trudge wearily up the trail.

Once we reach the slope near the high mountain lagoon, more beautiful than ever by virtue of being covered in a blanket of crystalline snow, I recheck the knots securing Solsol to the llama. Satisfied, I slap the beast's hindquarters.

"Ha!" I shout.

He bleats, clops to the top of the slope, his human cargo affixed securely. I gather myself, take a deep breath and scramble up behind him. Amazingly, despite the snow, ice and altitude, I don't slide back to the bottom of the slope.

When we reach the hut, I notice that the other llama is gone, too. Hungry, bored, cold and tired, they probably both ran off together. It was a miracle that the bigger llama came to me. The smaller llama evidently trotted down the mountainside unnoticed.

Maybe he'll wait for us at the tampu, I ponder hopefully.

I carefully untie the frozen girl, slide her gently off the llama's back then drag her inside. I tug her cloak across the uneven stone floor, shove her through the narrow opening, squeeze through after her, slide her through the tunnel into the Room of Death.

"Thank the gods!" Pispis exclaims, "You've found my sister."

"Pispis," I say sadly, "I don't know if Solsol's going to make it, I . . ."

Pispis scrutinizes her older sister's stiff frost-covered body and face.

"Solsol? It's me, Pispis." She pleads, her emerald eyes gleaming with tears. "Please wake up."

Though revivification seems hopeless, I'm determined to at least make an earnest attempt. Tatáy told me stories of children who came back to life after being frozen for many hours, even overnight. I pull out two soft warm alpaca blankets and place one underneath then another over Solsol then plug up the hole in the ceiling. Our body heat warm the small room up quickly.

"Pispis, crawl under this blanket with your sister," I say. "Cuddle up close while I rub her feet and hands. We have to warm her."

"All right," Pispis says. She snuggles close to her beloved sibling.

I reach under the blanket and start gently massaging Solsol's limbs, frozen stiff and and lifeless; I detect no vital signs. My heart sinks but I continue massaging despite the hopelessness of the situation. Outwardly I maintain a peaceful, hopeful facade, but inside I'm cursing the Machukuna.

What have I ever done to deserve this? Why aren't you helping us? I think, hoping they will pick up my desperate musings. But, as usual, the giants do not respond when I need them the most.

After several minutes, Pispis rolls out from under the blanket and kneels over her sister, a look of grim determination on her fair face. She hold her hands over her sister's torso; her palms grow pink then transform into a glowing shade of scarlet. I've never seen anything like this, not even from the shaman in our village. Pispis puts her hands underneath the blanket onto her sister's belly. Eyes an ominous shade of mossy green, she depresses and massages her sister's abdomen.

"I beseech Urcaguey, the Serpent God, symbol of chaos and force of darkness," she intones, her voice a low growl. "whose cold blood now flows through my sister's veins, to show yourself now."

A yellow-eyed serpent arises in a hazy brown mist from the unconscious girl's lower torso, its red forked tongue flicking in and out between its fangs.

"Solsol now inhabits the glorious lower world of *ukhu pacha.* " Urcaguey hisses, modulating each syllable slowly, sensually, "Accept your sister's fate."

Pispis places her perfect pink lips upon her sister's icy ear and continues to massage her stomach.

"Wake up, Solsol," Pispis whispers, "Please, sister. Blink if you can hear me."

Solsol's body remains cold and stiff; her still-open eyes show no signs of life. Pispis and I glance at each other in despair, neither of us willing to admit defeat. Not yet. We continue to massage her icy, unyielding flesh.

"If you can hear me," Pispis says, "you must try to rouse yourself. Wake up, Solsol."

Pispis's hands seem almost aflame as she massages her sister's torso while I halfheartedly rub her ice cold feet and hands. I feel myself sinking into the depths of despair.

We have to face the sad facts: she's as cold as the minute I dragged her into the cave, I determine sadly.

"It's too late. You must accept the will of the serpent deities of the underworld," the snake hisses, coiling around Solsol's chest, arms and legs. "Remember, you are, as are all Cloud Warriors, servants of the serpent gods."

Emerald eyes ablaze, Pispis holds up her scorching hands, takes a swipe at the snake god; the creature evades her grasp, rattles its tail and bares its fangs. Pispis looks away then snatches the serpent's neck in midair; its scaly skin sizzles in her scalding palms; it writhes and whips its tail and in moments becomes slack-jawed, forked tongue hanging from its mouth. Satisfied that the serpent is unconscious, if not dead, Pispis grabs the snake's tail, smashes its head upon the stone floor and jagged cave walls until its spine is bloody and exposed.

"Cloud Warriors are no one's servants—not the Incas, not their cursed priests or *mamaconas,*" Pispis growls, "and certainly not the servant of a dead snake." She tosses the dead creature across the floor, where it crumples against a wall. She blithely inspects her scarlet hands; her pink lips curl into a satisfied smile. "The serpent will make a nutritious meal," Pispis says nonchalantly. "when we get back down the mountain."

She claps her hands then returns to warming and kneading her sister's body.

I inspect the mutilated snake then cut off its scaly head, to ensure it doesn't somehow spring back to life. Turn my attention to Solsol, I resume rubbing her icy limbs, which seem warmer now. *Or is it just my imagination?* I press my ear against the girl's chest and wait.

Thump . . .

"Pispis, I hear something," I say, not sure whether I actually heard a heartbeat or imagined it. "Keep massaging her."

I say a short silent prayer to Mama Quilla.

Oh, protector of women I pray *and wife of Inti, please help your daughters in our hour of need.*

I hold my ear against Solsol's torso again. Nothing. I must have imagined the earlier pulse. I lift my head up and gaze at Pispis. The whites of her emerald eyes are bloodshot and welling with tears; all I can do is shake my head sadly.

"Don't give up, Solsol!" Pispis shouts. She beats her fists against her sister's chest so violently that I'm sure the poor girl's ribs will shatter, "Fight, sister, fight. You will not leave me here alone!"

For several minutes, I scrutinize Solsol's chalky face and her body jerking up and down from the force of her sister's desperate blows. Finally I can tolerate no more.

"That's enough," I say. Pispis ignores me and continues to pummel her sister's torso. "I said, that's enough." I grab her arms then gently pull her away from her lifeless sibling. Pispis brings her knees to her chest, covers her face with her hands, rocks back and forth and sobs violently. "You have to be quiet now," I insist.

She stifles her tears. I'm determined to end this anguish by releasing Solsol's spirit to the Cloud Warrior serpent gods.

But before I do, I put an ear to the girl's chest one last time.

CHAPTER TWENTY FOUR

1511 A.D.
Piajajalca
Chachapoyas

Arms and thigh muscles bulging, bronze skin glowing in the first rays of the early morning sun, the stout Lucanas carriers raise the sumptuous royal conveyance, all eyes upon Prince Tito.

"Cloud Warrior savages defy the will of the mighty Inca Empire by controlling commerce and taxing all goods shipped over these remote mountain passes. Piajajalca is land rightfully belonging to the sacred Inca Empire. Spare only the chieftain, which we will punish as a warning to others. Every other Cloud Warrior male or female, young and old, must perish in the name of Inti the Sun God!"

"In the name of Tatáy Inti!" the Inca warriors shout.

The high priest, Mayta summons the Salqa wind; it blows in from the bowels of the earth, bringing the great mystery of life and beauty of existence, the purity of an honorable death and the ecstasy of victory.

After energetically chomping on fresh coca leaves, the warriors feel the green energy coursing through their veins, the wild wind blowing upon their faces. They dutifully trudge up the steep mountain slope, thick as locusts.

A young boy soldier, no more than fifteen, shoots Taquiri an anxious smile.

"What is your name, young man?" Taquiri asks.

"Hankanpuma," the boy says shyly.

"Brilliant Puma?" Taquiri asks.

"Yes," Hankanpuma answers, "It is a name that I'd hoped to live up to one day."

"I'm sure you will." Taquiri says.

The Sun God raises his golden head higher over the east. The Machukuna vanish for they only appear in moonlight.

"So death will be swift at the hands of the Cloud Warriors?" Hankanpuma asks, chewing his coca thoughtfully. "And that is enough to be grateful for?"

Taquiri gasps for breath as the climb becomes steeper and warriors push from the rear to scale the mountain even faster.

"Yes," he replies, eyeing the boy as though he were his son, his own little dove. "The Cloud Warriors blows are swift and merciful. Do not be afraid, urpicháy.*"*

"Añaychay, Tatáy," the boy thanks his new friend, addressing him as father. He chew his coca more vigorously now, his lips curled into a brave smile, "I will welcome my journey to hanan pacha, *the heaven of my ancestors." As they scramble over a giant boulder, he asks hesitantly, ". . . is it true what they say about the Cloud Warriors? That they are giants with serpent eyes, red hair and beards woollier than an alpaca's?"*

"We will learn the truth soon enough, my dove."

"Yes," said the boy, green-flecked brown eyes gleaming in the early morning light, teeth green-gray from diligent coca chewing "We will learn soon enough."

"Let the blood of the Cloud Warriors flow down the mountainside into the Great River! We will make all rivers Blood River!" shouts the Inca prince, thrusting his sword forward. His carriers manage to keep the royal litter level as they feverishly ascend rocky slopes, bodies gleaming with sweat.

The front line of Inca warriors crawl swiftly over large rocks and thorny brush. The fragrant white blossoms of the lacinia bush poke their heads up to catch the first rays of sun, unaware that they will meet their doom under army sandals; once crushed, the flowers fill the air with a fragrance only the gods could have created. This may be the last aroma, many soldiers will experience in this physical realm of kay pacha.

The drummers pound war drums—the heartbeat of the gods; all chant the Inca War Song:

"We will drink from the skull of the traitor,
We will adorn ourselves with a necklace of his teeth,
We will play the melody of the pinkulla with flutes made from his bones,
We will beat the drum made from his skin
Thus we will dance."

CHAPTER TWENTY FIVE

Handlers enter the corral and immediately release trapped animals too young to be safely shorn. Specially trained shearers lovingly pet and whisper a soothing prayer into the vicuñas's twitching ears, then pick them up one by one, gently placing them on their sides upon white cloths spread on the ground just outside the fence. Using razor sharp obsidian blades, the men take less than five minutes to relieve the vicuñas of their precious wool. After struggling to get on their two-toed feet, the *vicuñas* happily bolt into the wilderness after a light pat on their shorn rump. Women nimbly pick through the fleece, removing debris: burrs, leaves, bits of dirt and gravel then roll and stuff the cleaned wool neatly into large sacks.

Shearing, cleaning and packing finally done, musicians bring out their instruments and Quiteños dance and sing late into the evening, many masked or dressed in makeshift *vicuña* costumes in honor of the sacred animals.

The dwarf rides on the litter to Quito, accompanied as usual by the Inca Sapa and Prince Atahualpa and followed by thousands of exhausted Quiteños carrying heavy sacks of freshly shorn wool.

"The gods must have been pleased," Chimbo says, "since the Cotopaxi Volcano did not erupt during the *chacu*."

"Most importantly," the Inca Huayna Capac says, "is that you enjoyed yourself, Chimbo."

"It was good to get away from the city for a while," the dwarf declares, deep dimples emerging on both cheeks as he smiles appreciatively. "Thank you, my father, my dove."

The prince rolls his eyes and sighs.

"Why must you coddle this half-man, Father?" the eternally vexed Atahualpa spits. "He's more useless than a woman."

"He's more valuable than you know," the emperor answers calmly. "As long as he's alive and happy, what's left of the Confederation—the rebels and their allies that almost defeated your troops due to Chimbo's leadership will not rise up against us. We cannot afford another bloody war, my son."

"I, for one, would rather corral *vicuña*," Chimbo adds, "than wage war."

"I'm a warrior," Atahualpa growls, "not a lowly shepherd."

"You are young, my son. You will learn in time." the Inca Sapa says, "I made a lot of mistakes at your age and I'm still learning from men far wiser than I. Chimbo has taught me many things, mainly, that being a great leader means that you must be flexible, be light of spirit and be many things to many people—a peacemaker, a warrior, a diplomat, a judge, an accountant and sometimes, yes, even a lowly shepherd."

CHAPTER TWENTY SIX

Çupay, the god of death and ruler of *ukhu pacha*—the underworld and his minions torment the new arrival.

"You made the right choice, maiden," he snarls through his grotesque set of pointed teeth, "You could have had the sky, sun, moon, stars, planets, everything that the heavenly world of *hanan pacha* had to offer. But you chose to come to us here in *ukhu pacha.*"

Red and yellow eyes glowering, he punches her chest though it doesn't phase her because Solsol is no longer connected to her earthly body therefore devoid of all sensation, including pain; it's a numbness she's never experienced before. With a vague notion that what Supay is saying about giving up *hanan pacha* is true, she can't remember if that's a bad thing or not.

"Good choish, yesh, yesh, yesh," one of Supay's vile minions lisps, nodding enthusiastically. Spittle flies out of his mouth with each sputtered word. Overgrown horns spiral out of his bald head; greasy, smelling globules ooze from filthy yellow pores. Solsol wishes he would shut up; his voice grates on her, like the squeal of a llama being sacrificed. "Good choish," he lisps again, slime splashing onto the new arrival's cheeks.

She wants to tell both creatures that she hates them and that they should go to the hellish realm of *ukhu pacha*; then she realizes that they are already there—a vast sickening arctic darkness which smells of rotting fish. *How did I get here?* She asks herself. She falls back into the freezing abyss that is now her mind, unable to even remember the question.

A serpent slithers over her benumbed body. He rattles, hisses and threatens her with his venomous fangs. Too apathetic to

147

respond, Solsol feels no fear, no hatred just a deep abiding exhaustion.

A strange pressure emanates from her chest; it seems to correspond with someone pounding on a door in the far, far distance; a familiar voice is yelling her name from a million universes away. It's someone she recognizes, if she could just remember her name; it's on the tip of her tongue. But there is only one word she remembers.

Capacocha.

Reverberating through the foggy wilderness of her mind, she only vaguely remembers what it means.

She sees herself running away from the Inca priest; *kay pacha*, the physical world, swirls in a drunken orgy around her. She wasn't ready to leave this physical world of people, family, friends, animals and plants, despite the Inca's religious training and sweet promises from the *mamaconas* who endlessly expounded upon the rewards of *hanan pacha*—a warm, sunny place where the Sun God, Mama Quilla and Illapa, the god of thunder and lightning reside, where she and her sister would be well fed, happy and be revered for all eternity as Daughters of the Sun. But she never really believed these things.

My sister, she thinks—the words impart just the tiniest particle of warmth, which enters her bowels, splashes in her empty stomach then flows into heart. She must know her own sister's name but the more she tries to think of it, the more it eludes her.

"Solsol," her sister's voice says from far far away, *"Please, wake up, Solsol."*

I'm trying, she wants to scream but not even one tiny sound emits from her parched mouth.

Creatures of all shapes, sizes, species and colors approach her —undulating worms, snakes and horned lackeys pull her to the edge of an arctic sea filled with icebergs and glaciers the size of the tallest Andes mountains. A giant sea spider, all legs and no body, scurries out of the water, massages her belly with his bright yellow proboscis then drags her through the waves into an underwater cave which leads to a universe where the agony of glacial cold is celebrated in a bizarre series of ceremonies and rituals where she is the empress of the dead. She floats helplessly in the icy water; sea creatures and serpents hiss, cheer, writhe and dance as they commit, evidently for her amusement, unspeakable acts of depravity: beheadings, tentacles scooping out eyeballs, arm and leg amputations and bizarre inter-species sex acts accompanied by dissonant music so loud, it makes her ears bleed.

I have to get away, she thinks.

A kaleidoscope of sapphire-colored butterflies flutter around a pregnant woman who appears out of nowhere, her crotch covered in dull green gray leaves, her eyes kind the color of freshly tilled springtime soil. She pulls potatoes from her naked breasts and coca leaves from her armpits.

Pachamama—earth mother and time goddess, Solsol prays silently, *help me.*

Drooling demons swarm around *Pachamama,* pawing on and lightly tickling her enormous belly, grabbing potatoes and coca and stuffing them into their gaping maws. *Pachamama* calmly nods at Solsol.

"You may go back to *kay pacha* now but you will suffer enormous pain," the earth goddess intones, the phrase sung instead of spoken.

Pachamama's words are puzzling and incomprehensible. *How could I ever suffer more than I'm suffering now*, she wonders, head pounding as if being beaten by a club. Slowly, Solsol drifts to the water's surface then floats upon the soft ripples of an underground stream. Overhead, fine hairlike roots hang from the black earth, soaking in the mineral rich water. She clenches her fists, lifts her arms and points her toes, spiraling slowly through the rich soil like a potato sprout pushing its way to a surface where a warming golden sphere of joy greets her. Her hands unfold, transforming into dainty green leaves, soaking in Father Sun's nourishment.

She tries to pry open her eyelids but they won't budge, like a flower bud not yet ready to bloom. Someone lifts her head and pours water through her slightly parted lips. The water is refreshingly sweet and cool. *More,* she thinks, *more.*

"Solsol," the voice says, "Can you hear me? It's me, Pispis. Nod if you can hear me."

Pispis, Solsol thinks, the figure of someone quite familiar comes to mind as water thaws and filters throughout the muscles, veins and capillaries of her rigid body, *Pispis, my sister.* Her eyes flood with salty tears; she tries to move her head but the muscles in her neck are as hard and unyielding as a palm-wood ax.

She remembers the sight of the hated Inca priest preparing to smash her sister's skull with a jewel encrusted ax used especially for performing the Inca rite of *capacocha,* snow floating in a whisper of white all around them. She remembers running away, blood surging like molten lava through her veins as the lower priest gives chase; she stops and turns when she feels she's far enough ahead of him.

"The priests are slow and clumsy," Solsol yells to her sister in the Chachapoyas language that the *mamaconas* ordered her to forget, "Run, Pispis! Run!"

When Pispis doesn't respond, she realizes it's too late; the high priest has already drugged her beloved sibling with a noxious potion making her unable to resist *capacocha* in any way. Even now, the thought makes her want to sob, but she can't; instead, her body twitches once as if suddenly falling off a cliff. Somebody says something then pours more water between her parched lips and the hydrating liquid trickles down her raw throat.

A small wood fire crackles, heating chapped skin, aching bones, and blistered fingers and toes that burn and sting as they thaw—a cold naked agony like no other. Then she remembers Pachamama's formerly incomprehensible warning. *You may go back to* kay pacha *now but you will suffer enormous pain.* It all makes sense now.

Numb and unable to cry out, Solsol's certain that if she could it would make the intense aching more bearable. Her mother, Sangama told her that one should ride pain like a wave; she wonders how that's done, having never been to the ocean and wonders if that applies to the agony of reawakening. A detached part of her frets about Çupay and his demons who are searching for her, their new Queen of the Dead; she perceives their demoniacal howls of protestation growing louder, closing in on her.

CHAPTER TWENTY SEVEN

1511 A.D.
Piajajalca
Chachapoyas

Cloud Warrior captain Chuqui Sota, his wife and newborn snuggle under thick wool blankets; silvery embers glow in the fireplace. Only half asleep, he sits up when he hears an odd rustling in the distance.

"What's that?" he whispers, lightly shaking his wife from her slumber.

"Go back to sleep, urpicháy, *my handsome dove," his wife says with a yawn, her lush auburn hair partially covering her face, "It is only Lord Wind telling you to go back to sleep."*

"No," he insists, his rugged face twisted in worry. "I definitely heard something." He stretches, jumps out of bed, loads two logs into the fireplace, chooses a sword hanging on the wall carefully sharpened the night before and swings it, his massive arm muscles bulging. The wind howls; a tree branch snaps and falls with a thump nearby. He sighs. "Maybe you're right, my dove, but I want to check anyway." He unlatches the door, steps out into the cold air; a gust of wind blows his long dark blond hair. He pokes his head back into his family's two story stone hut, earned by Sota's knack for skillful negotiation in the merchant trade. "Lock the door behind me, dear wife."

Karwasisa rubs her eyes, crawls out of bed, stands at the door as her husband walks into the dark, adjusts the latch, creeps back into bed, pulls thick wool blankets overhead, gathers her infant daughter to her bosom and dozes off.

Sota brandishes his sword, meticulously scrutinizing every corner of the Piajajalca compound. He spies a sleeping sentry and lightly kicks him awake; the sentry's eyes pop open.

"Falling asleep at your post," he scolds, "is punishable by death."

"I assure you, Captain Sota," the young sentry sputters, "I was only resting my eyes. All is well."

Sota studies the guard skeptically then continues to roam the village, staring into the pitch black night. It will be a matter of minutes before the inky sky transforms into a gray dawn then brilliant blue. From experience, he knows this is the most dangerous time for enemy attacks, especially from the Incas, who only fight during daylight hours—the only time their Sun God, Inti aids them in battle.

The Cloud Warrior hears someone breathing; he turns his head and sees the whites of a warrior's eyes.

"INCA!" Sota bellows. The sentry blows into his large pututu; the sound permeates every corner of Piajajalca. Mothers with children stay locked up in their huts but hundreds of Cloud Warriors young and old, male and female stream from the confines of their homes, armed and ready for battle. "Hurry!" Captain Sota orders as he duels with heavily tattooed Inca devils, swarming like ants into the compound. "We're surrounded!"

A stout silver-haired Cloud Warrior matron with sparkling blue eyes, races out of her hut, waving a club and an ax. She notes the Inca warriors pouring into the compound by the hundreds.

"We will journey together to the land of our ancestors," she yells to her husband of many years, who follows her out of their

home, *"dove of my heart."*

"Yes, my urpicháy,*" her gray-haired husband shouts back. Though a grandfather, he's a giant of a man; he knocks down several Inca warriors with an oversize battle ax and they crumble to the ground like sacrificial llamas. "But we will take some of these savages with us first."*

Hyperventilating, Karwasisa crouches with her baby and surveys her household's many weapons. She's itching to enter the fray and defend her homeland but unable to do so now that she has the new baby.

"Goddess of War," the young mother prays, amid screams, groans and war whoops shattering her world, "Give my people the strength of all our ancestors to vanquish our enemies."

Outside, the silver-haired matron clubs a soldier under his chin then swings her ax, severing his head before his body hits the ground. Her husband, finding no need for a club, simply wields his sword, as dozens of enemy warriors surround him. An Inca soldier clubs him; another one stabs him in the back. His wife clubs the Inca who felled her man then stabs him before she herself is beaten and stabbed. She shudders, collapses onto her fallen spouse then grasps his hand with her dying breath.

The early morning fog brings an eeriness to the high mountain town, now a bloody battlefield as wave after wave of Inca warriors sprint into Piajajalca, slaughtering all in their path, until hundreds of corpses from both sides strew the compound. Cloud Warriors continue to jump into the melee, brandishing swords and clubs, cursing and butchering the invaders despite their own injuries.

An Inca warrior, his face covered in red and black tattoos bashes in the young mother's door with a enormous spiked club. Karwasisa presses her bundle to her bosom and huddles against a far wall. The warrior smiles sadistically, knowing that after he's finished here, he will go to the next hut, then the next—a low danger mission, conveniently assigned to him by the emperor, a distant cousin. He lifts his barbed cudgel overhead; Karwasisa jumps out of the way, pulls out a long sharp obsidian blade from underneath the bundle where her baby should have been, plunges the knife into the warrior's ribs, skewers his liver and twists the weapon with both hands for good measure. He gazes at her wide eyed, drops the cudgel then collapses with a loud groan.

Karwasisa picks up her infant hidden under a pile of blankets next to her bed; she realizes more Incas will be coming soon to finish off Cloud Warrior women and children hiding in their homes; her only hope for survival is to run for the safety of the Great Jungle. She peeks out the door and witnesses the devastation —corpses of both Cloud Warriors and Incas everywhere, covered with gashes, dirt and blood. She quickly surveys the battlefield to find her husband; he's swinging his ax, cutting down dozens of Incas though his face is bloodied and arms and legs covered in lacerations. Karwasisa is overwhelmed with longing and love for her selfless mate but realizes that despite her husband's effort, he will probably not survive the unrelenting onslaught of Incas and neither will anyone else in Piajajalca. Chuqui Sota told her many times, that no matter what, he wanted the baby and her to survive and if that meant fleeing into the jungle, then that's what he wanted her to do.

May the gods reward my husband for his mettle, *she prays.*

She notices a serpentine fissure in the conflict between two parallel rows of stone huts; this may be her only and last chance to escape; she takes a deep breath, becomes the Serpent Goddess and stealthily slithers away.

CHAPTER TWENTY EIGHT

1522 A.D.
Coastal city of Tumbes
Inca Empire

Tumbes natives load and unload goods from hundreds of sturdy balsa ships moored in a small harbor of the bustling port city. The rest of the city's residents busy themselves constructing houses and ship's offices and widening their already broad streets. They don't notice the immense white sails imprinted with large red crosses billowing in the breeze.

A vast wooden ship, by far the largest vessel they've ever seen, sails into the harbor.

"*Mantega el rumbo!*" the ship's thin, bearded captain yells to his crew, "Steady as she goes!"

Several ragged-looking sailors scramble to trim the sails.

"*Echar anclas!*" the helmsman shouts. "Drop anchor!"

As soon as the Spaniards secure their boat, generous natives, including their esteemed *cacique*—the mayor, fill rafts with gifts of dried llama, exotic fruits, dried fish, jugs of fresh water and *chicha*.

Inca guards guide two messengers to Emperor Huayna Capac holding court in the Quito palace throne room, surrounded by visitors and petitioners from all over the empire. Chimbo Sancto stands on a stool beside the royal, doling out sage advice as needed. An elderly man with a deeply wrinkled face from a distant high mountain province bows before the sovereign.

"This land has been in my family for generations, my shepherd," the man says wearily, holding up a *quipu*, a set of knotted strings used for record keeping, "and my neighbor says that it belongs to him."

"It seems to me," Chimbo whispers in the royal ear, "that this land dispute should be decided by the mayor of this man's village. Ask him if he has consulted his local authority before coming here."

Huayna Capac nods; he almost always agrees with the half-man's advice.

"Have you consulted your local *cacique* on this matter?" the emperor asks.

"No, my Shepherd," the villager responds, his face flush with embarrassment, "I thought that you would treat me more fairly since the local government seems to be quite prone to corruption."

"Corruption?" the emperor says, "How so?"

"The mayor takes bribes," the villager says, "from greedy men who want my land."

"Do you have proof?" the emperor says.

"No, my emperor," the villager says, hanging his head, "but this type of thing is happening more and more frequently, not just to me, but to other hardworking *runakuna*."

"Go to your *cacique*," Huayna Capac says, "and tell him that the Inca Sapa himself said that if he is found to be taking bribes or involved in other contemptible acts of corruption, that he will be dealt with by his emperor quite severely. Then present your case to him. I'm sure you will be treated fairly. If not, return to Quito and I promise to take up the matter myself."

The ancient villager's face glows with gratitude.

"Thank you, my shepherd, my dove, my father," the man says as he backs out of the throne room, head bowed, "Son of Inti. May the gods bestow their eternal blessings upon you."

The old man limps away and the emperor claps his hands.

"Who is next?" the Inca Sapa asks.

One of the guards, head bowed, cuts into the long line of petitioners.

"Excuse me, my great shepherd," he says with a low bow. "It's a matter of urgency, Son of Inti," he says, "Two *chasquis* with important news from the empire's port city of Tumbes."

Huayna Capac scrutinizes the white feathered *chasquis* laden with heavy backpacks then claps his hands twice.

"Step forward," the emperor commands.

The messengers take two mincing steps forward; their heavy sacks jingle as they walk.

"With your permission, my shepherd," one of the messengers says, eye lowered, pointing at his companion's then at his own heavy load.

The emperor gazes at Chimbo; the dwarf shrugs.

"You have permission to relieve yourself of your burdens," the emperor says.

The messengers lower then open their sacks; cut diamonds spill onto the highly polished palace floor along with fine-toothed combs, tempered steel knives inside fine leather sheaths, an iron ax and a vest of chain mail.

The dwarf steps off the stool, walks to the edge of the dais, holds out his arms; a guard picks him up and places him on the floor next to the extraordinary treasure. Chimbo picks up the chain mail vest, puts it on and models it for the court. The throne room explodes with laughter as the metal vest drags on the floor. Next he picks up an iron ax and scrutinizes it carefully.

"It is harder than any of our stones or metals! And sharper, too." the dwarf exclaims, admiring the blade. He hands it to the guard who then hands it to the emperor who seems impressed with its razor sharp blade, impressive heft and superb craftsmanship.

"What manner of ax is this?" the emperor asks.

"The bearded strangers say that is made from. . ." one of the messengers says, hesitates, because he's forgotten the words. He holds up a finger, peers at the colored strings of the *quipu* tied around his waist, scrutinizes it briefly, finds what he's looking for, smiles brightly then slowly pronounces the strange words, "*acero forjado.*"[1]

"*Acero forjado?*" the emperor repeats, eyebrows raised. "What is that?"

"I'm not sure, my shepherd," the messenger says, "But the group of bearded white men who arrived on the *ganbo,* the largest ship that any of us has ever seen, seemed to treasure it, saying that it is virtually indestructible because its composed of special metals, which is then fired and beaten."

---

1 forged steel

"Some of the men let us inspect the gleaming metal on their bodies, too." the second messenger adds, "They called it . . . *armadura*."[1]

"They carried something they called an . . . *arcabuz*[2]," the other *chasqui* adds hesitantly, pronouncing each syllable slowly, "a weapon that thunders as it shoots deadly fire."

From the skeptical look on his face, it's obvious that Huayna Capac believes this to be a gross exaggeration. *A weapon that thunders as it shoots deadly fire?* he thinks, shaking his head. *No, this is not possible.*

"And what do these men want?" the emperor asks.

"We're not sure, my shepherd," the first *chasqui* says.

"But," the second messenger asserts, pointing at the gifts bestowed upon them by the foreigners, "they were friendly to the residents of Tumbes. We assume that they are men of goodwill."

"And they might even be . . . if you will forgive me, my emperor, " the first *chasqui* says uncertainly, " . . . gods."

---

1   armor

2   harquebus

CHAPTER TWENTY NINE

Solsol's body lurches spasmodically.

"Did you see that, T'ica?" Pispis asks wide-eyed.

I rub my eyes but am loathe to be optimistic. The convulsion could mean Solsol's muscles and nerves are twitching involuntarily as they thaw but it could very well mean something else; her body is stiffening in death: rigor mortis. I witnessed this phenomenon several years ago, a few hours after my beloved grandmother died. Though Tatáy tried to enlighten me on the reason for grandmother's eerie twitches, I refused to accept his explanation. Grief-stricken, I kept vigil over grandmother's corpse for three days. As her body began to deteriorate, Mamáy pulled me away, washed my tear-stained face and filthy hair, untangled and neatly braided my thick blond tresses, fed me hot potato vegetable soup and tucked me into bed. Afterward, I slept for two days straight.

I lift Solsol's head and carefully trickle water into her mouth hoping that the hydration might revive her though the poor girl seems to have neither a swallow nor a choke reflex—not a good sign. Though some water does seep into her throat, the majority runs out of her mouth, forming a small puddle on the cave floor. I set the water flask aside and sadly cradle the unconscious girl. Pispis lightly taps her sister's cheeks.

"Solsol," she says, "Can you hear me? It's me, Pispis. Nod if you can hear me."

The girl remains motionless; Pispis sobs as she strokes her sister's hair and long slender arms. I notice Solsol's gray skin is turning a light pink. Or perhaps it's just the light playing tricks on my eyes.

The girl's body lurches again, this time, violently; her eyes pop open; she stares straight ahead beholding a horrific sight no one else can see. She screeches as if being chased by hordes of demons.

"Solsol!" Pispis cries, "Solsol! It's me, Pispis, your sister."

Solsol moves her cracked lips frantically, thrusting her tongue in and out, utterances garbled, nonsensical while her eyes glow eerily in the dim light. I place her into her sister's arms who caresses her howling sibling, still oblivious to her current surroundings. I wonder if my fears about the girl going insane after returning from death have been realized. I press the water flask against her lips again.

"Drink," I says gently, "You need to drink." At first Solsol chokes on the water but I persist. "You want to get better, don't you?" The girl cocks her head, looks at me blankly, grabs the flask and sucks down every last drop.

The next morning is chilly, sunny and cloudless, the sky a perfect Andean blue. I lead the way as we slog down the snowy trail. Listlessly chewing a large wad of coca, Solsol is perched on the larger white and tan llama, gawking at the landscape as if she's in a world she's never seen before. I stop, turn and peer at the half-crazed maiden.

"Keep chewing," I tell her, "Faster. Father Coca will nourish and energize you but you must chew vigorously." Solsol shoots me a dull look but nods then chews a fraction faster. "Good girl. Very good." I say. I'm going to have to be satisfied with that tiny improvement for now.

"You are safe here with us, Solsol." Pispis assures her stuporous sister who she swaddled head to toe in thick woolen blankets. She finds her sister's hand under the blankets and presses it against her cheek. "Your hands are warm!" Pispis announces triumphantly. Solsol nods, pulls her hand back under the blanket then adjusts her position so she's sitting perfectly square upon the llama's back—a good sign. The beast is also burdened by the provisions sack. Although the total weight is probably too heavy, the llama clops forward bravely sensing he's carrying precious cargo. For all their faults, Incas are quite adept at breeding large gentle animals who are able to withstand heavy loads, high altitudes and the harshest of conditions. Pispis is careful to stay by her sister's side in case she has to restore her to an upright position. "We won't let anyone harm you. I promise." She pats her sister's thigh lovingly.

Solsol's eyelashes flutter in acknowledgment; she mutters unintelligibly and continues to gawk at the snowy landscape. The gravely ill girl should be in bed but we have no choice; we must move on before provisions run out. In addition, the savage high mountain weather and extreme altitude can be endured by man or beast for only so long.

I extract a wad of gray green leaves from my bag and tilt my head in Solsol's direction.

"Today we must call upon Father Coca for his blessings." I announce. "to help nourish Solsol so she can drink and eat. We must keep ourselves strong."

I blow over the gray green leaves, saying a short silent prayer, *we beseech your help, Father Coca,* as I visualize a successful journey to the *tampu* then back to my family's village. I crumble a few leaves onto the snow as a libation to Pachamama and Goddess

Mountain then stuff half of the wad into my mouth along with a piece of *llipt'a*. I hand an equal amount to Pispis, who dutifully tucks the coca leaves into her mouth and chews with reverence. She smiles, no doubt grateful for the almost instant boost of energy necessary to withstand this harsh trip then holds up a piece of llama jerky.

"Solsol, you need nourishment." Pispis says. "Just take one bite."

Solsol shakes her head, touches her forehead and holds her stomach.

"Don't force her to eat; it will all go to waste, believe me," I say, recalling my own terrible bout with *soroche*—altitude sickness. "We must get to a lower elevation as quickly as possible." I gaze uneasily at the sky; thick gray clouds seem to have blown in from nowhere. "Goddess Mountain is fickle and will conjure up another snow storm soon. Our llama won't survive another blizzard and neither will we. When we get to the *tampu,* we'll cook and stuff ourselves and let the llama graze to his heart's content. Hopefully we'll find the other llama there as well. We have more than enough food for another day or two but then we must focus on getting off the mountain altogether."

"But what if more Inca priests come?" Pispis asks uneasily.

I shoot Pispis a little smile then pull back on the llama's reins.

"Whoa," I say. The llama stops; I nuzzle the beast's woolly neck, "Good boy."

I hand Pispis the llama's reins; she takes them uncertainly. I take a few steps forward, look off into the distance and point. "See that white rock down there?" I ask, "The one that's balanced on that large boulder about 500 yards downhill?"

"Um . . ." Pispis says, squinting, "I think so."

I pull off the sling strapped around my forehead, extract a small smooth stone from my pocket, load my weapon, then spin it overhead—its hypnotic whirring and pulsing seems to rattle Pispis, who's never witnessed my prowess—not even when I killed the Inca priest who had almost cracked her head open with an ax. Solsol appears to be puzzled by the demonstration but thankfully not alarmed.

Eyebrows knitted in intense concentration, I focus then let the projectile fly. The stone zeroes in on the small white rock, ricochets then hurtles into the vast gorge below. I smile confidently —years of daily practice has paid off. I knot the sling around my forehead then take the llama's reins back from Pispis, mouth open in astonishment, emerald eyes glowing but I don't pay too much attention to that. I need to focus on leading the group safely to the *tampu* and pray fervently that it will be unoccupied upon our arrival.

CHAPTER THIRTY

Chimbo Sancto stands next to the emperor's bed, tears running down his chubby cheeks. Like so many Quiteños, including royals and many of the emperor's favorite concubines, the Inca Sapa Huayna Capac is dying from a plague the likes of which no one has ever witnessed. Skin covered in oozing welts, he's delirious with a high fever and for days has come in and out of consciousness. His eyelids pop open; he squints at Chimbo.

"Why are there three of you?" the emperor rasps with a weak smile. He blinks rapidly trying to focus, apparently conscious enough to know that he's seeing double . . . and triple.

"Drink, *urchipáy,* my dove," Chimbo insists. He holds a cup of medicinal herb-infused *chicha* to Huayna Capac's cracked lips. For days, the emperor has steadfastly refused sustenance, including water, *chicha* and medicine; today is no exception. "Drink. Please."

The emperor shakes his head and points at his throat then with a low groan, opens his mouth wide, revealing a grotesquely swollen tongue, gums and uvula. In fact, his entire throat is so infected, it won't be long before he succumbs to suffocation.

A petite young servant carries in a tray containing a myriad of clay jars.

"I brought more medicine," she whispers. Eyeing the emperor with alarm, she notes that whatever small part of his skin isn't covered in oozing welts, is pale gray-green.

"Tell the queen," Chimbo orders, "that she must come now. The emperor doesn't have much time."

The servant girl seems to be frozen to the spot.

"Our esteemed shepherd of the sun is not dying, is he?" she manages to squeak, forehead furrowed, eyes glistening with tears.

"Go!" the dwarf urges. "Quickly now!"

The girl sets down the tray on a low table then races into the corridor, the slap of her sandals echoing off the walls, on a mission to find Rahua Occlo, the reigning, reclusive Queen of the Incas and sister/wife of the emperor.

Chimbo Sancto, Atahualpa, the widowed Queen Rahua Occlo, daughter Princess Chuqui Huipa and an assortment of high priests and physicians surround the emperor's sick bed, including two of the queen's brothers, Xauxigualpa and Amurimachi. Huayna Capac is semi-conscious, his breathing labored. But he suddenly awakens, still feverish but surprisingly, acutely aware of his surroundings.

"Where is my son, Ninan Cuyochi?" the emperor croaks. "For he is next in line to take the royal fringe. I must speak to him."

Everybody in the room knows that Ninan contracted this deadly plague around the same time the emperor did. Prince Cuyochi is not dead yet but struggling to stay alive. No one has the courage to inform the emperor of his heir's desperate battle with the speckled monster, believing that the shock would instantly drive him to his demise.

"Father," Prince Atahualpa replies earnestly, "there is no need to name a successor now because you will recover from this illness, just like you have always recovered, even from the most serious of war wounds. Do you remember?"

"It has been foretold for many years that black-bearded men from a far away land," Huayna rasps, obviously agitated, "would sail to our shores. The prediction has come true now. Honor them as well as you honor our own ancestors. Do you hear me, Atahualpa?"

The emperor tries to push himself up on his elbows but it's no use. Instead he closes his eyes and all color drains from his face until it becomes lily white. He takes a final gasp, mouth open as if screaming. The physician checks the emperor's neck for a pulse and puts an ear to his chest. Queen Rahua Occlo's breathing grows quick and shallow, her skin unnaturally pale.

"Do something!" she commands.

"I'm so sorry," the physicians say as he shakes his head.

Queen Rahua Occlo and Princess Chuqui Huipa's keening pervade every corner of the Quito palace, so grief-stricken, they don't notice the guards entering the room.

Atahualpa points at Chimbo Sancto. With a nod he directs the guards to arrest the dwarf: former leader of the rebel empire, honorary eldest son of the deceased emperor and Inca of the Heart.

CHAPTER THIRTY ONE

Wafts of smoke curl into the sky as we near the *tampu*. After so much hiking, I have been daydreaming about resting my weary feet in the comfort of the cozy hut; I also planned to prepare a feast fit for the gods on the earthen wood stove. Now this.

"It looks like we have company," I announce listlessly.

Pispis regards the smoke, bites her lower lip and covers her face with her hands. Solsol is slumped over the llama, who is bleating, clopping and spitting. Without at least one good night's rest, the beast could end up collapsing for want of grazing and fresh water and Solsol will undoubtedly perish, our heroic efforts to save her wasted.

Pispis and Solsol stayed at the *tampu* after being led there by the Inca priests; the girls were chosen for the dubious honor of *capacocha*—human child sacrifice and had been educated and fed like Inca royalty since the horrible day they were kidnapped from their family's village and forced to reside in the Temple of the Sun. *Mamaconas*—Inca high priestesses, teachers and mentors— expected them to comply with the strict rules and rituals of the Inca religion. Most of the young girls, including Pispis and Solsol were miserable; they mourned their families, refusing to eat, unable to sleep and prone to frequent crying spells. In recent months, Pispis and Solsol were plied with alcohol and hallucinogenic drugs with the intention of making them docile, spelling the end of their days in the physical realm of *kay pacha*.

But the Inca's sacred ritual was foiled—first by Solsol, who unbeknownst to her younger sister had regurgitated much of the alcohol and drugs meant to keep her tractable. When they arrived near the mountain peak, Solsol saw her chance to escape and took it. Pispis vaguely remembers her sister calling her after the high priest pushed her to her knees at the sacrificial platform overlooking Humantay Lagoon. She recalls the high priest forcing a vile liquid down her throat, intoxicating her to the extent that the world spun around her in a dreadful rainbow of colors and sounds, making her unable to cut through the drugged fog to save herself. The last thing she remembered before waking up in the Room of Death was a stunning view of the sparkling aquamarine Humantay Lagoon. She wondered if this was the lovely Upper World, *hanan pacha* that the *mamaconas* had promised—then she blacked out.

It crosses Pispis's mind that maybe the gods are amused by this turn of events and will bless them with good fortune. Or maybe the gods are cursing them and the occupied *tampu* is only the start of a string of unlucky events which will forever curse our lives.

"What are we going to do now?" the girl asks, wringing her hands.

Shading my eyes with my hand, I peer at the *tampu* and in the process, catch sight of a tiny old woman hiking up the switchback trail; she doesn't seem to be aware of our presence yet. I silently point her out to Pispis then put a finger to my lips. Since we're at Mistress Mountain's tree line now, I guide Pispis, the llama and Solsol behind a thicket of bushes adjacent to the trail, remove the sling from my forehead and wait.

In the stark late afternoon sun, the Ancient One seems as wrinkled, bent and gnarled as a Keñua tree; she's carrying a large sturdy woven basket and leading an enormous, broad-chested albino llama with a long elegant neck and carefully groomed woolly mane.

I have never seen a llama this big. I muse. *It must have been specially bred by the Incas which means, the old lady must be associated with the Empire.* The thought sends shivers up my spine.

The old crone steps off the trail into a lightly wooded area, harvests some plants, her basket overflowing with an assortment of leafy wild herbs and flowers. Since we're well hidden behind brush and trees, she remains unaware of our presence, steps past us and continues ascend the trail.

Waiting until the old lady's gone a bit farther, I sneak up behind her then quickly lash my sling around her neck, twist and tighten it. She drops her basket and releases her llama's reins; the beast bleats, pulls back its ears, juts its neck out, purses its lips then spits a wide spray of saliva all over my face. I elbow the beast's snout; it pulls back its head, bleats then trots up the trail. The Ancient One desperately tugs at my improvised noose, choking and gasping for breath. I must make a decision now. If I release the old crone, she might very well run back to the *tampu,* unleashing Inca warriors or priests that may be resting there and who would be quite pleased to capture us; undoubtedly, they would force us back up Mistress Mountain and make us the centerpiece of *capacocha.* If I kill the old lady, the Incas will wonder where she went, conjure up their wrathful gods to search for her and end up capturing our little contingent anyway. But what if the old woman is just a simple *runakuna* making a pilgrimage?

The seemingly frail old lady spins around inside the sling, faces me, knees me in the stomach. Hard. I groan, double over, releasing the sling in the process. The surprisingly sinewy matron clasps her hands and crashes them down in one swift motion upon the nape of my neck. I collapse, the world spinning around me, panting for breath. She places a knee on my back, unsheathes a knife and holds its razor sharp blade to the side of my neck.

"Who are you?" she growls.

"Don't hurt her!" Pispis yells, stepping out from the thicket of trees.

"Step back and drop your weapons," the Ancient One snarls "Or I swear, I'll slit your friend's throat right here and now."

"I don't have any weapons," Pispis says. She puts her hands up and turns around slowly to prove it. "See?"

The Ancient One must have been a beauty in her day with slanted dark brown eyes, a regal nose and shiny onyx-colored oval fingernails; her fine straight hair is parted in the middle and twisted into a spool of spun silver at the nape of her neck.

"What are *you* doing here?" I demand, knife still poised on my neck. "You weren't here a week ago."

"You are a cheeky little assassin," the old lady snarls, "aren't you?" She compresses the blade until I can feel it nick my neck's tender skin; this woman is serious about killing me if she has to.

"It's just we three girls and the llama." Pispis insists. She pulls the beast's reins; he clops into the open, Solsol still slumped over his back. "See?"

"We're just *runakuna*, like yourself. " I say, then hesitate, not knowing how much I should tell this woman about our recent misadventures, " . . . We're just returning from a pilgrimage to Mistress Mountain."

"Liars!" the Ancient One growls, "You're bandits, specially trained by your barbaric yellow-haired tribe to attack, rob and murder innocent *runakuna*."

"I know that's what it seems like," I say meekly, "But we have no weapons save for my sling and a knife my father gave me."

The Ancient One searches my waist, finds my blade, pulls it out of its sheath and tosses it on the ground.

"So, you were planning to kill me with that?" the old crone rasps.

"No," I say, "I swear . . . "

"The Inca priests, " Pispis explains, "were going to sacrifice my sister and me at the Humantay Lagoon. But we escaped."

"You escaped *capacocha?*" the old crone says.

"Yes," I rasp, " and it wasn't easy. I would tell you the story but if you're with the Incas . . ."

"I'm not with the Incas!" the Ancient One says. ". . . Well, not exactly."

"What does that mean?" Pispis asks, "Either you're with the Incas or you're not."

"Then where did you get the giant llama?" I ask, tasting the dirt my lips are pressed into.

"So you think the Incas are the only ones capable of breeding giant llamas?" the old lady asks. "You give them too much credit. The Incas are warmongers, not animal breeders." She scrutinizes the very ill Solsol, still slumped over the llama.

"What's the matter with her?" she asks.

"After running away from the high priests, my sister almost froze to death in a blizzard, " Pispis explains, "T'ica here," she

174

says, pointing at me, "found her freezing to death in the snow. We worked together to save her." her voice breaks into a high pitiful peep, "We don't know if she'll ever recover fully."

The Ancient One pulls the knife away from my throat, puts it back in her sheaf hung on a thick cloth belt around her waist, stands and dusts off her tunic; she scoops up the herbs and delicate mountain flowers that tumbled out of her basket, keeping a wary eye on me, her erstwhile attacker. She steps toward the stand of trees, pets our llama then inspects Solsol by pulling back her eyelids, touching her skin and checking her pulse.

"She's alive," the Ancient One whispers, a look of grave concern darkening her face, "but just barely."

"Can you help her?" I ask.

"Doubtful," the old woman states. "Let's take her to the *tampu* and see what we can do. But first, somebody needs to fetch my llama."

"What's his name?" Pispis asks.

"Achiq." the Ancient One answers.

Pispis puts two fingers in her mouth, blows a long earsplitting whistle then energetically hikes up the trail.

"Achiq! Achiq!" she yells at the top of her young powerful lungs.

I get up on my feet and shake my head.

If there are any Incas within fifty miles, I think, *they would surely be alerted by Pispis's whistle and loud voice.*

The Ancient One grabs our llama's reins, lithely pads down the trail as if walking with the paws of Goddess Puma. I hesitate for a moment, thinking this could be a trap. The old lady turns around, hands on her hips.

"Are you coming or not?" she asks impatiently, pointing at Solsol's limp body, "We have no time to waste."

CHAPTER THIRTY TWO

After following the high priest Villac Umu into to the deceased's bed chamber, two mummification experts and their apprentices wrap him tightly onto a stretcher, carry him down the palace corridor and scurry toward a steep narrow staircase leading to a large cellar; clerestory windows line its four wall and rays of sun keep the room brightly lit until sunset. They disrobe the dead royal then place him on a large stone slab. The older gray-haired mummification expert extracts a knife from a leather pouch. He opens the corpse's belly with a small scalpel; the incision oozes clear liquid and blood. He parts the slit open with his hands, slips his knife into the open abdomen, cuts out the liver then places it in a large clay pot. He repeats the process with the deceased's kidneys, lungs, intestines, etc. Finally, he forces open the upper torso, severing veins, arteries and valves connected to the heart, plucks out the muscular organ then holds it up to the light.

"It's important to extract all internal organs intact and in this instance, particularly the heart." he explains to the young apprentices, who observe the process solemnly. He gingerly places the emperor's heart in a separate clay pot filled with a variety of strong smelling herbs and salt. "The emperor's body will travel to Cuzco, but his heart will remain here with his beloved Quiteños, whom he treasures above all others."

Apprentices fill the empty cavity with salt and herbs, stitch it back together, place the emperor's knees to his chest, right arm crossed over left, eyes cast down then bring it to the palace courtyard to desiccate in the dry high mountain air.

Weeks later artisans apply layers of flesh-colored makeup to disguise hideous pock marks spawned by the plague, style hair and darken eyelashes and eyebrows then arrange fine clothes and gold and silver jewelry over the mummy. Apprentices fasten the royal mummy onto a funeral litter elaborately adorned with feathers and gold.

Dressed in elaborate tunics, headdresses, jewelry and capes, Queen Rahua Occlo, Princess Chuqui Huipa ride directly behind the mummy's litter, lesser royals and nobles ride behind them, two by two, side by side. Curiously, Atahualpa rides at the end of the line and doesn't appear to be suitably attired for a state funeral, wearing a coarsely woven tunic more appropriate for planting potatoes or, ironically, shepherding llamas.

Coarse thick hair in disarray and donning a shapeless filthy corn meal sack, Chimbo Sancto trudges at the end of the funeral cortege, hands tied behind his back like a common criminal; he's sullen and angry, not at Atahualpa but at himself. He knows he should have predicted this unfortunate scenario when the emperor fell desperately ill. However, his sincere affection and allegiance for the emperor blinded him to the prospect that he could die under the care of dozens of highly skilled Inca physicians. Now, he must pay the price for being overly optimistic and underestimating the speed at which Atahualpa would take the opportunity to arrest him.

The widowed *coya* waves at Atahualpa to bring his litter to the front of the funeral cortege. He notes her signal with a tilt of his head, then orders his carriers to move next to the queen.

"Are you sure this is necessary, Atahualpa?" the queen mother states. She cranes her neck then points at the pitiful dwarf stumbling on foot at the rear.

"He angered the gods by dishonoring our traditions and taking advantage of my aging father," Atahualpa says. "Tatáy Inti, our

Sun God demands obeisance and punishes those who suggest otherwise. Would you have the gods visit even more misfortune upon the empire than they already have?"

"No," the queen says, "but I just thought . . ."

Atahualpa stops her with a dismissive wave of his hand.

"The gods and our ancestors will not be mocked, widowed *coya*." the prince says. He gazes down upon the six litter carriers waiting patiently below him, broad shoulder muscles bulging under the weight of the litter. "Back to the palace," he barks.

The carriers turn the litter and proceed north.

"Wait!" the shocked queen mother cries out; the prince's carriers stumble to a halt. "Will you not be joining the funeral cortege for the entire journey, Atahualpa? This is your father after all."

"History tells us that provinces of great empires are prone to rebellion after the death of a ruler," Atahualpa answers stoically, "Until a new emperor is definitively decided upon, the empire is quite vulnerable. As you must know, the period of interregnum is quite unstable."

"The council is working on this decision as fast as they can, my prince," the queen states.

"It will only be a matter of days, at most a few weeks," Princess Chuqui Huipa adds, toying with a strand of her thick raven hair, "until the proper rituals are observed and the gods consulted. Soon you will be officially announced as the new emperor."

"This is not necessarily an honor that I covet," Atahualpa

replies stiffly.

"It is your duty," Princess Chuqui insists, "to accept the scarlet fringe if bestowed upon you, otherwise, my brother Huascar would be named emperor. And I would have to marry that drunken toad."

"Not necessarily an honor that you would covet then?" Atahualpa asks impishly.

"I would sooner," the princess says indignantly, "marry Çupay —the very devil himself."

"Then," Atahualpa says. "you must appreciate my reluctance to accept the fringe." When he points, the litter carriers move the prince's litter next to the mummified remains of his father. "Only one that has carried the weight of leadership for so long can understand its hardships. Isn't that right, Father?" the prince asks the mummy, who, of course, remains mute. Atahualpa shakes his head ruefully.

"And what will happen to Chimbo Sancto?" Queen Rahua Occlo asks.

"Under the circumstances, your concern as the widowed *coya* of the Inca empire should rest solely with the fate of the empire," Prince Atahualpa spits, "not with the fate of that useless half-man. We can only hope the gods will spare what remains of our plague-ridden empire for the sin of suffering the conceits of this cock-eyed heretic."

Rahua Occlo is taken aback. Atahualpa is right, to an extent. The plague has certainly taken its toll, not just upon members of the royal family but on the general population as well. Royal *quipumayocs*—Inca accountants working with population enumerators, estimate that well over twenty percent of the population has thus far sickened and died over the course of a few short months; the plague strikes hundreds of additional citizens every day. Pock-marked corpses seem to be piling up in mounds everywhere but no one, not even the high priests and Inca physicians, who futilely attempted to save the emperor have a remedy for this arbitrary curse from the gods.

Despite the epidemic, residents of the royal palace, servants and nobles alike, developed quite a bit of affection for the ebullient, irreverent Chimbo, except, of course, for Atahualpa who continues to despise him with a passion, frequently referring to him as: the pocket-sized embarrassment, the flea-sized heretic and blood sucking parasite. Nevertheless the dwarf helped make the palace a joyful place, where lively political and theological discussions and challenges could take place without fear of retribution. The late emperor greatly appreciated the intellectual stimulation, especially in his old age where repartee became much preferred over military battle.

"We can not journey without you, Prince Atahualpa," Princess Chuqui Huipa states with a pout.

"And why not?" Atahualpa asks.

"Because," the princess whines, "there are too many dangers along the way."

"Who will protect us from hostile tribes," the widowed *coya* adds, "rebels or even rogue government factions we might very well encounter? The journey to Cuzco is long and treacherous since we must travel over remote mountainous terrain. Without you, we are easy targets. "

"As you can see," Atahualpa responds with a wave of his hand, "the funeral cortege is guarded by hundreds of the empire's most trusted and highly trained warriors."

"But your vast military expertise," Princess Chuqui Huipa adds, "would be our very best protection from such hostile elements."

"I will do my best to join the funeral celebration in Tumibamba, my beloved father's birth place, " Atahualpa says firmly. "Until then, there is much I must attend to in Quito."

With a clap of the prince's hands, litter carriers tote him toward the royal palace; the queen and princess crane their necks and watch him fade into the distance. They can only pray that the gods of the Inca empire will protect them in their hour of mourning and perilous period of interregnum.

CHAPTER THIRTY THREE

The Ancient One covers the sick girl with a thick blanket. Pispis and I sit on the floor next to her. I glance intermittently at the door, sure that Incas will burst through any second and cut us to pieces.

"Royals and commoners alike are no longer in any condition to scale the likes of Mistress Mountain, much less perform their sacred sacrificial rites. The gods have abandoned the Inca Empire." The Ancient One presses her lips together and nods. "Jap, jap, jap, jap, jap, jap," she says smacking her lips with each 'jap'. "Pestilence time; world reversal."

"*Pisti Timpu.*" I murmur remembering what the village shaman told me. "But the Incas were just here a few days ago."

Pispis nods apprehensively—the memory of the forced marched up Mistress Salkantay Mountain still all-too-fresh.

"Things change very rapidly in *kay pacha,* this physical realm," the Ancient One says, nonchalantly, "Don't worry, my doves. We are safe." She claps her hands, strolls to the corner stove, pokes the smoldering embers and adds a few more logs.

Her collection of assorted pots set upon shelves cover an adjacent wall; she pulls down a small black jar, opens it; the stale smokey air of the *tampu* fills with the pungent, powerful smell of an herbal liniment. "Go to the stream and fill a flask with water," she orders Pispis, "And don't dawdle!"

Pispis grabs a flask then runs outside. Lord Inti smiles down upon her in the late afternoon sun.

"*Inti Tatáy,*" she prays, "thank you for the crisp clean air and sunshine."

She runs past the rear of the *tampu*, where three llamas are munching contentedly on the lush grasses of the *puno*. The brown llama that escaped from the peak had clopped down to the *tampu*, as hoped; he stands next to the larger tan and white llama that carried Solsol. The Ancient One's giant albino, Achiq keeps its distance; he seems to have no interest in cultivating a friendly relationship with the others.

Pispis arrives at the lush green banks of the stream, quickly fills the flask and sprints back to the *tampu*.

The Ancient One bends over the semi-conscious Solsol and dabs the aromatic ointment under her nose.

"Jap, jap, jap, jap, jap, jap. Dehydration." she says, continuing her habit of nodding and smacking her lips loudly. When Pispis runs back in breathlessly with the water flask, Solsol wakes with a start; she is wild-eyed, on the verge of hysteria. The Ancient One regards the smoldering fire, flicks her finger and the flames magically reignite. She begins a hypnotic chant with long low guttural clicks and hums, squats, lifts up Solsol's head then touches the flask to the girl's lips. Her eyelids fluttering, Solsol sips the cool mountain water. The Ancient One continues to chant, her thick onyx-colored fingernails gleaming in the firelight. She lightly anoints the girl's forehead with the herbal liniment. Her thirst quenched for now, Solsol lies back.

"Is she going to be alright?" Pispis asks, her voice trembling.

The Ancient One stands, straightens her spine, steps to the herbal shelf and pulls down a large silver cup embossed with an unsettling image of a scowling man sporting a hooked nose. She eyes her collection of potions, spots a tall slender jug, lifts it from the shelf, pulls out the cork with her perfect white teeth and pours a strong smelling liquid into the odd silver cup. "Jap, jap, jap, jap,

jap, jap." she utters to no one in particular. She inhales the brew's powerful scent then smiles. I recognize the smell of the potent purple liquid from where I sit.

It's aha, I think, *a powerful potion only specially trained sorcerers and shamans know how to brew.*

"Jap, jap, jap, jap, jap, jap," the old woman says, squinting and tilting her head as if able to read my thoughts. She chuckles, reaches out to lightly pinch our cheeks. "Purple maize, quinoa," she informs us, "various herbs and . . . a special fruit. Secret recipe." She blows over the top of the brew, pours some drops on the floor, dips her fingers in the cup, then sprinkles the air with fine droplets as she chants, invoking blessings from the Earth Goddess, Sacred Places, Goddess Salkantay Mountain.

"Pachamama, Tirakuna, Apu Salkantay," she prays softly, pausing for a moment to concentrate on what she wants, standard practice for a successful *phukay*—an offering to the gods, "I beseech you to *fully* restore this yellow-hair, this *runakuna,* this *munay warmikuna,* to us here in *kay pacha."*

Our Sonqo village shaman gave a dose of sacred *aha* to my dying grandmother and said the appropriate prayers, too, but she perished soon after anyway. Tatáy said it was simply her time to soar to the upper world—*hanan pacha* and no amount of medicine or magic could have changed that. I choke back my tears at the memory; I fervently pray the old crone will fare better with the gravely ill Solsol.

The Ancient One kneels, places a hand behind Solsol's head, trickles a stream of the sparkling purple brew into her mouth then lays the girl's head down on the straw bed. She hands the silver cup with the embossed image of the scowling man to me; I don't know what to do with it but I grasp it with both hands.

The old woman lifts her hands which transform into countless twinkling stars; she sways and chants. Solsol becomes drenched in a river of sweat and cosmic light; she coughs, hacks, spits and shudders. When the old crone lowers her hands, the universe of stars vanishes in an instant.

"Jap, jap, jap, jap, jap, jap," she notes cheerfully, nodding emphatically with each syllable.

Solsol's pale gray skin slowly becomes pink then radiant; it's then that I notice that the formerly scowling man's face embossed on the silver cup is now smiling.

CHAPTER THIRTY FOUR

1511 A.D.
Piajajalca
Chachapoyas

The early morning fog brings an eeriness to the high mountain stronghold now a bloody Inca and Cloud Warrior battlefield. Piajajalca residents as young as twelve jump into the melee, slinging swords and clubs, cursing the invaders, despite serious injuries, determined to defend their homeland to the death.

Taquiri has heard it said that it takes twenty Inca warriors to kill one Cloud Warrior; now that he sees the size of these savages, he understands why. An immense bearded man looms over the diminutive Taquiri, laughs huskily then thrusts his blade. Taquiri hops out of the way, then swings his padded shield, knocking the sword from the man's massive hand. With no desire to continue the brawl, Taquiri races out of Piajajalca, past dozens of circular huts with their odd cone-shaped thatched roofs. On the way out, he notices his new friend, the boy soldier, Hankanpuma—Brilliant Puma, a talented archer who's drawing a bead on a Cloud Warrior; the arrow hits the muscular red-haired man in the back and he slumps to the ground.

"Come with me," Taquiri yells, trying to be heard over the din of screaming, moaning and cursing.

Hankanpuma lowers his bow.

"Where are we going?" the boy yells, a mixture of confusion and fear on his youthful face.

"To safety," Taquiri says, trembling uncontrollably.

The boy soldier nods; together they bound east into the rainforest.

Taquiri knows the consequences of deserting the Inca army: weeks of public humiliation and torture in the Cuzco town square, followed by dismemberment, disembowelment then finally death by burning. Being burned to ash means he would be unable journey to the heavenly realm of hanan pacha, *important because that's where he would join his wife and son—if they've been killed, something he's not yet sure of.*

But he's willing to chance desertion anyway especially since he's stashed three poison darts in a leather pouch under his tunic, soaked in the powerful toxin of the golden frog. He'd made friends with a Choco Embera native, named Maicu from the northern rainforest who'd been kidnapped, hauled back to Cuzco and conscripted into the Inca army so that he could instruct weapon makers in the manufacture of poison arrows and darts. Taquiri learned the highly specialized craft well before Maicu had somehow managed to escape, along with scores of his precious golden dart frogs, presumably to the wilds of the jungle. Before his captain assigned him to other weapon-making duties, Taquiri managed to pilfer the poison darts. Maicu had assured him the darts would remain lethal for at least two years. If Taquiri ever got captured for desertion, he planned to stab himself in the neck and after three minutes of intense agony, journey to hanan pacha.

CHAPTER THIRTY FIVE

Hundreds of priests, dancers, actors and musicians untiringly celebrate and reenact the dead emperor's life; professional mourners shriek and wail. Alongside the Inca road, citizens emulate professional mourners, determined not to be seen as traitorously indifferent to the sovereign's passing; their shrill cries fill the air with such intensity that birds are knocked out of the sky, leaving the cobblestone road strewn with their feathered carnage.

Over the high plains, a sedate procession of the emperor's sons and brothers bearing the funeral litter on their shoulders precedes the widowed Queen Rahua Occlo and her daughter, Princess Chuqui. Huayna Capac's heart has already been deposited in the Temple of the Sun in Quito, symbolizing that although his body will reside in Cuzco, the emperor's heart would always be with the people of the northern empire.

Joining the celebration from distant and not-so-distant provinces, Daughters of the Sun will be sacrificed in honor of the dead monarch, some in Cuzco, others at designated sites along the way. Many coastal sun virgins, unused to the rarefied heights of Andean highland towns, will die en route from altitude sickness; Inca accountants, record unexcused absences on color-coded knotted strings—*quipus*. Since their records are renowned for accuracy, making graft exceedingly rare, *quipumayocs* are exceedingly unpopular with corrupt bureaucrat and *runakuna* alike. Rebellious provinces often make alliances with other disgruntled tribes and together proclaim their contempt for the empire's increasingly onerous religious demands and high taxes by orchestrating armed rebellions, most of which end in bitter defeat.

* * *

The funeral cortege arrives in Tumibamba, the dead emperor's birth place and site of a royal estate, complete with a palace, lavish gardens and a sumptuous Sun Temple built before his death to his exacting specifications; mourners will remain here for a month.

Despite lack of sleep and exhaustion from endless hours of travel, funeral attendees rise before dawn and gather in the colossal intricately landscaped square in front of the palace where high priests take turns reciting poems praising the dead Inca's long list of accomplishments.

Attendants pour endless cups of *chicha* for all funeral attendees. Even poor local children fight to get to the front of the line, waving crude gourds.

"My turn!" a cherry-cheeked girl of five yells.

"No!" another young boy yells, "My turn!"

High priest Villac Umu carries a tightly bundled newborn into the square, near a freshly excavated pit. He holds the infant overhead, chanting praises to the Sun God until Inti finally smiles upon devotees with the day's first rays of light. He drops the infant into its final resting place; attendees chant in unison.

"Inti, our most sacred Sun God, bless us, your children of the sun and grant us everlasting life!"

Local clerics stand next to solemn young mothers from vanquished provinces who carry infants also intended for *capacocha* to prove allegiance to the empire and to ensure the deceased Inca will have company in his journey to the upper world, *hanan pacha;* many conquered tribes would rather comply than face the dire consequences rained down upon them by the Incas.

The queen mother and princess watch aloofly, perched on low plush thrones on a wide dais set back from the top step of the Tumibamba palace.

"I would rather be buried alive," Chuqui Huipa whispers in her mother's ear, as dancers twirl to the hypnotic beat of drums and singers yodel, "than marry that devil Huascar. At least then, my suffering would be over."

"I have no intention," Queen mother Rahua Occlo whispers back, "of granting such permission. And Huascar cannot assume the throne without it."

"How do you plan to refuse him, Mother," Chuqui asks, sipping from her ornate gold goblet. "without getting us killed, that is?"

Villac Umu escorts a fourteen year old virgin, bleary-eyed and barely able to walk the endless steps to the sacrificial platform positioned in front of the queen mother and princess. Wearing a close fitting cap covered in pristine white feathers, with plumes set ear to ear in a fan-shape, she is beautiful, well-nourished, clothed and bejeweled in the bold royal fashion of scarlet, bright blue and gold, in stark contrast to her *runakuna* contemporaries in the crowd, who don threadbare tunics over gaunt, under-nourished bodies. Increasingly onerous taxes to support endless wars and lavish royal lifestyles continue to impoverish many provinces, however those who offer their most perfect young children to the Inca gods are rewarded with extra rations and prestigious bureaucratic appointments.

"Our future lies with the gods, *urchipáy*, my dove." the queen mother replies to Princess Chuqui. The queen gulps the remainder of her *chicha* from a large gold and silver goblet. A servant refills it instantly. "And I trust the gods will aid us in our time of need."

When the Daughter of the Sun kneels, devotees of all ages stagger about the Tumibamba Square, swilling endless cups of *chicha,* anxiously awaiting the Inca sacrament. Others wander the streets to find nearby copper-lined canals in which their over-filled bladders can be drained.

The high priest turns his palms to the heavens invoking the cheers of the inebriated crowd. An assistant hands him a golden spiked club, which he lifts overhead bringing the crowd's roar to a fevered crescendo. Villac Umu shudders then brings the club down upon the virgin's skull, dispatching her to *hanan pacha* instantly; the crowd's shouts can be heard from the highest peaks of the Inca Empire's sacred mountains.

CHAPTER THIRTY SIX

After an early breakfast stew of *ch'uño* mixed with wild *ullucus,* a root vegetable that the Ancient One found growing near the *tampu,* the sisters play a hand clapping game while they sing a song about whom they will marry and how many children they will have. The formerly desperately ill Solsol now looks and acts perfectly normal; even more miraculous is that she hasn't lost any body parts to frostbite, not even a tip of a finger or a toe. While the sisters continue to play, I gather up our few belongings for the final leg of our journey down the mountain. The Ancient One hands me a large cloth bundle of exotic dried fruit, dates and nuts.

"This will give you nourishment when you most need it." the Ancient One proclaims, "Jap, jap, jap, jap, jap, jap."

She uncorks several jars, pouring out various trinkets onto a coarse black cloth: tropical seeds, coca seeds, unspun wool, incense, fool's gold, shells and a tiny starfish. She folds the cloth, steps to the stove, emits a high pitched chant in the same strange language she invoked yesterday, scowls, throws the packet in the fire, where it hisses then quickly burns to ash. She smooths her silver hair, bares her perfect teeth in a broad smile and claps.

"You will be safe now, my doves," the Ancient One says, "if you remember one thing. *Tirakuna,* the powerful sacred places are our nurturers but they are capable of punishing *runakuna* and royalty alike for their moral lapses. This is what's happening to the Incas now and not just because of *capacocha.* Child sacrifice is merely one of thousands of transgressions against their own people for which the Incas and their minions must pay, the greedy inbred bastards." The Ancient One puts a hand over her mouth then giggles like a young girl. "Forgive my strong language, girls but this is how it always is with the ruling classes; they grow paranoid and dissatisfied with their lives, craving more and more dominance until people rise up and challenge them or until the gods rain down catastrophes upon them in ways they never imagined. I've been around long enough to see these things for myself." She lifts the lids off of several clay storage jars and sniffs each one. "Now the people mourn the warmonger, Inca Emperor Huayna Capac, who, the last I heard, is suffering from the plague like any other man; he could be dead now for all I know. The royals are now searching desperately for a cure, fearing they could be next." She stuffs a large woven bag with a variety of medicinal herbs and hands it to me.

"The emperor is ill?" I ask, peeking into the bag. "I thought he was a god."

"T'ica, the truth is. We are all gods, each in our own way." The Ancient One pats the bag which she just handed me. "Your village of Sonqo will be visited by the speckled monster," she says, "but do not be afraid. You will know what to do."

"But," I protest, "I don't know anything."

The Ancient One lightly touches my hand.

"You are more powerful," the Ancient One says, "than you know." The old lady fills a flask with *aha*, the powerful potion that cured Solsol, and hands it to me. "Have a safe journey."

"You're not coming with us?" Pispis asks.

With a twinkle in her eyes, the Ancient One shoves another couple of logs onto the fire then reclines on the straw mattress; she taps the bed, bidding us to make ourselves comfortable there.

"Have you heard about Pachacutiq Inca Yupanqui?" she asks.

I shrug and shake my head.

"Pachacutiq was the ninth Inca Emperor," Solsol says, "We learned about him when we studied at the Temple of the Sun."

"His real name was . . ." Pispis adds, "Cusi Yupanqui and his father was Inca Viracocha. When the savage Chankas invaded Cuzco, the Inca Viracocha fled but the brave Pachacutiq stood and fought."

"It is said that the Chankas were defeated so badly," Solsol adds "because stones rose up to fight on Cusi Yupanqui's side. After that, he was known as Pachacutiq—he who overturns time and space."

"After defeating the Chankas, Pachacutiq rebuilt Cuzco, including the Temple of the Sun into a magnificent architectural wonder." Pispis recites. "Many local and regional leaders—the *curacas*—did not hesitate to acknowledge Pachacutiq's skills and referred to him as Sovereign Lord, Child of the Sun God."

"Jap, jap, jap, jap, jap, jap," the Ancient One says, waving a gnarled forefinger, "The *mamaconas* taught you Daughters of the Sun well. But though Pachacutiq is greatly revered," she continues, "there are things you were not taught. For instance, he set a precedent by being ruthless toward otherwise peaceful independent tribes who refused to give up their sovereignty and freedom to become part of the Inca Empire; his cruelty also extended to his own flesh and blood: he murdered two of his brothers and two of his own sons due to paranoia that they might be seeking to overthrow him. As if that wasn't bad enough, his viciousness extended to the Daughters of the Sun—like you two sisters. The holy high priestess, Ccacca Mama along with her young charges found the true secrets of the universe. After those secrets were discovered, Pachacutiq, due to a combination of paranoia, innumerable atrocities and advanced age found himself unable to attain the spiritual enlightenment of the high priestesses. In fact, he considered the enlightened Daughters of the Sun a threat to his dominion over the Inca Empire. Wide-spread *capacocha* of the enlightened young women started in earnest then. Pachacutiq, the crazy old sovereign, also thought he could stave off the ravages of old age and even death by sacrificing and drinking the blood of innocents. He also insisted that conquered tribes prove their loyalty to the empire by handing over their most beautiful young children; refusal meant retribution in which all rebels and their families would be annihilated."

The old woman pauses and stares at her young listeners.

"And what about our tribe, the Cloud Warriors?" Pispis asks.

"You will be happy to know," the Ancient One answers, "that Pachacutiq lost many wars against the vicious Cloud Warriors. Even today, they are a force to be reckoned with."

Solsol and Pispis beam with pride.

"When we return to our family," says Pispis, "we will fight the Incas, too."

"As you should," the Ancient One continues, "if there are any Incas left by that time."

"Because of the speckled monster," I ask, *"Pisti Timpu?"*

The Ancient One nods.

"T'ica, my dove, enlightened *runakuna* know," she says, "that feasting on knowledge is even more important than eating. I will tell you girls a tale that will explain many things to you."

She takes a deep breath, closes her eyes, her silver mane glimmering in the firelight.

"Cusi Coyllur Ñusta—Princess Joyful Star was renowned for her stunning beauty, intelligence, kindness and generosity. A wildly successful, handsome young Inca general, Apu Ollantay fell in love with her as did almost every young man in the Empire. When Ollantay was sure that the princess felt the same way about him, he asked her father, Emperor Pachacutiq for her hand in marriage. But the emperor had other plans for his royal daughter, insisting that she marry one of her full brothers to ensure the purity of the Inca blood line. When she refused, the emperor imprisoned her in a place she'd never be found."

"His marriage proposal rejected by the emperor and the princess gone, Ollantay enlisted his faithful mountain troops, the Antis who waged war upon the Inca Emperor because he had always treated them parsimoniously, though they had always fought valiantly for their sovereign."

"After a decade, Apu Ollantay lost the rebel war but by that time, the sick, aging and cruel Emperor Pachacutiq finally died and named his heir to the throne, his son, Tupac Yupanqui. Though the new emperor could have massacred Apu Ollantay and his troops, he wisely decided to be merciful and pardoned them, even reinstating Ollantay's status as general."

"Though elated that he and his troops had been pardoned, Ollantay still longed for his beloved Cusi Coyllur Ñusta—his Joyful Star but none seemed to know her whereabouts. The general assumed that Pachacutiq murdered her, as his ruthlessness had been demonstrated many times before, even to his own offspring."

"That's so sad," Pispis declares. She dries her tears on her tunic sleeve.

Solsol and I sniff and wipe away our tears, too.

"Jap, jap, jap, jap, jap, jap," the Ancient One says, "very sad indeed but the tale is not over yet."

Our eyes light up in anticipation; the Ancient One stabs the air with a gnarled finger.

"At that time, a young maiden, Yma Sumac resided with other miserable Daughters of the Sun in the Qorincancha located in Cuzco. Yma was considered a charity case—an orphan mercifully sheltered and educated by the dedicated high priestesses of the temple. The beautiful orphan was expected to become a high priestess and live the rest of her days in the temple, though she consistently refused to do so, much to the consternation of the *mamaconas*. She would go for daily walks in the sumptuous courtyard and garden of the Qorincancha which, as Solsol and Pispis know first hand, is filled with meticulously crafted life-sized silver and gold corn plants, shepherds, llamas, jaguars, guinea pigs, monkeys, birds and even butterflies and insects, gifts bequeathed by the now deceased Pachacutiq himself."

"When Yma was around ten years old, she became aware of a soft, barely audible moaning emanating from a place in the courtyard that she could not pinpoint. Though discouraged by the matron of the Daughters of the Sun, Ccacca Mama, Yma Sumac's interest in this mystery persisted. Pitu Salla, a young girl, also a Sun Daughter was assigned to keep an eye on Yma. What the *mamaconas* did not know was, due to Pitu Salla's highly evolved powers of perception, she quickly discovered the secret behind the mournful vocalizations. She waited until the high priestesses were fast asleep, surreptitiously leading Yma through the dark courtyard, lighting the way with a torch. She pushed back a thicket of bushes, fixed her torch and pressed a spot on a nondescript boulder; it swung open. Upon entering the secret cave, they discovered a beautiful but emaciated woman lying senseless on the ground, a snake twining itself around her waist. They gave the woman food and water and once she recovered her senses, Cusi Coyllur Ñusta—Joyful Star informed Yma Sumac that she was not an orphan but her very own daughter and that of Apu Ollantay. Not even Tupac Yupanqui knew that his dead father, Pachacutiq had imprisoned his dear sister there for all those years. Joyful Star reunited with her brother, now the emperor; with her husband, the handsome general, Apu Ollantay; and with her precious daughter, Yma Sumac, who had been taken away from her at birth. All took their rightful place as royalty beside the Inca emperor."

"Whatever happened to Pitu Salla?" I ask, "The Daughter of the Sun who helped reunite Yma Sumac with her family?"

The Ancient One gazes deep into our eyes then raises her hands. Her wrinkled skin smooths; she is young and stunningly beautiful. A vast universe of stars, planets, comets, asteroids and cosmic light lift them into the heavens then plunge them into an inter-dimensional nexus inside the depths of Lake Titicaca where they find Pachamama in all her fecund beauty: her lungs are the rainforest, her arms the herbs, trees and plants. She sits cross-legged, her lower limbs form the bottom of a large lake in which water flows from the snowy Andes and where fish and turtles swim. Anacondas slither around her feet, condors fly overhead, a family of pumas rests on her belly.

Machula aulanchis—familial ancestors reside there, too. My beloved grandmother is once again youthful, my grandfather, handsome and strong; my father's brother and sister-in-law—Uncle Tupakusi and Aunt Asiri, who died in an attempt to make the pilgrimage to Apu Salkantay are there, too, happy and whole.

Our bellies fill with pure knowledge, contract then empty as if giving birth. We gaze skyward at Mama Quilla; she holds the moon in her hand, her large slanted eyes, full pink lips, pearly teeth and crown of intricately cast silver embedded with dozens of perfect sapphires glimmer in the night sky.

"I have borne witness to your travails, my doves," the Moon Goddess says, her voice as soft and soothing as a summer cloud.

Mama Quilla's tears rain down upon a lush meadow flush with undulating stems, flowers, seed pods and leaves of exotic herbs and plants. The goddess's silvery dewdrops pour into our outstretched palms, forming a pendant embossed with the image of the Moon Goddess.

We are transported back to the *tampu,* where we search for the Ancient One; she is nowhere to be seen.

CHAPTER THIRTY SEVEN

Prince Atahualpa arrives in Tumibamba aloft an elegant litter followed by an entourage of a dozen warriors. The favored but mixed-blood son of the deceased Inca has become an increasingly imposing figure, especially since his father's death; tall, ruggedly handsome with smooth skin, untouched by the ravages of the speckled monster. The litter carriers set him down in front of the Tumibamba palace. He climbs the steep flight of steps leading to the dais where his stepmother, Queen Rahua and her daughter are sitting on their low gilded thrones indulging in drinks concocted from exotic fruits brought in by runners from the wilds of the eastern jungle. The widowed queen waves at him.

"Atahualpa," the queen mother coos affectionately, "I was afraid you might not come."

"I have much to attend to in Quito." Atahualpa says breathlessly, "There are rumors of bearded strangers riding enormous beasts, playing havoc with coastal provinces. I came as soon as I could."

"Bearded strangers?" Chuqui asks with a dismissive chuckle. "Enormous beasts? You of all people know the savages of the coastal provinces are prone to gross exaggeration."

"Rumors often have their roots in truth." Atahualpa retorts politely but firmly, "Therefore, I will be unable to travel with the funeral entourage any farther."

"Huascar will be furious if you do not come to Cuzco." Rahua Occlo says, "I beseech you to delegate your competent generals to investigate these untoward rumors and come with us. It is your filial duty."

Atahualpa sighs, presses his full lips together then gazes at the queen.

"I must regretfully inform you," he says calmly, "that six members of the sacred council were murdered two nights ago in Quito. The assassins came under cover of darkness. Thus far, we've been unable to apprehend or even identify them."

Princess Chuqui angrily spews a mouthful of her exotic drink.

"Huascar must have had a hand in this!" she cries, "That madman is capable of anything."

"All the more reason," the queen mother says, "for you to accompany us to Cuzco, Atahualpa."

"Huascar needs your blessing," Atahualpa says, "to marry the beautiful Princess Chuqui. Without nuptials of pure royal blood, there can be no coronation."

"I will never give my blessing to such a union," Queen Rahua Occlo asserts. "Never."

Atahualpa eyes his carriers and warriors at the foot of the stairs; the corners of his eyes seem to sag from exhaustion.

"I must take my leave now," he says, "I will send messengers as necessary." He begins to walk down the steps, stops then turns to address the queen and princess. "One more thing; where is that insufferable gnome my father was so fond of?"

"If you're referring to Chimbo Sancto," Princess Chuqui says, "he's in the Tumibamba dungeon."

The widowed queen nods in affirmation.

"Make sure you keep him well fed," the prince says, "because I intend to make a tasty morsel of him when he's thrown into the Dungeon of Horrors in Cuzco."

* * *

After a month of frenetic grieving and devotion to the mummified Son of the Sun God, the warrior emperor Huayna Capac, provincial *runakuna*, many reeling from exhaustion and too much *chicha* line the Inca road weeping, blubbering and waving farewell to the queen mother, her daughter and the funeral cortege.

The funeral travels south to Cuzco along the meticulously cobble-stoned Chinchaysuyo Road at the foot the Andes Mountains. Locals gather to lament the passing of the emperor; they stand alongside village priests, who pray and wail as they openly sacrifice llamas, food and hundreds of children.

"This beautiful child," a diminutive villager shouts at the passing funeral procession, "is the daughter of our village mayor." He points at the plump impassive child dressed in a colorful tunic kneeling in front of him. "Our Daughter of the Sun will accompany the emperor on his journey to *hanan pacha*."

A larger man standing next to the tiny priest holds a crude stone mace with a palm wood handle and strikes the girl's skull. She falls to the ground; a cloud of dust rises around her lifeless body. Local performers dance maniacally around the newly sacrificed child, throwing flower petals and singing her praises for dying so well.

The queen mother and princess's litters don't stop or slow down for this display of fealty to the late emperor; they simply acknowledge the sacrifice with bored nods and carry on.

The funeral party approaches the Apurimac bridge near Cuzco; a *chasqui* unexpectedly arrives, a royal *quipu* slung over his shoulder.

"I have been ordered by Prince Huascar," the messenger announces, dark eyes lowered, brow knitted, "to deliver this message directly to the hands of the queen mother."

He displays the *quipu* for all to see, then hands it to Rahua Occlo. She scrutinizes the knotted rope for a moment; a look of bewilderment spreads over her face.

"What is the meaning of this?" Queen Rahua asks testily, as she deciphers the *quipu*. "'All pall bearers must hasten ahead to Limatambo?'"

"Yes, my queen," the *chasqui* says, head and eyes still lowered.

"But it is traditional," the queen mother protests, "that my retinue of close family members ans I always stay together during the funeral procession."

"Yes, my *coya*," the messenger says with a helpless shrug, the fluffy white feather inserted in his headband billowing in the breeze.

"What do you make of this Colla Topa?" the queen mother asks.

Colla Topa, a member of the Quito imperial council, is the highest ranking of the many half brothers acting as pallbearers, an act of considerable religious significance, however light the burden of the desiccated royal mummy may be.

"With your blessing, queen mother," Colla Topa responds, "my brothers and I will gladly comply with Huascar's request."

Princess Chuqui shudders at the thought; she gnaws on a large wad of coca in an attempt to calm her frayed nerves.

"I don't like this," she whispers to her mother.

"And neither do I," the queen says, "Are you sure about this, Colla?"

"We will see you soon in Cuzco, my queen," Colla assures her with a confident smile.

He and the other pallbearers place the royal mummy in the hands of able-bodied cousins, servants and guards then set off down the dusty road forking off to Limatambo.

The old, serpent-eyed Villac Umu approaches the queen, his thin face more haggard and drawn than usual.

"Something's afoot here, my queen," the priest says. "Why must Huascar disrupt our royal funeral procession when we are so close to Cuzco?"

Rahua Occlo puts a finger to her lips, mulling over the priest's thoughts then spots one of her most trusted guards, Quizquiz. She beckons him with a wave; when he approaches the queen, she points at Colla and his brothers already hiking toward Limatambo.

"Quizquiz," the widowed *coya* says, "Follow them to Limatambo. But don't get caught doing so. And, do not take any action, no matter the circumstances. Can you do that?"

"Yes, my queen," Quizquiz says with a deep bow. "I will hasten to investigate and disclose my findings to you in a timely fashion."

"Mother," Princess Chuqui asks, "Where is Chimbo Sancto?"

The queen mother surveys the rear of the procession, forehead furrowed.

"The dwarf is gone, evidently escaped," Rahua Occlo says, with a pleased grin, "May the gods protect him."

Colla Topa and his brothers approach Limatambo, where dozens of armed Huascar loyalists are lined up in front of the local *tampu*—a large way station, where approved travelers, (mostly soldiers), can stop, eat, bathe and sleep.

"Are you Prince Topa?" one of Huascar's minion's, Tupac Atao asks, feigning an air of friendliness. The man is short, stocky and reeks of cheap alcohol.

"Yes," Colla responds, "What is this all about?"

"Arrest them!" Atao shouts.

Huascar's lackeys slam their swords against Colla and his brothers's heads, knocking them unconscious but careful not to kill them. Next they bind their hands and feet and string each upside down from nearby trees, posts and rocky outcrops.

Quizquiz witnesses the coup from behind an array of boulders knowing there's nothing he could do even if he had permission to do so.

Colla Topa's lips are split open, dripping blood, his eyes swollen shut; he is all but unrecognizable from the punishment doled out by Huascar's drunken henchmen who laugh sadistically with each kick, punch and smack.

"Tell me about the conspiracy devised by that bastard, Atahualpa against Prince Huascar, the only legitimate heir to the Inca throne," Atao asks for the hundredth time, "and your death will be swift and painless."

"I know nothing of a conspiracy," Colla Topa says, "I swear it in the name of Inti, Viracocha and all the gods and goddesses of the Inca empire."

The broad side of a battle ax meets Colla's temple, knocking him unconscious. Atao throws a jug of water on his face intended to revive him so he can withstand further torture. Colla sputters and chokes; Atao beats him again.

Condors swoop over the mutilated bodies hanging by their ankles; one bird pecks at Colla's bloodied face; he moans and the bird hops away. Colla and his brothers are left to die slowly in Limatambo for the sin of not confessing to a conspiracy that does not exist.

After witnessing the entirety of the henchmen's atrocities, Quizquiz runs to intercept the funeral procession before it reaches Cuzco. When Rahua Occlo sees the look of panic on Quizquiz's face, she knows what must have happened.

"My beloved *coya*," Quizquiz says, with a bow so low, that his forehead touches the ground, "Colla Topa is gone, along with all his brothers. Tortured and murdered by Huascar's henchmen."

Princess Chuqui shrieks until her face flushes crimson.

"My brothers!" she screeches, "Oh, my beloved brothers!" Attendants try to calm her by proffering *chicha* and coca but the distraught princess knocks the chalice and the coca leaves onto the dusty ground.

The queen mother recognizes her responsibility to remain calm even under these dire circumstances. She recites a silent prayer to the Moon Goddess to give her strength then gazes into Quizquiz's black eyes.

"I'll need your help, loyal friend," the queen says pointing at the funeral cortege behind her, "to inform the others."

"Yes," Quizquiz says, "I understand."

Quizquiz runs alongside the funeral procession alerting dancers, singers, musicians, mourners, Daughters of the Sun and leaders of powerful provinces of the necessity of gathering around the queen's litter. A former llama herder, Quizquiz deftly corrals then apprises them of Huascar's villainy.

"My lords and ladies, go back to your provinces," the queen mother pronounces, "and prepare for battle. We must all pray for the salvation of the Inca Empire."

"And what of your safety and that of your daughter?" a simply dressed dignitary from the northern jungles asks, a look of grave concern on his kind brown face.

"My daughter and I will be safe," Queen Rahua answers, "at least for the time being. My intention is to talk to Huascar and save him from this madness. I hope my efforts will not be in vain."

"Yes, my *coya,* my widowed queen," the dignitary says as he climbs onto his litter; dozens of frightened like-minded provincial leaders do the same. "I trust our empire will survive this calamity."

"It's in the hands of the gods now," the queen says, her eyes flooded with tears as she ponders the loss of beloved family members. "We must entrust our future to them now."

Most of the members of the funeral cortege disperse north onto the Chinchaysuyo road. What's left, including the queen and princess, the mummified emperor and his litter carriers continue south into Cuzco.

CHAPTER THIRTY EIGHT

Though her mind is lucid, Solsol's body is still too weak to walk the long distance to my village, so she rides Achiq, the giant albino llama left behind when the Ancient One vanished into the ether; the beast seems to have little difficulty carrying her. The two other llamas carry what's left of our provisions.

After several hours, our legs rubbery from exhaustion, we reach the outskirts of Sonqo; I recognize and greet every hill, plain, ridge, rock, outcrop, lake or stream; true *runakuna* know that each possess a name and unique personality. A prominent bald hill named Apu Antaqaqa, dotted with mysterious ancient ruins and caves, large and small, addresses us.

"Go back," Antaqaqa bellows, voice echoing throughout the region, "*Pachaq hap'isgan.*"

"*Pachaq hap'isgan.*" I repeat worriedly, "Who is ill, Apu Antaqaqa?"

Antaqaqa is silent but in the distance the blast of Sonqo's village *pututu*, a conch shell used to alert villagers of impending danger, penetrates the atmosphere.

"What's the matter, T'ica?" Pispis asks. "And what's that sound?"

Solsol awakes, rubs her eyes, slides off Achiq then strokes his neck.

"Are we lost?" she asks.

I remember the Ancient One's ominous prediction: *Your village will be visited by the speckled monster.* My body's tingling from head to toe and I feel faint; I point at the bald hill.

"We'll take shelter here, my doves," I say, keeping my voice as calm as possible, "in one of Apu Antaqaqa's caves. Let's plan to spend more than one night here. Take the llamas, unburden them. There is a small creek behind the hill; the water there is clean. Let the llamas drink their fill then let them graze. Eat the rest of our provisions. I must go to my village alone now."

"We will go with you," Pispis asserts, "of course."

"Yes, T'ica," Solsol insists, "We must stay together."

I hand the moon goddess pendant to Pispis.

"This will protect you." I say. "Pray for Mama Quilla's assistance."

I race to Sonqo without looking back.

The *pututu* player, Mallki is tall, strong with long lean arms and sturdy legs befitting his name which means tree: his dark brown eyes are bloodshot. Usually a cheerful young man, I've never seen him so distressed.

"T'ica," Mallki says, choking back his tears, "The village is under quarantine. Almost everybody is sick or dying. My mother, father, sister, brother—they're all gone. Why did the gods take them from me?"

"I'm so sorry, Mallki," I say, "What happened?"

"It's the plague," he says with a shudder, "It's wiped out almost half of our village."

"And what of my family?" I ask.

I close my eyes and brace myself for the worst.

"I don't know," Mallki says. "But you can't go in there. The speckled monster will take you."

"But I have medicine that might help those who have not yet perished."

I show him my flask filled with *aha.* The young man's body sways; he seems as frail as a newborn llama. Then without a word, he waves me through.

Dead bodies, all but unrecognizable from the hideous pock marks covering them, are strewn on the dusty ground between huts. I spy our ancient village shaman sitting cross-legged and leaning against his hovel, his back to me; I run to him.

"Apu Shaman," I squeak. Curiously, he doesn't seem to hear me, so I touch him lightly; his body keels over and kicks up a small cloud of dust when it hits the ground.

In a daze, I stumble over a half dozen more corpses before I reach my family's hut; the village reeks of death and disease. I prepare for the worst, take a deep breath and remind myself that no matter what happens, I will see my loved ones again in *hanan pacha,* the divine upper world.

"Mama Quilla, Pachamama," I pray fervently before entering, "Give me strength."

I push open the thick wooden door, stick my head inside and look around; there's a large pot of vegetable stew poised over the ashy remnants of a wood fire but my family is nowhere to be seen. I ruminate on their whereabouts for a moment: *my parents are wise, perceptive* runakuna*; they know that space and time are isomorphic. They may have foreseen this tragedy and decided to leave before the plague hit the village.* I don't want to contemplate the other possibility: that my family is already dead, hastily buried in a shallow grave or worse yet, left to rot in the open—like the shaman. My chest heaves when I picture my baby brother still and lifeless then recall what Pachamama said to Mamáy during the leaf divining ceremony the shaman conducted before I left on my journey.

Your milk is rich and nourishing; your baby will grow to adulthood.

So my baby brother is still alive. But the Earth Goddess said nothing about my parents' longevity.

Where could they be? I ask myself.

My father was fond of saying that he has distant relatives living in the jungle; he'd visit them once a year, right after the fields were plowed and crops sown. However, he always insisted that the rest of us remain in the village to look after the newly planted crops. I was in charge of keeping the birds away by throwing small stones at the little bandits; Mamáy was responsible for keeping the irrigation system in working order. His annual forays into the jungle were met with protests and tears because the forest is rife with poisonous snakes, insects, frogs and eels, blood-thirsty piranha, caiman, deadly plants and, worst of all, cannibals.

"Don't cry, my precious little doves. There may be a time when we'll need to flee from our village into the jungle," he would say as he held us tight and chewed his coca leaves, "A true *runakuna* prepares for his family's security. He doesn't sit around all day getting drunk with friends until harvest season. I've built a boat so we can travel rapidly down the Great River when needed; only I know where it is hidden. I've almost finished a nice shelter in the remote village of our relatives—just in case."

Then he'd turn and walk east, toward the Great Jungle, singing sad songs of lost love, the long ear flaps of his colorful cap, which he knitted himself, fluttering softly in the breeze.

My bittersweet recollections of Tatáy are interrupted when the *cacique* of Sonqo, Mayor Yanamayu stumbles into the hut, wild-eyed, feverish, lips and face covered with pock marks.

"Help me," he rasps then curls up on the floor.

My first inclination is to send the pitiful man away; I never really liked the vain, power-hungry village leader and especially despised his impudent son, Eqeqo; his family never liked me either.

After finishing chores, I relax on a large smooth rock next to a gurgling creek, enjoying a warm summer day. My pet parrot, Yana suddenly becomes agitated, flapping her wings frantically.

"Run!" she squawks.

Five village boys appear, creating a semi-circle around me, making sucking noises, holding their crotches—no one is over the age of fifteen, the youngest eight.

"Come on, T'ica, my beautiful white dove," Eqeqo yells, exposing himself by lifting the front of his tunic. "Don't you want to marry me?"

I scramble to my feet then turn quickly to make my escape, leaping over the creek and onto a path toward a grove of saplings and thick brush. The boys try to hop over the creek, too, but, their short legs and clumsy feet slip on smooth, wet rocks, plunging them headlong into the water. I hear them cursing and shouting.

A village boy named Hastu appears from out of nowhere and tackles me; he'd been lying in ambush in the bushes. I hit the ground face first, then Hastu rips the sandals off my feet. I roll onto my back then lightly touch my bloody upper lip.

"Look," he screeches, holding my footwear overhead. "Look how big T'ica's feet are!"

"Give them back," I demand. My sandals are new, lovingly crafted by Tatáy; I'm not going to let the village troublemakers steal them or toss them over a steep cliff, where they'd be lost forever. "Give them back right now!"

Hastu lumbers off, whooping, shouting and still holding my sandals. Legs churning, I charge ahead, grab the neckline of his tunic, shove my arms under his sweaty armpits, spin him several times until he drops my sandals then jettison him into a thicket of thorny bushes. I pick up and slip on my sandals then sprint away. The village troublemakers try to pull their pudgy friend out of the spiny undergrowth.

"Ouch," Hastu shouts, kicking them away, "You're making it worse! I'll do it myself."

After considerable yowling, the boy finally frees himself. His friends run away, occasionally turning to taunt their chubby friend limping behind them as he plucks thorns out of his fleshy butt.

"Hurry!" Eqeqo teases as the other boys roar with laughter, "Before T'ica throws you into the sticker bushes again!"

Huarachicho is *a puberty ceremony for young males in their early teens. Ceremonies and races test everything from speed, strength, flexibility and endurance. Even though I'm a girl, I unofficially participate on the sidelines and easily beat all the boys at every race. Near the end of the festivities, the boys receive breech-cloths then their parents form two rows forcing their sons to run the gauntlet as they pummel them with sticks and knotted ropes, in an effort to toughen them up.*

Fair is fair, so I decide to be the first one to run through; I evade almost every barbarous stroke. The boys run as fast as they can but fail to elude the merciless drubbing; they exit the gauntlet limping or holding bruised and bloodied ankles, calves and toes. When Eqeqo starts crying his father, Mayor Yanamayu greets him with a wiry stick and whips him mercilessly; the soft spoiled boy whoops and screeches all the way back to his family's hut.

The next evening, the mayor comes uninvited to my family's hut, stepping into the household without first politely asking permission, per village custom.

"Your daughter made the boys look bad at the Huarachicho,*" he complains to Tatáy.*

Squatting in the far corner of the hut, I keep my eyes down and continue weaving a colorful textile I plan to fashion into a new tunic. Thank the gods, Mamáy isn't there; she's occupied with bringing a pot of stew to a pregnant neighbor's house, whom she suspects isn't eating enough; she doesn't approve of my penchant of competing with the village boys.

"I will talk to my daughter," Tatáy replies, shooting the mayor an icy stare.

Seconds later, the flustered mayor grunts then stomps out of our hut without uttering a polite farewell.

I know that it took a great deal of restraint for Tatáy not to say more to the indignant mayor: that this was his own fault for spoiling his cry-baby son—taboo in our village society, where only the most resilient survive. All village children—except for the likes of Eqeqo—work hard, contribute to the survival of the village and the household..

"Ususi?" Tatáy asks, using the formal Runasimi term for daughter.

"Yes, Tatáy?" I answer without looking up.

"That man is nishu luku,*" he says.*

"Yes, Tatáy," I reply, trying to suppress a giggle, "That man is extremely crazy."

Despite all the bad blood between our families, I recognize that I have no other choice but to help the sick man. But first, I want information.

"Do you know where my family is?" I ask softly. He's glassy-eyed, delirious, mute; his sickly pungent smell fills the hut. "Do you know where my family is, Mayor Yanamayu?" I repeat but it's no use. I sigh, uncork my flask and, with some effort, pull the pudgy man into a semi-sitting position. "Open your mouth wide," I tell him. "I'm going to give you medicine."

The mayor's cracked lips drop open, his tongue is blanketed in the same oozing pock marks covering his body, the sight of which makes me feel queasy but I squirt a bit of the medicine into his foul-smelling maul anyway. He swallows, moans, shudders then collapses, smacking his left temple on the rough-hewn wooden floor. At first, I consider with horror that the *aha* might have killed him but after a few moments, he starts snoring; I breathe a sigh of relief. The herbal concoction seems to have brought my repugnant patient some measure of relief—whether it will cure him remains to be seen. Nevertheless, I fervently pray to Viracocha, the god of the universe for his speedy recovery, if for no other reason than he might be the only person who knows where my family went. With some effort, I roll him onto a coarse woolen blanket; I smile at the memory of my parents cuddling close underneath its warmth, my father whispering words of affection to his beloved wife.

"Sleep well, my beautiful dove." Tatáy would say, "May Mama Quilla protect you and our family always."

Mayor Yanamayu mumbles, grunts, snorts, wheezes and snuffles, still feverish but sound asleep. I decide to leave the snorer behind for a while to see who else I can help and perhaps even find a villager who is healthy enough to give me information about my family. I decide to go to the mayor's hut first; Eqeqo and his mother might know where my loved ones went.

CHAPTER THIRTY NINE

Pulling a sack of provisions in with them, Pispis and Solsol crawl into Apu Antaqaqa's most inconspicuous cave, its interior warm and dry. After enjoying a handful of dried fruit and nuts, they pull blankets over their weary bodies and fall asleep almost instantly.

Solsol awakens to the sounds of the llamas' curious high pitched sobs.

"Wake up," she says to her sister.

Pispis blinks, rubs her eyes, sits up and listens to the bleating.

"I must go to the llamas," she whispers.

Pispis crawls toward the cave's mouth; Solsol grabs her sister's arm, pulls her into the dark then puts a finger to her lips. Two men walk past wearing meticulously crafted leather sandals and red and white checkered tunics of the Inca army, followed by a blur of llama hooves.

Our llamas! Pispis mouths despairingly.

Solsol buries her face in her hands; she's so attached to the llamas, especially Achiq, with his shaggy white neck, soothing gait and patient nature. The thought that their animals have been stolen by the Incas is unbearable.

The warriors' plodding footsteps and the clop of llama hooves fade into the distance. The sisters slide to the back of the cave.

"We have to get them." Solsol whispers.

"I know," Pispis says, "But how?"

I step back into my family's hut after scurrying around the village to help as many sick as possible. The mortality rate for most households is quite high—over fifty percent.

"Thank you for your help, T'ica," the mayor says.

After sleeping for several hours, his fever is nearly gone, formerly gray skin now russet brown.

"I stopped by your family's hut." I say.

"And?" he asks anxiously.

"You're a lucky man," I say, "I gave Eqeqo and your wife the medicine. They were *nishu gravi.*"

"I know," the mayor says, "Gravely ill, like I was."

"They're asleep now. I hope they'll be better when they awake but I can't promise anything."

"Thank you," he says, his eyes wet with tears of gratitude. "May the gods bless you."

"*Hamusayki*, Mamáy?" a female voice calls outside the hut's entrance, politely asking if she can enter.

"*Haampu!*" I call out in welcome, hoping to see someone who isn't gravely ill for once.

Carrying a baby, a slim beautiful woman named Umiña with light brown hair, green eyes and lush dark eyelashes ducks into the hut; she's from northern Peru, somewhere near Chachapoyas, or so I heard. Umiña met her husband, a handsome Sonqo villager two years ago on a merchant trip up north.

I clear my throat, suggesting that the mayor should probably go back to his own hut now. He reaches out for my hand; I help him up and he heads to the door, turns and bows.

"Thank you again, T'ica," he says, his voice sounding a bit gravelly. He straightens his tunic, smooths back his messy thatch of black hair and steps outside; though a bit unsteady on his feet, he seems well enough to find his way back home alone.

The young mother hands me her baby, who, except for a few faint pock mark scars on his chubby cheeks, appears healthy. He reminds me of my baby brother.

"And how are you feeling little Wawa?" I coo. The baby, like all village infants under two, doesn't have a formal name yet—just Wawa. The baby grabs my finger, kicks his chubby little feet, coos and grins. I uncork my medicinal flask, administer a tiny drop of *aha* into the tiny patient's rosy mouth then say a silent prayer to Pachamama, asking that the medicine prevent the baby from getting worse. I hand the child back to his mother. I feel the need to get to know this woman better, especially under the dire circumstances of the plague. "How is your husband, Umiña?" I ask.

"I don't know," the young woman replies shaking her head as she rises. "He went on a merchant trip up north. I'm worried about him," she says as her infant nuzzles her bosom. "I heard the sickness came from there."

"Keep yourself and the baby clean and well fed," I say with an encouraging smile. "Say your prayers and don't worry too much. Do you have enough food?"

The young mother glances at the huge pot of cold soup.

"I think so," Umiña fibs.

"Take as much as you want, my dove. Since you're nursing, you must eat enough for two."

The young mother hands her baby back to me, picks up some kindling near Mamáy's stove and spreads it under the soup pot; the smoldering ashes ignite the dry tinder quickly; she picks up the gourd that Tatáy fashioned into a ladle, stirs the pot, stomach growling, mouth curved into a big smile.

After eating her fill, Umiña utters a stream of thanks and compliments before returning to her home, baby strapped to her back. After she leaves, I'm so exhausted, I drift off then awake with a start when I realize I've forgotten about Pispis and Solsol. I stand, dust myself off, tighten the plaited sling around my forehead and check my tunic pocket to make sure I have enough stone projectiles. Satisfied with the state of my simple munitions, I step out of the hut and sprint toward Apu Antaqaqa.

I slow my pace when I spy two unfamiliar men from afar with our three llamas. True *runakuna* can recognize each other from a great distance but these men are not villagers. They're wearing red and white checkered tunics, armed with shields, daggers, bronze halberds and tight-fitting bronze helmets fitted with large yellow feathers at the fore, golden cuffs around their wrists and scarlet fringes below their knees; these are all signs that they are not *aucac runa*—low ranking foot soldiers; they're undoubtedly high ranking Inca officers or even generals—*kamayuk* or *hatun apu*.

I recall my father's words: *the Incas only promote their most blood-thirsty warriors; those wearing yellow feathers could also be in command of a large battalion.*

Achiq, the over-sized albino, raises his muzzle, pulls back his lips, sniffs the air then starts squealing when he perceives my essence. I hide behind a large formation of boulders and pray the beast won't drag the officers in my direction.

"What's the matter with you, *machu* llama?" the older Inca officer asks Achiq. "Are you hungry?"

"Maybe he's thirsty," the younger Inca says.

"Yes," the older officer agrees, "That's probably it. Let's find water."

I know the chances of killing both men are very low, even with my expert sling skills. I might be able to maim or even kill one of the men using the element of surprise but then the remaining warrior would be on high alert before I could load, whirl, aim and fling another projectile. I wonder if these men harmed Pispis and Solsol in any way; my heart breaks at the thought but until I inspect the caves at Apu Antaqaqa there's no way of knowing what, if anything, has happened to them. I breathe deeply to banish these gloomy thoughts and attempt to focus on the task at hand.

Achiq squeals and pulls the soldiers toward the immense boulder formation that I'm hiding behind. I attempt to formulate some sort of defensive plan but the situation seems hopeless; sneaking away won't work if the stubborn Achiq keeps on dragging the soldiers toward my smell. And, it's impossible for almost anyone to outrun two highly trained Inca warriors.

"Mama Quilla, Goddess of the Moon," I pray "Pachamama, Goddess of the Earth, protect me, your daughter. "

You are more powerful than you know, the voice of the Ancient One echoes in my mind, *nature is on your side.*

I try to imagine what that could mean in this bleak situation since the Incas are heavily armed and highly trained warriors. In contrast, I only have a sling useful for one shot at a time. *Nature is on your side.* I muse on the story of the old emperor Pachacuti who vanquished the mighty Chankas tribe due to stones transforming into warriors and fighting for him. *Obviously just a myth,* I think disconsolately. Heart pounding, I note two immense parallel boulder formations with several smaller boulders balanced on top. If I can climb up the rear of one undetected, I might have a chance to roll a large rock on the men if the llamas pull them into the narrow path in between formations. That's assuming I have the strength to push the huge rocks down the slope.

I scale the boulder and hide behind a large egg-shaped rock. Meanwhile, Achiq, grunting and squealing, seems determined to drag the warriors into the long narrow path below.

Good boy, Achiq, I think, *good boy.*

The other llamas seem content to clop behind the warriors who are now situated directly below me, catching their breaths, leaning against cool smooth stone, unaware of any danger.

"Those priests and those girls could be anywhere," the older Inca officer says after squirting a long stream of purple *chicha* into his mouth from his simple army issue flask.

"Highly unusual situation," the younger man says, nodding. "They probably all froze to death. Nobody was expecting snow and cold weather so late in the season."

"If they froze to death at Apu Salkantay Mountain, " the older man says, "Somebody would have found their bodies."

"Maybe they were eaten by pumas," the younger man suggests.

"No," the older man says, "Pumas wouldn't go that high to eat frozen carcasses. Plus, they certainly wouldn't attack a group of four; the priests would have been able to fight an animal attack off since they were armed."

"Depends on how large and hungry the animal was," the younger officer says.

So they really are looking for Pispis and Solsol, I think, my worst nightmare realized.

The wind blows steadily, whistling softly, obscuring my grunts as I push on the egg-shaped boulder, unable to get a foothold on the smooth rock with my worn out sandals. Though there are other boulders, this one appears to be the easiest to shove. My brow wet, I try again but the stubborn rock refuses to budge so I mull over all my options. I could still try to sneak away but once alerted, the Inca warriors would run after me; few civilians can outrun Inca soldiers, so that won't work, especially since once captured, only the gods know what they would do to me. I brighten up at the thought that the llamas would lead me to the Solsol and Pispis, if I could somehow eliminate these men.

I remove the sling tied around my forehead, dig into my tunic pocket, pull out a rock and load my weapon. As I prepare to twirl it overhead, I'm pelted from behind by a sprinkle of pebbles. I peer downhill, amazed to see Pispis and Solsol standing at the foot of the boulder formation, undetected by the warriors. I acknowledge the girls with a nod, press my forefinger to my lips and motion them to climb up. They scale the boulder swiftly, their green eyes and pale hair glowing in the late afternoon sun. Maybe with their help, we can roll down the boulder. I re-tie the sling around my forehead, place the stone back inside my pocket, point at the stubborn rock, I've been trying to push then hold up three fingers.

The girls nod, understanding what I mean and place their hands against the huge egg-shaped rock. I start the silent countdown, holding up a finger for each number: *One . . . two . . . three . . .* we struggle to push the firmly wedged boulder but it still won't budge. Solsol lies on her back and places her feet on the rock; her sister follows suit. I remain standing to control the trajectory of our giant body-crushing rock. On the silent count of three, the boulder loosens and teeters precariously; dirt and pebbles slide downhill but, the Inca officers have let their guard down, focused on guzzling *chicha*. I press my lips together; the sisters pray to their serpent gods to give them strength. We shove the tottering boulder again. With a loud crunch, it suddenly gives way then bounces downhill faster than I could have imagined, slamming into and crushing the older Inca officer. Thank the gods, our llamas sprint away unharmed. The younger surviving warrior beholds the source of the assassination.

"You!" he yells.

He scrambles up the face of the boulder, wielding a bronze battle ax which glints in the late afternoon sun. Pispis and Solsol jaws drop open; they seem paralyzed by fear. I press against another large rock.

"Pispis! Solsol!" I yell. "Help me!"

The sisters scramble to their feet, quickly lining up next to me. There's no time to push with legs; we use our shoulders, sandals sliding over the rocky surface. The warrior realizes what we're attempting to do and scurries to the right. With one final push and a collective groan, the boulder gives way, plunging erratically down the rocky hillside; only the gods know which way it will go. The boulder glances off the man's feathered helmet sending his body cartwheeling down the slope; his face smacks against solid rock so brutally, it makes me wince. Helmet crushed, face, arms and legs a mass of bruises and bloody gashes, we hear him moaning on the narrow path below us; he's badly injured but not dead, at least not yet.

I eye the girls uneasily.

"We have to finish him," Pispis says, eyes glistening, jaw set, "We have no choice."

Solsol nods, tears welling in her emerald eyes. I load my sling and pray.

CHAPTER FORTY

Legs churning below a tan fringed tunic, large woven bag and *quipu* strapped shoulder to waist, a royal Inca *chasqui* stops when he notices Mallki and Mayor Yanamayu, who are standing outside the plague-ravaged Sonqo village.

"I understand that Sonqo was invaded by the speckled monster," the messenger says.

"Yes," Mallki says, "I lost my whole family. The village is under quarantine for now."

The mayor sticks out his chin and shows the messenger his pock marked face and neck.

"I almost died, " he says, "but my family and I were saved by our very own village girl, T'ica. You see, she has a potion . . . "

Eyes open wide, jaw clenched, Mallki nudges the mayor. The young man knows that telling royal *chasquis* anything, good or bad, almost always ends in disaster because of their connection to the Inca Empire.

"She prayed over us," Mallki says, sticking out his lower lip and cocking his head, "nothing more."

"What's this about a potion?" the messenger demands, taking off his *quipu.*

"Oh, it was nothing," Mayor Yanamayu says unconvincingly.

"What was the girl's name again?" the *chasqui* asks. "The girl with the potion?" He strokes the *quipu* preparing to tie whatever Yanamayu says into its multiple strings.

The mayor looks at the ground, shuffles his feet; he needs a moment to turn this to his political advantage.

"If I tell you," he says with an avaricious squint and shrug, palms up, "what do I get in return?"

Since no one seems to know how the speckled monster visits its victims and because I want to check on the condition of those who I already treated in Sonqo, I leave Pispis and Solsol at the Apu Antaqaqa cave.

"Your baby looks healthy, Umiña," I say, "All the spots are gone from his little face." I gaze adoringly at the cherub. "Yes, you look much better now, don't you?" He gurgles, grins and wiggles his tiny toes.

"Your medicine," Umiña responds placidly, "and your prayers have saved us."

"Pachamama and Mama Quilla are with us," I say.

"All the gods are with us," the young mother affirms.

"Have you heard from your husband?" I ask.

Umiña holds her forehead.

"No and now food is scarce with so few to work the fields." she says. "Supplies will run out very soon."

"What will you do?" I ask.

"I'm not sure," she says. "My husband could come back soon or . . . he may never arrive."

"I'm preparing to travel north with two young Cloud Warrior girls who were kidnapped by the Incas." I inform her. "It's too long a story to explain now but we hope to find their parents in Chachapoyas; I will search for my family afterward."

Umiña's emerald eyes cast a glow over her baby; she points at a large sack, stuffed with provisions then holds up an intricately knotted *quipu*—granting permission to travel on the Inca Royal Road.

"I know the way, " the young mother says.

After a night camping in a makeshift shelter fashioned from blankets laid over bushes and saplings in a unobtrusive forest clearing, we awake, anxious to start hiking again; though hungry we decide to set off without eating because we are still so close to the Inca capital of Cuzco.

After hiking for half a day, we arrive at Llacpacta Pass. Umiña stops and points east over a vast misty canyon.

"Look, my doves," she says, "Over there."

We peer into the distance until thatched-roof stone dwellings surrounded by verdant terraces come into focus: it's an oasis suspended in the clouds.

"Machu Pichu," I say softly.

"Built by the Inca Emperor." Umiña says, "For what purpose, no one knows for sure."

Pispis and Solsol gape at the site, wisps of long blond hair blowing softly in the wind; they turn their emerald eyes upon Umiña and me.

"When Daughters of the Sun are taken to Machu Pichu,"

Solsol says wistfully, holding her sister's hand, "they never return."

* * *

A rope bridge sways over the rushing waters of the Urubamba River; the span appears to be too flimsy and unstable to hold even one person, much less our group of four accompanied by three pack llamas.

Each year, over a thousand men, women and children from four local communities volunteer to replace the bridge; they pound, twist, weave and braid bale after bale of native grasses creating ropes thicker than a man's arm. Musicians bring their instruments, leading the workers in song; dancers twirl to the simple folk songs. Finally, the sturdy grass cables are strung across the chasm, dangerous but satisfying work, the secret of which is passed down generation to generation. These *runakuna*—people of substance, work twelve to sixteen hour days until their masterpiece is finished, gather their belongings then bid sad farewells to friends they only see once a year. My family helped build their share of community bridges, but not this one. I scrutinize the tattered bridge closely.

"This bridge should have been replaced months ago," I say warily.

"The plague." Umiña surmises, "Many people died or were too sick to work on the bridge this year. It should be safe to cross for our small group."

The young mother tip toes across the bridge, leading a llama behind her; she stops, turns and waves at us from the middle of the span; Wawa is strapped to her back, his little head bobbing up and down with each dainty step. "Don't look down and think of something happy," she shouts.

As a true *runakuna,* I have never really been afraid of anything, not even heights, but this is different; the wind blows and the bridge sways erratically, as if Lord Wind is chiding me: *you wanted more than to be a* munay warmikuna, *now is your chance.*

I can't imagine why I ever wanted to be more than a woman of substance now, if such a thing is even possible.

"I'm coming!" I shout.

"Think of happy things!" Umiña calls out again. "And don't look down."

Thinking of happy things eludes me for the moment; I can't recall why I ever wanted anything more than to be with my handsome father, kind mother and sweet baby brother. After all I've been through, I treasure my family more than all the riches of the Inca Empire.

Achiq and I step onto the swinging rope bridge; the giant albino is not fond of this idea, pulling back its long neck and bleating in protest.

"Come, Achiq," I coax, "Come on. Be a good boy." I tug on his reins, take a deep breath and reflect on happy childhood memories:

I am six years old when I discover a cochineal, an insect that produces bright red dye. It sits in between the spines of a prickly pear cactus.

"I found one!" I call out excitedly to Tatay.

"Be careful, T'ica!" my father warns. "Do not let the cactus prick your tender fingers, my dove or you will be done for the day."

He nimbly picks three insects off a nearby cactus and stuffs them into a tattered pouch.

With the bright light of Lord Inti bearing down on me, I carefully knock the insect off the cactus and onto the ground with a stick, scoop it up and stuff it in my own little sack.

"Got one!" I peep.

I proudly gather dozens of the cochineals without once pricking my fingers on pernicious cacti spines.

Ch'illca is a green leafy plant with white flowers, which when boiled with *collpa*—a mineral compound, produces a bright shade of green; the perfect color for depicting snake and lizard designs that I'm obsessed with incorporating into my weaves, much to my parents' dismay who believe *runakuna* should stick with colorful geometric patterns and depictions of the Sun God, condors, llamas or alpacas, not cold-blooded serpents.

Father and I pick *q'olle* flowers from a small, low lying tree to make yellow. We will boil alpaca yarn with its blooms, achieving a variety of sunny shades depending on the length of time the wool remains in the solution. I intend to boil the wool until it turns a brilliant yellow.

Once home, I carefully spread my cochineal insects on a flat stone to dry in the sun. After a few hours, I help Mamáy grind them into a fine powder, an easy job since the insects are soft and pliable. We boil the ground insects in a large pot hung over a low fire with just the right amount of llama urine and copper to achieve the desired shade: deep purple—my favorite color.

I dye another batch of wool bright green, the next batch yellow, the next purple, carefully hanging each dyed batch out to dry.

Mamáy helps me spin the wool into long lengths of colorful yarn then sits next to me as I learn how to weave.

"Daughter," Mamáy complains as she squats next to my loom, "Your design is very intricate, too advanced for a beginner weaver and even for an experienced one, like me. I don't know if we can do this."

But I have no such doubts, envisioning what I want, praying to weave with the hands of Mamaoello, the goddess who taught *runakuna* how to spin and weave.

My hawk-eyed mother sighs impatiently and nitpicks every little mistake.

"No, no," Mamáy complains, "I already told you, the yarn goes under . . ." she touches my hand and helps me guide the yarn so that the intended design can be achieved, "then you pull it through like this."

I gaze at her skeptically.

"Are you sure?" I ask.

"Why must you question everything I do?" Mamáy asks, playfully smacking me on the thigh.

"Sorry, Mamáy."

After days of constant criticism, I begin to comprehend the weaving process and Mamáy finally compliments my woven cloth. With her and Goddess Mamaoella's guidance, I produce a deep purple tunic, with primitive smiling green lizards and snakes and sunny yellow butterflies. It will prove to be the envy of every little girl in Sonqo.

I smile wistfully at the memory, then look up; I've reached the other side of the swaying rope bridge. Behind me, Solsol and Pispis practically fly over the span, pulling our llamas behind them.

"That wasn't so bad," Solsol says breathlessly.

Evidently unhappy about being forced to cross the rickety bridge, the dark brown llama stares angrily at Pispis, pulls back its neck, spits in her face then clops furiously down the road.

"Come back!" Pispis yells, as she wipes llama spittle off her face with her sleeve. "I'm sorry!"

She races after the animal, trips, gets back up, dusts herself off, darts after the beast again, grabs his reins.

Lost in thought, my heart aching, I pause to pet Achiq. Fond recollections of creating textiles with my family bring an intense longing to see them again, though I don't know whether they are sick, dead, alive, lost in the jungle or held captive by cannibals or by the Incas. If they're still alive, they're undoubtedly as worried about my fate as I am about theirs.

"Come on!" Umiña says, abruptly ripping me from my musings, "We have a long way to go."

Before we resume our journey, a Machukuna materializes on the Royal Inca Road in front of us.

"They're coming," a Child of the Moon whispers a concerned look on his giant face; he slowly fades away. From the unchanged looks on my fellow traveler's faces, I'm the only one who saw him.

Umiña's pricks her ears and listens intently.

"Do you hear that?" she asks.

"Hear what?" Solsol asks.

"From the other side of the bridge." I whisper, holding a hand to my ear. "Listen."

The faint sound of footfalls echo in the clear mountain air becoming louder and more distinct by the second.

Warriors approach the rope bridge led by an Inca general, wearing an ornate feathered bronze helmet.

"Run as fast and as far as you can then when you get tired, find a place to hide." I yell. I face Umiña. "Don't let anything happen to that baby. I can take care of myself." Umiña, Solsol and Pispis look at each other but seem frozen in place. "Run, I tell you!"

They bolt down the road, llamas bleating, baby wailing, his cries choppy but growing fainter the farther they run.

I pull out my knife, hurtle to the bridge then frantically saw on one of four main grass cables. Success! Lord Wind tosses the bridge wildly as a dozen warriors hesitate to step onto the treacherously lopsided span.

"Cross, you cowards!" The general barks.

A dozen warriors step onto the rickety structure; Lord Wind blows and they lose their equilibrium, plunging headlong into the Urubamba River, shrieking hysterically until they hit the cascading water below. Undeterred, more soldiers attempt to cross the bridge, balancing on three frayed cables with grim determination.

Though temperatures are cool, my brow is soaked in sweat as I slice the twisted strands of another cable. I gaze at the ferocious Inca officer on the other side then make the final cut; the mangled bridge spills more warriors screaming and cursing wildly into the rushing waters.

Two more cables to go, I think, my heart pounding so savagely, I feel that it will soon burst from my bosom altogether.

The intrepid Inca general wraps his feet, legs, arms and hands around a cable and climbs toward me. Dozens of warriors standing on the opposite embankment shoot arrows by the hundreds and propel innumerable rocks from slings; I manage to dodge the volleys but a stone manages to clip me above my right eyebrow. Though blood streams into my line of vision, I can't let it stop me so I slice blindly on the rope the Inca officer is clinging to. A few foolhardy warriors, frustrated by their futile attempts to strike me with stones and arrows attempt to climb across the crippled bridge like their general; a mighty gust of wind instantly thrusts them into the Urubamba River though the Inca general holds fast, despite Lord Wind's attempts to shake him loose.

The general slides hand over hand across the chasm as if he's done it a million times before. When he reaches the end of the rope, I thrust my blade at his throat but he holds on with fierce determination then grabs my wrist and my knife falls to the ground. I sink my teeth into his hand until I draw blood then kick him in the face. He smiles as if playing with a mere toy, swings his legs to and fro then propels himself onto land. I turn and sprint. He catches me in a few seconds, throws me to the ground and holds a knife to my throat.

"Tell me where the other golden-haired savages are hiding," he growls, "and I will make your death quick and painless."

"There are no other maidens," I fib.

I know I have no chance against this man who appears to be made of fired palm wood; all I can hope for right now is a chance to stall him long enough so my friends have the luxury of a long head start. "I don't know what you're talking about."

"Stupid girl! I just saw them!" the Inca officer rages, "The two younger ones killed the priests rather than having the honor of journeying to *hanan pacha*. Then they killed two high ranking officers who were looking for them."

"I don't know anybody like that," I fib again, "I swear."

"Never mind. I will find them with or without your help." His breath is putrid; the smell so strong it makes my eyes water. "When I take you back to Cuzco, you will be sentenced to the *samca-huasi*—the house of horrors where you will be locked up with vipers and hungry pumas," he growls into my ear. "Perhaps I'll stir up their blood lust by cutting you here . . ." He points the knife at my left breast and laughs sadistically. "Or maybe I will have a little fun with you first."

He reaches under my tunic and strokes my inner thigh; my stomach roils in disgust. I'm so frightened, so tired, so weak.

I can't fight back, I think, *he's too strong.*

You are more powerful than you know, the Ancient One's words reverberate inside my diminishing consciousness. *You must fight, T'ica. Fight. You know how to fight.*

Yes, I think, *Rumi Maki—my hands are made of stone.*

I elbow the knife out of his hand, grab his sweaty head, gouge my thumbs into his eye sockets, slam my head onto his forehead then knee him sharply in the groin. He howls, rolls off me, moaning in agony. When I stand, he grabs me by the ankle, drags me down, climbs on top of me with a sinister grin on his dark, scarred face. He inches his way up my body, pins my arms with his knees then chokes me with his powerful calloused hands; I gag as everything goes white.

Pachamama, Mama Quilla, Ancient One. I silently pray before I plunge into an abyss of unconsciousness. *Help . . . "*

I perceive a familiar whirring sound then in the next instant, a loud crack, like a piece of dried hardwood splitting in two. The Inca groans, collapses like a wet sack of *ch'uño*—freeze dried potatoes and blood seeps from the back of his skull onto my torso; with a shudder, I shove the man off me, gasping for breath, roll over, push myself to my knees and shake my head, wondering what just happened.

When I survey the trail, I notice Umiña holding a sling, a halo of pink circling her light brown hair, emerald eyes gleaming in the sun.

CHAPTER FORTY ONE

Umiña and I drag the Inca general's lifeless body to the edge of the chasm, heave him into the Urubamba River then throw his helmet in after him; both disappear instantly into the rushing waters. I notice my knife, take a few wobbly steps toward it, pick it up, blow off the dust and shove it into it's leather sheaf.

"*Yusul payki,* Umiña, " I say with deepest gratitude, my mind still reeling; I did not expect to survive the vicious assault, "Urpicháy *sonqoy.*"

"*Hinallatapas,*" she says with a warm smile and big hug. "And you, too, are the dove of my heart."

"Let's cut down the bridge now," I say.

I quickly cut through the third rope, then cleave through the fourth; what's left of the bridge swings to the opposite side with a resounding crash then slaps off the chasm walls several times before falling silent.

Pispis walks toward us leading the llamas as Solsol holds Wawa who is wailing hysterically; she hands the angry baby back to Umiña.

"He wouldn't stop crying," she says, "I think he's hungry."

"I don't think so." Umiña states confidently. To the girls' amazement, the baby stops wailing as soon as the young mother places him in her back carrier and ties it around her shoulders. She gazes at the sisters with a smile, "That was his, 'I want Mamáy to carry me.' cry."

"Oh," Solsol says. "It all sounds the same to me."

"You will learn one day when you're older and become a *munay warmikuna,*" Umiña says and turns her head toward her baby. "Won't they, Wawa?" The infant coos happily then, exhausted from wailing, falls fast asleep.

"My sister and I will both grow to be women of substance," Pispis says with a bright smile then gazes at the swollen bruise on my brow, wrought by a warrior's projectile. "What happened there?" she asks.

I'm reluctant to tell the girls about my recent life and death struggle; they've already gone through so much. I shrug.

"I fell," I fib.

"How?" Solsol asks.

"And what happened to the bridge?" Pispis asks. "And to the soldiers?"

"You girls ask a lot of questions," I say with a grin.

"But we want to know what happened," Solsol insists.

"Let's just say," I say slyly, "that we were able to convince the Inca warriors to leave us alone."

"Oh," Pispis and Solsol say in unison, apparently satisfied with my evasive answer. "We have a gift for you."

They hand me the moon goddess pendant, which they slipped a thin cord in a tiny hole nobody noticed before. Solsol ties the necklace loosely around my bruised and battered neck.

"Yusul payki," I say, suddenly so emotional, that I find myself fighting back tears of gratitude. "It's a lovely gift."

"We must go a little out of our way to the sacred hot springs," Umiña says after gazing at the sun to assess the approximate time, "It is there that T'ica's wounds will be healed by the sacred waters. Then we can continue north to Chachapoyas."

"I'm so weary, I don't think I can take another step." I say.

The young mother adjusts the cloth holding her baby, picks up one of the llama's reins and peers at me.

"Yes, you can," she says with determination. "And you must."

At the hot springs in Cocalmayo, situated next to the Urubamba River, the stars are just beginning to reflect off the crystal clear sacred water; there is a *quilla hunt'asqa*—full moon. The warm water soothes and cleanses my battered body.

Umiña plays with her baby, encouraging him to float on his back then flipping him over and holding his hands so he can keep his head above water. He holds his breath, dives into the water, turns and swims back to his mother like a little fish. She picks the chubby infant up and pats him on the back; he sputters and promptly blinks water from his big brown eyes.

"Good little Wawa," Umiña says as she nuzzles her child, "All *runakuna* must learn to swim. Isn't that right?"

Pispis and Solsol splash playfully, sink into the hot springs, close their eyes and press their weary backs against boulders worn silky smooth from centuries of water flowing over them.

I focus on the silvery orb above, lift my arms to the heavens; I'm waist deep in the warm healing water, moon goddess pendant glowing silvery blue from the hallow of my neck.

"*Kaypachiswaychis, Mama Quilla*," I chant. "Empower us, give us strength and vision. Let us burst from our earthly cocoon to discover our real selves."

General Hango, a stocky man with a hooked nose that seems to cover more than half his face, holds a hand up. His litter carrier and battalion stop; the officer listens intently as he stares into the black night.

"Do you hear that?" he asks the high priest sitting in the gold encrusted litter next to his. They listen attentively. Nothing.

"Your nerves are getting the best of you, Hango," Apu Chalco Yupanqui, Huascar's high priest says. "Let's move forward."

The litter carriers step forward, their human cargo swaying above them.

"Tell me, priest," the general asks, trying desperately to exhibit an air of calm as he searches for words of assurance, "what do you think about the tales of the young women who were able to kill two Inca priests, two Inca officers and an entire battalion of warriors at the Llacsa Pass Bridge? A sole survivor says there are powerful forces at work; that the women we seek are not simple *runakuna*."

"Only pure-blooded Incas have the power to summon the gods." the priest answers laconically, "You have no doubt of that, do you, General?"

"No doubt," General Hango sputters, "Certainly, no doubt at all."

The general has *rumi sonqo*, a heart of stone. Groomed from childhood to be nothing less than a ruthless, blood thirsty warrior, he follows orders to the letter; his infamy brought him up the Inca officer ranks quickly. But now, the well-known prophecy foretelling the end of the Inca Empire, starting with the plague, which has already decimated the population, has shaken him. Even his own elite warrior battalion took ill; at least half of them succumbed to the devastation of the speckled monster. Making matters worse, royals ordered these weakened survivors to march nocturnally to find these elusive maidens without benefit of Lord Inti's sacred sunlight to bestow strength, courage and victory upon them.

"We're almost there," Apu Chalco Yupanqui says. He points down a hill leading to the sacred hot springs of Cocalmayo.

Hango turns to face his battalion of five hundred warriors.

"Remember," he says, "the witch named T'ica is not to be harmed. We must convince her to come with us peacefully."

"Afterward," the priest says, "we can dispose of the others as we wish."

"But," Hango counters, "the princess said . . ."

"I am in command here, captain," the high priest interrupts, "I thought you understood that."

"Of course, Apu," Hango says, head bowed. "Of course."

The full moon descends from the heavens and illuminates the sky, water, boulders and vegetation. Once it alights upon the cliffs above the water, a figure steps out, shimmering brilliant blue and white and floats down to the water's edge.

"It's Mama Quilla," I murmur. The Moon Goddess pendant hanging from my neck glimmers blue and white, too.

"Kimat, Kimat, Kimat," Mama Quilla calls out, evoking the name of the queen of the underwater world. A raven-haired nymph breaks through the water, crowned with a halo of shiny dark green leaves and bright yellow primroses; long black lashes blink away water droplets that shine like diamonds in the Moon Goddess's glow. "Kimat, my sister, you have come," she says. "Arise."

The nymph arises, her skin luminescent with shades of green and brown; she brings a tempest with her: thick black clouds obscure the stars, the wind howls and hail pummels the earth, bouncing off boulders and tender human flesh alike. Umiña picks up her baby and with Solsol and Pispis hurriedly step out of the sacred hot springs, taking cover in a nearby cave.

Only I remain in the hot springs, arms still uplifted, impervious to the hail stones, which bounce painlessly off my skin and embed like moonstones in my wet hair.

Kimat, queen of the underwater world and Mama Quilla ascend to the top of a cliff and transform into two tender forms.

CHAPTER FORTY TWO

"We mean you no harm!" Hango barks from his lavish litter into the darkness near the sacred Cocalmayo hot springs. "We only need the one called T'ica to come with us to Cuzco." All is deadly silent, except for the breathing of the carriers patiently holding litters upon their broad shoulders. "Our emperor has already perished and many royals have taken ill; we understand that perhaps T'ica can cure them."

I wonder for a moment how word got out that I have the ability to cure the plague then it hits me: Sonqo's mayor must have bragged about how I cured him, the news got picked up by a local *chasqui*, who then delivered the message to Cuzco royals.

The fool, I think darkly. *I should have let him die.*

"Don't royals," I yell, "employ the services of the Kollahuayas, the magicians from Acamani?"

"In the past, the Kollahuayas were able to cure royalty of their ailments." the high priest interjects, "But the speckled monster is different—vicious and lethal with a stranglehold on the whole of the Inca Empire."

"Agree to come with us," Hango lies, "and the others can go where they will."

"Don't do it, T'ica!" Solsol yells, "The Incas are liars."

"Better to journey to *hanan pacha* now," Pispis says resolutely, "than to be enslaved or tortured by the Incas for months or even years to come."

Another luminous body—*runa kurku k'anchay* shimmers in the high cliffs overlooking the sacred hot springs and alights next to

Kimat and Mama Quilla; it looms over the soldiers who gaze at the majestic sight, knees quivering; they try desperately to keep their weapons from shaking in their hands. Inca law decrees that warriors who display outward signs of cowardice are to be executed immediately.

"Go back to Cuzco now," Pachamama pronounces. She hoists the youthful forms of Kimat and Mama Quilla, now infants, overhead. The earth goddess's voice is low and steady as she continues, "and I will let you live, General Hango. Disobey and you and the priest will make the tortuous journey to *ukhu pacha*—the dreaded underworld. Tonight."

"A magician's trick, nothing more," Apu Chalco Yupanqui whispers, "How they do it, I'm not quite sure, but it's quite clever."

The general steps boldly toward T'ica.

"Give me the girl," Hango states, "And we'll be on our way."

Pachamama lifts the infants overhead then releases them. They float down upon an escarpment and full grown jaguars materialize in their place, golden eyes sparkling, ears pulled back, thigh muscles twitching.

"Stay back, men." the general orders. His troops take a step back, weapons drawn; they know jaguars are powerful predators who often attack and eat villagers; for years, Inca emperors have tried in vain to exterminate them. "Are these *runa uturunca?*" General Hango asks the high priest.

"Shapeshifters?" the Inca priest scoffs. "Those are just wild animals, like any other. Or perhaps a convincing illusion."

"But if they are *runa uturunca*," the Inca officer continues, obviously shaken by the materialization of the felines, "they can't

247

be killed with our earthly weapons."

The ground begins to tremble and shake. It is a *pacha kuyuy*—an earthquake of enormous magnitude. Pachamama's earthen belly splits open into an endless abyss, swallowing the battalion of terrified warriors. The earth creaks and rumbles and Mother Earth spits them out again.

"Throw down your weapons now!" Pachamama roars. The regurgitated men scramble to their feet. "Now go back to your families and don't come back."

The warriors drop all weapons and race into the darkness; almost all are reluctant conscripts, glad to return to their respective provinces, hoping to find surviving family members after the decimation of the population by the plague.

The jaguars screech then leap from their stony perches, one onto Hango's litter, the other onto Apu Chalco Yupanqui's. The beasts wrap their powerful jaws around the Incas' necks, drag them to the edge of the litter then drop them upon the rocky ground below. Eight royal carriers stare wide-eyed at the moaning royals, lower their litters and run for their lives.

Their faces pasty white, the general and priest are in shock but still alive. When the beasts pounce upon their bellies, they do not die well; screaming, begging and thrashing like the hundreds of innocent men, women and children they've raped, tortured and killed in their misspent lives in the mercurial physical realm of *kay pacha.*

CHAPTER FORTY THREE

Half feline, half moon goddess, brilliant white fangs glimmering in the moonlight on one side of its face, a set of perfect human teeth on the other, the creature leaps onto a gnarled tree branch protruding from the cliff looming over the sacred thermal waters, roars, then soars, a silver streak in the raven black night until it reaches the moon.

The other jaguar dives into the sacred water, swimming lazily in a circle around me. I watch it cautiously, too exhausted to be frightened: I reach out and pet its noble head. The beast purrs then dives into the warm water. In a moment, the water nymph emerges, lets out a fierce growl, bats her thick eyelashes, turns and submerges into the healing waters, disappearing through the rocky cracks in the bottom of the pool, then after a few moment, reemerges with a coarsely woven bag full of thrashing fish, silvery in the light of the full moon.

"Trout!" I exclaim.

She swims to the edge of the sacred water and hands the bag to Umiña.

"*Yusul payki,*" Umiña says, thanking the water nymph. "*Urpicháy sonqo.*"

"And you are the dove of my heart. And remember," Kimat whispers, "where you find water, there I will be."

She dives and vanishes through the bottom of the pool once again.

Umiña and I push what remains of the dead general and the high priest into the black abyss created by the earthquake. Pachamama rumbles and with a jolt, seals the abyss.

"I see you have fully recovered, Solsol," Pachamama says her form invisible to us now.

"*Urpicháy sonqo.*" Solsol says, placing her hands over her heart.

The girl ruminates about her short but horrific time in the miserable underworld where, aided by Pachamama, she was able to escape and rejoin her sister in *kay pacha,* the earthly world.

A glittering white dove lands on Solsol's left shoulder, caresses her cheek then flutters off into the dark night.

I imagine Pachamama's deep brown eyes upon me.

"You have journeyed well, T'ica, my dove. Your parents and baby brother await your arrival in the jungle." she explains, "They are safe with the Chirihuanas."

The Chirihuanas? I thinks with a mixture of panic and confusion. *But they are cannibals.*

Yes, the goddess responds, apparently able to pluck thoughts from my mind. *Inca soldiers fear this tribe over all others. That is why your family is safe. When you arrive there, you will see.*

"But how do I find this tribe?" I ask aloud.

I imagine Pachamama's brown eyes fading then becoming one with the earth. I wonder if the Machukuna will be able to help me find my family in the depths of the vast jungle after escorting Pispis and Solsol to Chachapoyas—the land of the Cloud Warriors.

Pispis finds a flowering bush; she carefully twists off a yellow primrose then tosses it into the water. She jumps in after it, floating on her back, kicking lightly.

"I like the water nymph the best," the little girl trills, just like any child her age, happy and carefree despite the innumerable sorrows she's faced in her young life, "because I like to swim."

Bubbles emerge from the depths of the water, the shy water nymph surfaces, picks up the primrose, buries her nose in it, kisses Pispis lightly on the cheek, removes her delicate crown of intertwined yellow primroses and places it on the girl's head

"This is for you," Kimat says. She flips backward into the water and vanishes again.

After squealing in delight, Pispis touches her crown of primroses and does a back flip into the water, too.

We all decide to emerge from the sacred waters, dry off, then gather enough kindling to make a campfire, skewering the mountain trout with sticks and grilling the tender flesh slowly over the open fire. After gorging ourselves, we spread our blankets inside a nearby cave, lie down and fall asleep.

The siblings arise before dawn, energized by the nutritious evening meal and the notion that Mama Quilla, Pachamama and even Kimat, the Queen of the Underwater World really are with us. They snack on leftover grilled fish.

"The Inca will not give up." I whisper to Umiña, who has already tied her baby to her back. "They will keep on sending troops until they find us again."

"We will need to stay off the main road," Umiña says, "There are foot trails winding through the upper jungle and plenty of wild fruit there to sustain us."

* * *

Thriving in the unusually wet spring, swarms of mosquitoes assail our hands, feet and faces. Desperate for a solution, Umiña spies a small stream, digs her hands into the mud and spreads it over her face.

"Smear your faces, your feet, your hands with this," she says, "and keep the rest of your body covered."

We slap the muck onto our bodies. Afterward, I gently dab it onto the baby's face, though the blood sucking pests don't seem to be nearly as interested in him as the rest of us.

Pispis points at a spindly tree loaded with brown fuzzy oblongs with a hull that appears to be nearly as thick and tough as a coconut's.

"Look, *copoasu!*" Pispis yells. She twists the fruit off its branch, then smashes its hull against a small boulder; white pulpy seed sacks, which smell like ripe pineapple, appear. She pulls out a fruit sack and pops it into her mouth. "Hmm. Delicious!"

Solsol holds out her hand and Pispis places the luscious fruit in her sister's palm. She puts it into her mouth and moans in ecstasy. Next Pispis places a juicy sack into Umiña's waiting mouth, then another piece into mine.

"Excellent," Umiña exclaims. She puts a tiny piece into her baby's mouth; he squeals in delight.

Naked except for a tattered loin cloth, a tiny emaciated man steps into the clearing, his brown eyes sparkling. We stare at him wide-eyed, mouths dripping with fruit and at a complete loss for words. Pispis breaks the silence.

"Would you like some fruit?" she asks trying not to choke, "We have plenty."

"Thank you. But what makes you think I'm hungry," the man says with a serene gaze, "when I feed off the generous nourishment of Mother Moon, Father Sun and the stars?"

"Are you a *guacacue*?" I ask. "My father told me of diviners who walk naked through nature and stare at the sun to gain knowledge."

"You are a clever girl," the tiny man says impishly.

"Please join us," Umiña says as she plops cross-legged on the ground, "And share your coveted secrets of nature with us."

"Pachamama reveals all to those who will listen." he says, scrutinizing us with a beatific smile. He sits across from Umiña, his back straight, eyes lifted to the sky. The upper jungle grows silent, even the wildlife appears to stop foraging to hear his words. He gazes at the young mother then addresses her baby with a high friendly sing song voice. "*Hila nayra huahua*—first born son, you know of what I speak, don't you?"

Little Wawa coos, gurgles and kicks his tiny feet as if to say, *yes, of course, I know.*

"You are brave little doves." the man states, "Your journey through the rainforest will be long and arduous."

"We cannot travel on the main road," I explain, "though it is much easier in almost every way, it is quite treacherous, at least for us."

Staring at the sun, he nods; a hummingbird with gleaming ruby feathers flies onto his shoulder, then puts its tiny beak inside his ear as if relaying a message; the man listens to the creature intently. When finished, bird flies off, tiny wings whirring.

"Inca warriors are tracking you on the Royal Inca Road; perhaps you don't know that Emperor Huayna Capac has already expired."

"So we've been told." Umiña says.

"Yes," Chimbo says, "the entire population of the empire has been greatly affected."

"Half my village was wiped out by this dreadful plague." I say.

"Now succession to the throne is in contention by two half brothers: Atahualpa and Huascar," he explains. "These royals are *huacha-utek*, dangerous desperate men especially Huascar who is a murderous lunatic. Traveling through the forest also has its hazards; hostile natives often blow poison darts into necks of strangers; Inca warriors will be searching for you here, too."

"What else can we do?" I ask.

"There is a safer route on which you can only travel by connecting with *saiwachay*—energy connecting the three worlds of *hanan pacha, kay pacha* and *ukhu pacha:* the upper world, the surface world and the lower world—future, present and past." the explains, "If your hearts are open, I will show you how. But we must wait until nightfall."

"How do you know about what Inca royals are doing?" I ask, "I thought *guacacue* were only interested in nature and spiritual matters."

The man smiles benevolently.

"I have learned much about the true nature of life since I was forced into hiding," the little man says, "My name is Chimbo Sancto, loyal adviser to the late Emperor Huayna Capac. I, too, am running from the Incas."

* * *

After sunset, Chimbo raises his arms, palms facing the cloudless sky, bright with stars; dense whirlpools of chaotic energy fly off his fingertips into the cosmos.

"All must rid themselves of *hucha*." he says, "even *guacacue, like myself.*"

Filaments of white light flow into and accumulate in his right hand. He brings his palms together overhead and energy flows from his right hand to his left, flows down his left arm into his heart, pulsates a white light then disperses throughout his body.

"Now we must cleanse the llamas who serve you so well," he says." He turns to the beasts who have been contentedly munching on the lush grasses of the upper forest; a small silver bell with a llama motif handle materializes in his palm. He rings the bell next to the llamas' ears; small whirlpools of *hucha* fly off. "These beasts are content and know their place in *kay pacha*." He nuzzles the llamas' necks. "Good llamas," he trills, "Good boys." Each beast nuzzles him in return then nonchalantly continue to graze.

He turns to me next. I'm curious to discover what I can learn from this odd little man and intrigued by his ability to manipulate life and energy forces so effortlessly. *How could it be so easy?* But realize we have little choice but to continue our journey on a safer, more prudent path, whatever that might be; we have nothing to lose and everything to gain.

Starting at the top of my head, Chimbo lightly drums his fingertips, as if simulating a light rain; he continues down my torso, stomach, hips, legs, feet to the tips of my toes. Each tap creates a *ponqo*—a tiny whirlpool in my energy field, until I glimmer from head to toe. He steps back, raises his arms overhead again, palms facing the sky as white energy flows into his right hand. He clasps his palms together and, again, life force flows from his right hand, into his left, down his left arm, into his head where it radiates like a shining star then flows to the rest of his body.

Thus bathed in light, he places his hands lightly on my head, slowly fluttering his fingers in front of my body, gathering loosened whirlpools of *hucha,* which flicker and fizz in his hands. Then he repeats the procedure on my back, starting from my head, going down my spine. When he reaches my toes, he places his palms, filled with chaotic energy on the dark warm ground.

"Earth Mother, I beseech you to accept this *hucha* and transform it into infinite love and goodness," he prays.

Dust kicks up, creating a little vortex; Pachamama sucks the whirlpools of *hucha* deep into her belly, *ukhu pacha*—the lower world which connects with roots, underground streams, soil, minerals, suck up the energy and convert it into soothing light. We hold our breaths until the Earth Goddess brings the *hucha* back to *kay pacha,* the physical realm, then hurls it back to *hana pacha,* the heavenly upper realm. When it reaches the cosmos, it explodes into a massive meteor shower rocketing wildly across the void.

We ooh and aah, admiring the sensational spectacle of energy and light.

"The *hucha* is wild again," I say.

"Yes," the *guacacue* says, "but now it has found its purpose. Energy, even *hucha*, is neither good nor bad; it must be channeled to serve the universe's needs. "

"Oh!" Pispis cries out in awe as another burst of light showers down from the heavens. She holds Solsol's hand; the sisters can't believe their eyes. Umiña's baby coos then extends his chubby little fingers as though trying to catch the play of light.

Chimbo repeats the procedure starting again at my head then traveling to my toes, removing any remnants of *hucha* along the way. As before, after he gathers the chaotic energy, he places his palms on the ground, asks Pachamama to accept it; she pulls the chaos into the lower world, lets it resurface then hurls it into the cosmos, where it illuminates the night and finally dissipates.

With the last vestiges of *hucha* removed, I find myself embracing the past, present, future, *ukhu pacha, kay pacha and hanan pacha*—lower world, surface world and upper world. Chimbo gazes at me serenely then gives me a warm embrace.

"*Saiwachay* welcomes you and will soon connect you to the universe." he says, his voice sounding like thousands of leaves softly rustling in the breeze. "You will know what to do from there."

My condor glides lazily overhead, lands on my shoulder, flapping his giant wings; the bird has been gone since he guided me to Solsol's whereabouts on Apu Salkantay Mountain. Ecstatic to see him again, I hold out my hand; the condor jumps onto my palm, melting back into a hard shiny black clay bird-shaped *enqa,* which I place inside the pouch around my neck; I utter a short prayer of thanks to Pachamama for guiding my bird back to me.

The action of placing my *enqa* in its pouch seems to be the last piece of a complex cosmic puzzle; my body begins to shimmer, fingers, toes, arms, legs painlessly separate into millions of infinitesimal particles as do my internal organs. I perceive each particle tingle and diverge a scant millimeter from each other; after a short pause, the molecules scatter inches apart, then a few feet, yards, miles then millions of miles. *Saiwachay*—pure unadulterated life force embraces me and I in turn embrace it. Three worlds—upper, surface and lower connect as one pulsating glorious universe.

The tips of my toes are the only solid body part remaining; my earthly vessel is rapidly dissolving into the ether. I'm engaging upon a journey but to where, I do not know.

"Pachamama," I pray, "connect your filaments to mine, be my anchor as I soar."

I recall my father entertaining me as a child with his theories of the universe when we would gaze at glorious purple and orange sunsets after a hard day of plowing fields and planting potatoes and corn.

Never forget, T'ica, my beautiful dove: everything is connected to everything else; everything has consciousness.

CHAPTER FORTY FOUR

I spiral into the profound cold and silence of the cosmos and infinite timelessness, pushing myself into the embrace of Mama Tuta, goddess of the dark, the void, the stars and the night. Though unable to see her with my own physical eyes, I feel her presence.

I beseech your assistance, Mama Tuta, I pray. *Please show me my path.*

The law of the universe is harmony, Mama Tutu responds, her voice soft and low, *the law of life is to live well.*

Struck by an overwhelming desire to be in harmony with the universe, I yearn to exist in eternal bliss in the ether, my authentic spirit home. I dread returning to *kay pacha*—the physical realm where weariness, hunger, fear and simply staying alive are all but constant companions. My thoughts wander to family and friends: Tatáy, Mamáy, and my infant brother; Umiña and her baby; Solsol and Pispis and the llamas. How are they? Where are they? Do they need my help? What happened to the *guacacue*? The mere thought of life without family and friends crushes me.

No, I cannot exist without them, I think.

My heart soars in the knowledge of what I must do; I'm willing to lose everything, except for my loved ones—the very essence of a harmonious universe and living well.

I'm ready to go back now.

Pachamama appears in all her verdant glory and escorts me to the surface world of *kay pacha*. As I travel through the ether, my body's infinitesimal particles begin to vibrate then merge in the invisible world—*tiqsi*. Moments later, my physical structure fully materializes in *kay pacha* but in an unfamiliar location; my bones bear down upon me like lead weights; my mind is disconnected from all worlds—upper, surface and lower. I fight to keep my eyes open but it's not use; I curl up on a cool smooth surface; someone tenderly covers me with clouds of warm blankets before I fall into a deep sleep.

I groggily scrutinize my surroundings—a large subterranean tunnel with floors and walls of polished granite.

Where am I and how did I get here?

The last thing I remember is the *guacacue* removing *hucha* from my body. I'm dismayed to discover that my memory becomes more vague as I attempt to recall recent events.

So strange. Why can't I remember?

"Good morning, T'ica," a familiar voice says.

With a gasp, I turn, rub my eyes and gaze into the cerulean eyes of the pearly-toothed Machukuna, one of the group who insisted on my mission to the holy mountain of Salkantay in the first place. He smiles benevolently and makes a sweeping gesture to direct my attention to hundreds of other giant Children of the Moon standing behind him, their large ivory teeth gleaming in the warm, well lit subterranean facility.

"Good morning," I answer. The giants titter in response but not derisively; they are affectionate and even tender. *Gentle giants, gentle souls.* "My father told me that Machukuna," I say, "no longer exist in *kay pacha,* our physical realm."

"Before Inti the Sun God and *runakuna,* only Goddess Moon

and the Children of the Moon existed," the kind giant explains, veins pulsing iridescent blue beneath translucent skin. "But all that changed in the *pachakuti*—the time of great upheaval."

"It was Tatáy Inti's time to rule the earth," another giant continues, "But Machukuna could not survive in the searing sunlight. Some of us dove into deep waters, others hid in the trees. A few fled to the mountains and sought shelter in caves though even a small amount of sunlight proved fatal. At sunset, the Children of the Moon emerge from the spirit dimension from their small stone dwellings—*chullpas* built on countless Andean slopes, which all *runakuna* have seen. There they warm their bones by the red glow of the evening sky. With the full moon, our bones and flesh reanimate and we stroll on the sweet soil of *kay pacha*, tending the same fields that *runakuna* tend during the light of day." The Machukuna turns, throws out his arms and nods at his comrades. "The old world of the Children of the Moon still exists in a dimension parallel to *runakuna*."

The cave grows dimmer, looks of concern sweep over the giants' kind faces; they fade away.

"Wait!" I cry, "Don't go!"

My *enqa* stirs in its pouch, the tiny clay bird wriggles, jumps on my shoulder, quickly transforming into a full size condor once again. He squawks, flies down a tunnel passageway then flies back. I grope blindly in the dark, using the cold stone walls as a guide; the bird continues to soar back and forth, screeching impatiently. When I turn a corner, a thin shaft of sunlight pours through a tiny hole in the rock wall, helping to light the way; I climb several steps of carved stone which lead to a small portal; I crawl through, poke my head through another opening which leads outside. My condor soars off into the perfect blue sky.

I hear the murmur of male voices, maidens sobbing and a baby wailing, their voices growing closer. I duck back into the tunnel after seeing my friends trapped inside a cage atop a litter.

"We must find the one called T'ica," a gruff male voice grumbles, "She's the one who knows how to cure the plague. The royals are offering a huge reward to anyone who captures her alive."

"Huascar can keep his reward," another soldier adds, "We're lucky we captured her friends without getting annihilated."

Huascar, T'ica ruminates, *isn't this the dead emperor's sons, a desperate man who will fight against his brother for the royal fringe?*

"The one they call T'ica is a witch." a third soldiers says, voice trembling with nervousness, "A powerful one from what I hear. If you make her angry, she calls upon her gods . . . and there's no telling what they will do."

"I heard she's a shapeshifter," a fifth soldier teases, "who likes nothing better than to seduce the ignorant and transform into an ugly old crone in the middle of doing it." He moves his hips suggestively; the others groan at his vulgar joke then continue marching south to connect to the Royal Inca Road leading to Cuzco.

These Inca warriors fear me, I surmise. I crawl out of the tunnel then follow the litter, thick jungle foliage providing adequate cover.

"Did you hear that?" a nervous warrior asks anxiously.

In an instant, a projectile cracks open the back of his skull and he crumbles to the ground; another warrior checks the felled man's pulse.

"He's dead," he whispers, eyes blood shot with terror. A whirring sound and a stone strikes the warrior's right eye. He wails, sinks to his knees; another smacks his left temple and he collapses.

I zigzag through jungle foliage, finding high ground on a variety of boulders, loading my sling, aiming and shooting.

"In the name of all the gods and goddesses," a frightened warrior shouts, head bloodied by a glancing projectile blow, "it's the witch! We're doomed"

"Shut up!" an Inca lieutenant shouts, a large yellow feather at the top front of his helmet. He creeps into the jungle, sword in hand.

Four warriors lay dead upon the floor of the jungle. The Inca lieutenant returns with me, his sword pointed at my back.

"Which one of your friends should die for your treachery!" he snarls, "Four of my best men dead because of you."

The baby is wailing again; Umiña tries to sooth him to no avail.

"This was none of their doing," I say, "I should be the one to die. No one else."

"You are more valuable to me alive than dead, witch," the Inca lieutenant growls. "Now choose or I will kill all of them."

"I swear to you," I say, "you put a hand on my friends and the gods will curse you and your family in ways you never imagined."

Little Wawa wails even louder now.

"Shut that brat up!" the lieutenant barks, "Or I will kill that bawling little monkey right now."

He steps toward the litter cage; Umiña sobs and cradles her infant tight against her breast.

"No! Not the baby!" Solsol begs, "I confess that I killed the priests and soldiers. I'm not afraid to die."

"I cannot live without my sister," Pispis pleads between convulsive sobs, "Take us both then. Please."

The lieutenant cocks his head; the litter carriers lower their burden and the officer unlocks the cage.

"Behold the wrath of the all powerful Inca Empire," he says arrogantly, brandishing his sword, "upon the wretched, traitorous, snake-worshiping Cloud Warrior savages of the north."

Solsol hesitantly arises from her bench followed by Pispis.

"You don't have to do this," Umiña says to the sisters, "I am not afraid to journey to *hanan pacha* with my baby."

The lieutenant bangs the cage with the broadside of his sword.

"If you say one more word, whore!" the Inca leader shouts at Umiña, "I will skin that bastard of yours alive. Do you understand me?"

Umiña stares defiantly at the man as her baby whimpers softly.

I glance at the sisters then at the ground where a dead warrior's sword lays near my feet; the girls eyes sparkle in acknowledgment since they see the weapon, too. They step slowly out of the cage.

I snatch the weapon, stunned by its heft. I raise it overhead with two hands, swing it at the lieutenant's neck; he turns, blocks the strike with his sword. I realize instantly that I can't compete with this man in a sword fight, so I turn and race into the jungle, still holding onto my new weapon. The Inca runs after me, roaring and cursing. I know I can't outrun him but perhaps I can outmaneuver him.

"Run!" I yell to my friends as I seek a place to hide, "Run in different directions. He can't catch all of us."

My companions tumble out of the litter cage then dart into the dense foliage. The Lucanas litter carriers look on for a moment then run, too.

Umiña's baby starts wailing.

"I'll shut that brat up," the Inca shouts, as he walks toward the irritating sound, "if it's the last thing I do!"

Umiña runs, pressing the infant tight upon her breast but he just won't stop crying. Recognizing the hopelessness of the situation, the exhausted young mother plops down in front of a large tree, cradling her child. When the officer finds her, her emerald eyes are aglow, a pink halo frames her head.

"We are not afraid," Umiña says serenely.

The lieutenant smiles sardonically, lifts his sword. His eyes open wide as if startled; he chokes, touches his neck, drops his sword, then takes two wobbly side-way steps.

"Witch!" he croaks.

He collapses face down into dense vegetation, trembling convulsively.

After noisily whacking through thick foliage, Chimbo Sancto appears, holding a long bamboo blow gun. He inspects the mortally wounded warrior, thrashing and foaming at the mouth.

"Don't fight it, Inca," the dwarf *guacacue* advises. "Let the poison take you.

CHAPTER FORTY FIVE

Chimbo Sancto prances ahead of us, still in his filthy loincloth but head held high as any man who ever lived, elated to have saved his friends from the murderous Inca lieutenant. As we descend, our faithful llamas in tow, the Inca capital city glistens in the sun, its roads gently curved; clever architects designed the city in the form of a giant crouching puma.

Though my village of Sonqo is relatively close, less than fifty miles away, I never visited the Cuzco, due to Tatay's extreme distrust of the Incas.

"I still don't think this is a good idea." I say, "The Incas are trying to hunt us down."

"This will be the last place," Chimbo Sancto explains patiently, "that Inca warriors will be looking for us." He gazes at the Cloud Warrior sisters then at me. "Just remember to keep your heads covered." We adjust our hoods snugly over our conspicuously blond hair. Umiña's brown hair permits her the luxury of traveling without a head covering but she helps us tuck away our flowing locks. "Don't worry. I have friends in Cuzco. Princess Cura Occlo was quite fond of me as were a number of other Cuzco royals," the dwarf says.

"The princess was our friend, too," Solsol squeaks, "she used to play with us Daughters of the Sun at the Qorincancha."

"Cura Occlo," Pispis says, "is kind—unlike the rest of the royals."

"Especially Prince Huascar," Solsol says with a scowl, "Cura's half brother—he's a very bad man."

Though apprehensive, we stroll past the Saqsaywaman fortress, its walls erected from immense boulders in the imperial style. Most people say the stones were placed together with such precision, no mortar was needed; Tatáy told me that the ancient simply stacked gigantic bags of cement on top of each other then watered them down. But who knows for sure? The cyclopean citadel is heavily protected by hundreds of armed, fierce-looking Inca warriors, inside and out.

Pispis taps me then Umiña on our shoulders; she points out the shimmering gold and silver plated exterior walls of the Qorincancha located in the city's royal quarter, also the location of four royal palaces.

"Look," Pispis says, "The Temple of the Sun."

A flood of painful memories wash over the sisters recalling the harsh supervision of the *mamaconas*. I touch the Moon Goddess pendant at my neck.

"Don't worry, girls," I say, "Mama Quilla will protect us."

Captain Usna, a jagged purple scar across his forehead and carrying a huge paunch, eyes Princess Cura Occlo perched on a low golden throne, dressed in a simple white and red tunic.

"Lower your eyes, Captain Usna," Princess Cura Occlo says, "How dare you?"

The captain bows low, arms out-stretched, eyes down.

"Forgive me," he mumbles into the floor.

"My father, Shepherd of the Sun and Most Holy Emperor of the Inca Empire has perished from the plague in Quito, though only recently taken ill. Many Quiteños, royal and non-royals alike have died, too. However, the queen mother has sent assurances that she and my sister Chuqui are in fine health. In this unstable period of interregnum, the widowed *coya* has designated me to take command until further notice."

"But, I thought," the captain mumbles, "that your brother, Prince Huascar was supposed to be in command."

"As you well know, my brother is on a drunken whore-mongering rampage," the princess states, "somewhere in the provinces. So, I am the interim sovereign in Cuzco, therefore, you will respect me as such until further notice. Do you understand?"

"Yes," the captain whispers, "Of course."

"Now stand," the Princess asks. "and tell me what business you have here."

The captain straightens, his knees creaking audibly but careful to keep his eyes and head lowered in deference to the princess.

"Princess," the captain says, "we have word that General Hango and high priest, Apu Chalco Yupanqui have been murdered at the sacred hot springs in Cocalmayo by that group of . . . witches we've been looking for."

"Witches?" the princess scoffs.

"A vicious," the captain states, fear evident in his eyes, "powerful coven."

"Huascar and I talked about this. We only need the one called T'ica," the princess says, "because of her skills in curing the plague as she did in Sonqo. I don't understand why one little girl cannot be peacefully enticed to . . ." A guard, head bowed steps into the throne room, interrupting the princess's train of thought. She sighs impatiently. "Come forward," she says irritably. The guard steps onto the throne dais, whispers in her ear. Cura seems bewildered by his message. "Bring this . . . person in," she orders.

"Yes, princess," the guard says with a bow.

He waves a dwarf, naked save for a loincloth, into the room. The princess scrutinizes the filthy half man and shakes her head; she doesn't recognize the emaciated character in front of her.

"My princess," the dwarf says with a deep bow.

He lifts his chin then shoots her a dimpled grin.

"Chimbo Sancto?" the astonished princess asks.

"So you still remember your old friend?" the dwarf asks.

"Who could forget the famous, immensely entertaining Chimbo Sancto?" the princess declares warmly.

"At your service, princess," the dwarf says, "and that of the empire."

The little man waves the young ladies waiting in the corridor into the throne room; Pispis and Solsol enter first, followed by Umiña and child then me. When the princess recognizes the sisters, her eyes well with tears.

"Come to me, my doves," Cura says, her voice breaking with emotion.

The sisters scurry across the throne room, hop up on the dais and embrace their royal friend.

The captain steps forward, sword drawn.

"Those yellow-haired Cloud Warrior witches," the Captain Usna protests, "escaped *capacocha* by murdering two priests, then went on to slaughter innumerable warriors—some of my best men."

"If you don't want to be hung from your hair in the town square until condors feast on your eyes," the princess says, "only to live out the rest of your days begging for scraps of roasted maize, I suggest you lower your sword and step back right now, Captain."

Usna pats his paunch, lowers his sword then steps back, a scowl on his scarred face.

"As you wish, my princess," he murmurs.

"Out of my sight, Usna," the Princess says, waving him off, "before you exhaust my rapidly diminishing supply of benevolence."

The captain backs away from the throne, turns and storms out of the throne room, his immense belly leading the way.

We can only glance at the opulent walls of the Inca palace covered in breathtaking, stylized gold and silver images of the Sun God and dozens of other major and minor Inca deities as Princess Cura and her servants rush us down one lavishly decorated corridor after another toward the main bath house. When we arrive, attendants wait beside an immense granite bathtub filled with steaming bath water. We strip off our filthy, ragged attire as servants hold up plush towels for propriety's sake, then lead each of us, modesty intact, into the hot water.

"Take care to burn all those clothes," Cura orders, "They are beyond repair and could carry disease."

A timid servant girl wrinkles her nose, gathers our garments, holds them at arm's length then scurries into a corridor. Two other royal handmaidens remain.

"And, you, my faithful servants," the princess says,, "take a good look at my friends here, determine their sizes and select a wardrobe for them from my own reserve. Garments for our dear little Wawa and Chimbo Sancto should be retrieved from the . . . children's wardrobe collection." She blushes. "Forgive me, Lord Chimbo."

"I have long ago," the dwarf answers cheerfully, "ceased being offended by references to my diminutive stature. But thank you for your concern, Princess."

As the servants dash out of the bathing area, we dunk our heads, lean against the sides of the bath and relax while Umiña's baby pushes his chubby legs like a frog through the water. Except for Chimbo, none of us have ever enjoyed a warm indoor bath before.

The handmaidens return with piles of silky vicuña tunics crafted by the most esteemed weavers and seamstresses in the empire—the Daughters of the Sun. Another brings in several pairs of ornately crafted leather sandals—simple *runakuna* would never have the time or resources to craft such footwear for their own use.

"Are those for us?" Pispis squeaks excitedly.

"Seamstresses and sandal makers will make alterations tonight as needed." Cura says. She regards us pensively. "Soon we will travel by royal litter to Quito with the fastest Lucanas carriers in the empire. I have already sent a message via *chasqui* to ask the queen mother's permission to do so; I await her affirmation in hopes that we will soon be on our way. It is too dangerous to remain in Cuzco much longer."

Servants fuss over us, presenting trays of food we might not have tasted yet and filling sturdy hammered silver and gold chalices with sweet *chicha* as we sit on plush floor cushions around a low wooden table groaning with roasted llama, skewered guinea pig, baked fish, savory quinoa, vegetable and potato soups, fresh sweet tropical fruits of all sizes and colors, and *mazamorra morada*— sweet purple maize pudding. Princess Cura sits between Solsol and Pispis; the old friends laugh, tease, tell jokes and play guessing games in between stuffing themselves until their stomachs ache.

"Do you hear that?" Cura asks, her brow furrowed with concern.

We grow silent. The low doleful pitch of a *pututu* permeates the palace walls.

"What could that mean?" Pispis asks.

"Probably nothing good," Solsol whispers.

A distraught *chasqui* races into the dining hall, gasping for breath, holding an intricately tied *quipu.* He immediately notices the princess and bows deeply.

"They're dead!" he moans, his eyes cast down.

"Who?" Cura asks, irritated that the delightful meal and camaraderie with her young friends has been interrupted. "Who's dead?"

"I . . . I don't know how to tell you but . . ." the young man stutters.

"Give me the *quipu*," the princess demands impatiently. "I'm fully capable of deciphering the message myself."

The young *chasqui* hands her the mass of carefully knotted strings. Cura examines the *quipu;* dread and incredulity sweep over her lovely face, which seconds ago had been glowing with happiness and camaraderie in the company of long lost friends. Her vision blurs in a veil of hot tears. When he notes the princess struggling to accept the message knotted on the *quipu*, the *chasqui* decides to speak; but to Cura, his voice is distant and distorted as if stuck in a void million of miles away.

"Your brothers were ordered by Huascar to go to Limatambo and there they were . . ." he becomes so overcome with emotion, he can't bring himself to say the last dreaded words. "I'm so sorry, princess," the chasqui says. "The people of the Empire grieve with you."

Cura inspects the *quipu* again, her face drenched in tears.

"The Queen Mother also denies permission for us to head to Quito," the princess read, her voice breaking, "We are to await her imminent arrival in Cuzco along with that of my father's funeral procession."

CHAPTER FORTY SIX

Prince Huascar storms down the corridors of the royal palace, accompanied by a retinue of a dozen guards, Captain Usna and Quetzal, the prince's new smarmy high priest. The prince's face is set in a perpetual scowl, making his uneven features seem even more unpleasant; he dons over-sized earrings which could be mistaken for small gold dinner plates if they weren't hanging from his grotesquely distended earlobes.

In an expansive bedchamber, Cura Occlo sits cross legged on a low bed and rolls dice onto a large wooden bed tray, a much needed diversion for the royal who is grieving the assassination of ten brothers; little does she know, this is only the beginning of Huascar's dirty tricks. Umiña, sitting across from her new royal friend, scrutinizes the princess's roll.

"I win!" she declares.

"Again?" The princess says with mock exasperation and a giggle; she slides a dozen seashells to her opponent's side.

Solsol and I are locked in concentration over a complex Inca board game, using beans as counters. Pispis spins a top which whirs endlessly on the polished granite floor. Nearby, Chimbo rocks little Wawa in a carved wooden cradle depicting a jaguar mother nursing two newborn cubs.

The baby frowns then begins to wail.

"Umiña," the dwarf says, "I think your baby is hungry." He leans over the cradle, picks up the infant, "Are you hungry, little Wawa?"

Huascar and his minions burst through the bedchamber door. Captain Usna points at Solsol and Pispis. Chimbo hands the baby to Umiña and the rest of the maidens scramble to their feet, looking for a quick way out; guards block the door, their only exit.

"These are the Cloud Warrior witches," the captain says, "who dishonored the gods and the emperor when they escaped *capacocha* and murdered our priests and warriors with their witchcraft." Usna slowly circles the sisters, his sword drawn. Solsol and Pispis remain stoic, expressionless, utterly enervated from the continual struggle to stay alive. "Typical savages; our noble high priestesses devoted themselves to their religious training to no avail. And what did the empire get in return? Not only disdain for the honor they were so graciously awarded but assassination of the most celebrated clergy and officers of our time."

Huascar scrutinizes the girls; he puts a finger under Solsol's chin.

"Lovely girl," the prince says lecherously. She glares at him; her emerald eyes darken ominously. The unnerved royal steps back, fully aware of the Cloud Warrior's power to summon their serpent gods.

"What do you want, brother?" Cura Occlo asks.

Huascar raises his eyebrows, tilts his head; his grotesque earrings jangle.

"I see you're feeling better, sister," he says. "since you're able to keep yourself and your friends amused in your hour of grief." He catches sight of Chimbo Sancto, rolls his eyes and frowns. "A dwarf? Really, sister? Your taste in companions is quite intriguing."

"Whom I chose to keep company with," the princess says

contemptuously, "is none of your business."

"Arrest these people," Huascar says to Usna.

"Yes, Heir Apparent to the Royal Fringe," the captain says.

The pot-bellied Captain Usna wrinkles his scarred forehead and squints at his guards who tie coarse ropes around the sisters' wrists though Umiña's and my hands remain free.

"Heir Apparent?" the princess scoffs, "The deceased emperor's high council in Quito has already performed the ceremony of divination; our brother Prince Ninan Cuyochi has been confirmed as the heir to the fringe. Executors have already left Quito and are scheduled to arrive in Cuzco in a matter of weeks to make arrangements for the official coronation."

"You must not have gotten the message. Ninan died of the plague shortly after your father," the Inca captain states, holding up an official knotted *quipu,* "*Chasquis* from the northern empire informed your father's executors when the funeral party arrived at the emperor's palace in Tumibamba."

"Ninan's dead?" the princess says. "That can't be."

"And father's high council in Quito," Huascar says with a smirk, "has been . . . how can I say this delicately? . . . replaced. Permanently." He shoots Quetzal and the captain a sidelong glance; they chuckle, their mouths twisted into evil smirks.

"Dozens of my brothers, at least the ones you haven't murdered in cold blood," Cura growls, "will be more than happy to destroy you before they let you usurp the empire. Especially Atahualpa who spent years on the battlefield while you've never even picked up a sword."

"A good administrator delegates combat duties," Huascar responds blithely, "to those better suited for the task. And have you forgotten that Atahualpa is a bastard, born to a Quito princess without an ounce of Inca blood coursing through her insurgent veins?" he sneers. "I will deal with Atahualpa the Bastard in my own time. Besides, it seems my fraternal popularity has greatly increased since dispersing virgins and prestigious administrative offices to forty faithful brothers, not to mention assorted powerful warlords."

"The gods' wrath will rain down upon you in ways you never imagined." the princess hisses, "You will pay dearly for this unholy usurpation. "

"I have also demanded the immediate return of the late emperor's harem and entire household back here to Cuzco." Huascar says blithely, "Queen Rahua Occlo, my dear sister Chuqui Huipa and their servants will arrive here along with father's funeral cortege very soon. I expect to receive mother's blessing to marry shortly."

"The Queen Mother will never give permission for a murdering usurper to marry her beloved Chuqui," Cura says. "And without a wedding of pure blood, there can be no formal coronation."

"Well, I could marry you then," Huascar taunts, baring yellow, uneven teeth.

"I can only thank the gods," Cura says with a shudder, "that I'm not your full sister, Huascar."

The mad prince gazes at his manicured nails, strolls over to his half sister then strokes her bosom salaciously. Cura glares at him then gruffly pushes his hand away. The prince puts his fingers around her neck then squeezes his hands like a vise.

"Then I will take you as my concubine, dear sister." he says, his mouth poised over her nose, "along with whomever else I please."

I pull my knife from its sheaf and attempt to get to Huascar; guards push me back with ease.

"Stop!" Cura manages to croak though her face is red and turning purple. "Please."

When her eyes roll back in her head, Huascar cackles, releases his grip then pushes her to the floor.

"Take these witches to the dungeon," Captain Usna orders. "And don't forget the dwarf."

"No!" Princess Cura pleads. She coughs, rubs her bruised neck then struggles to her feet. "Don't take them. I beg you. I promise they will harm no one." She glares at Huascar. "You could stop this. I demand you stop this. You know very well that T'ica can cure the plague!" Cura turns and points at me. "And her friends can assist her in this task. They might be the only hope for our empire."

"Your weak little ploy," Huascar scoffs, "does not persuade me in the least, dear sister."

"But," Cura insists, "I don't understand. These people are the ones we've been looking for. Don't be a fool, brother."

Umiña, head held high faces the princess; a dim halo of golden light encircles her head.

"It is important to die well, my princess." she says with a

beatific smile. "People of the Chachapoyas do not beg for their lives no matter the circumstance." She glances at her friends then at Captain Usna. "We will go with you now."

CHAPTER FORTY SEVEN

At the Sacsayhuayman fortress, thousands of Cuzco mourners, musicians, dancers, singers and actors meet the greatly truncated funeral party then lead them to the enormous square in front of the Temple of the Sun, frenetically continuing the celebration and commemoration of the dead Emperor Huayna Capac's life.

Scowling and drunk as usual, Huascar waits for his mother and sister in his garishly bejeweled, feathered and canopied litter. When he sees them, he whips his litter carriers with studded leather lashes.

"Hurry you fools!" the prince slurs as *chicha* sloshes out of his silver goblet. "Over there! To the queen mother!"

Rahua Occlo and Chuqui notice the drunkard's litter but due to the crowd, are unable to execute an evasive maneuver.

"Oh no!" Chuqui cries, as her brother's litter advances.

"Stay calm, daughter," her royal mother advises, "We must be cordial and pretend we know nothing of Huascar's recent atrocities."

"But he tortured and murdered ten of my brothers in cold blood," Chuqui shrieks, trying to be heard over the wailing of mourners.

"And if you don't do as I suggest," the queen mother hisses, "we could be next."

Chuqui spits out a pasty wad of depleted coca then inserts a fresh gray green sheaf along with a large piece of *llipt'a* into her jaw; she chews vigorously, praying that Father Coca will heal her broken heart.

"Mother!" Huascar says, saluting the queen drunkenly, "Finally, you and my beautiful sister, soon to be my future wife *and* empress of Tawantinsuyu, the Inca Empire have arrived."

"May Inti Tatáy bless you, my son," the queen mother says maintaining a dignified countenance, though her blood boils at the sight of her murderous offspring. The queen mother leans over and hisses in her daughter's ear, "Greet your brother. And smile!"

"May Inti bless you, brother," Princess Chuqui says, forcing her mouth into a smile, though just looking at Prince Huascar's drunken countenance makes her stomach turn.

The prince squints at the rapidly setting sun.

"Festivities will grind to a halt within the hour." he slurs, "Just as Lord Inti needs his repose, so we need ours. I am staying at the royal estate in Calca. My emissary will arrive at dawn here tomorrow to take care of . . . business. I trust you will be in the throne room to greet him, Mother. Chuqui, you will be staying at your usual accommodations at the royal palace . . . until after the wedding of course."

The thought of sleeping with this toad makes Chuqui squeamish; she struggles to suppress her urge to vomit. But, in deference to her mother and knowing full well the scope of her brother's brutality, she tips her head.

"And what of our sister, Cura Occlo?" Chuqui asks, bracing herself to hear that he murdered her, too, but praying with every fiber of her being that he hasn't.

"Princess Cura is at the royal palace at the moment," Huascar mumbles, "the cold fish."

The queen and Chuqui glance at each other uneasily. Huascar

has been attracted to Cura since they were children. He would often corner her in her bedroom, trying to force himself on her. Cura was able to fight him off when he was still a youth, but after reaching adolescence, Huascar became more aggressive. After complaining bitterly to her father, Emperor Huayna Capac, he posted guards at Cura's bedroom door, terrible insult for Huascar who always considered himself exempt from all social mores.

"If we are to stay at the royal palace here in Cuzco," the queen mother says. "I trust we will be safe there?"

"Why wouldn't you be safe?" Huascar slurs.

He stands unsteadily in his litter, lifts his chalice, puts it to his lips, chugs down the remaining *chicha,* then tosses the empty vessel into the milling throng where it slams onto an innocent bystander's forehead, knocking him cold and sending him sprawling on the crowded street. Huascar points at the unconscious man lying on the street, indicating that he should be carried away.

Two guards pick up the injured man, whisking him away from the throng. When they return, the prince keels over in a drunken stupor and ends up on the floor of the litter. The head litter carrier, a strong Lucanas native gazes at the queen mother then puts a finger to his lips; he and five other carriers have ugly whip lashes on their backs, faces, torsos and extremities.

"Let him sleep," he whispers, in halting *Incasimi*, a look of desperation on his face. "We will take prince . . . to Calca now."

CHAPTER FORTY EIGHT

As promised, the soft-spoken emissary arrives at dawn, dressed in a simple white tunic and no jewelry probably at Huascar's insistence, who is unreasonably paranoid of any display of vanity that could be interpreted as an act of subversion. The emissary bows then hands the queen mother a royal *quipu,* its strings intertwined with fine threads of silver and gold and expertly knotted with the exact details of the proposed royal nuptials and subsequent coronation.

Queen Rahua Occlo is remarkably calm; however Princess Chuqui sits on an adjacent throne, her eyes red from weeping, sleep deprived and mentally exhausted. Her half sister, Princess Cura stands next to her, wearing a brave face, but inside, terrified of any meeting with Huascar or his emissaries and the calamity it may bring.

The emissary indicates a braided string of pure spun gold.

"All one must do, my queen, is tie your royal signature knot here" he says, "affirming your blessings for the royal nuptials, after which, we can proceed with Huascar's coronation."

The queen mother blithely scrutinizes the *quipu,* her lips move as she deciphers each knotted string. She loops a gilded strand around her forefinger and admires it as it shimmers under a beam of early morning sunlight.

"Excellent craftsmanship," the queen says as she continues to admire the gilded strings, "A true work of art." She cocks her head, smacks her lips then tosses it on the floor. "Though he is my own flesh and blood, " the queen mother hisses, "I will never allow that homicidal, fratricidal usurper marry my Chuqui."

"But, *coya,* I beseech you to reconsider," the dumbfounded emissary argues, knowing that his own life might very well in jeopardy as the bearer of bad tidings to the madman who would be emperor, "as your son is in no condition to accept a rejection of this magnitude."

"And neither is he in any condition," the queen mother says, "to be emperor of Tawantinsuyu or any other empire."

"My queen," the emissary pleads, "I beg of you. I fear retaliation will be swift and cruel."

"Leaders from all over the empire have already been notified," the queen mother articulates resolutely, "that upon my untimely death or that of my daughter that Cuzco will be attacked, ransacked, Huascar loyalists massacred and buildings burned to the ground. If the prince happens to escape this initial purge, he will be hunted like an animal, forced to hide in the bitter cold of the high mountains or the sweltering jungle, subsisting on roots and berries. Knowing my son, the coddled weakling wouldn't last a fortnight. If Huascar's murderous ambitions persist, which I assume they will despite all rational reasons not to, royal executors would offer an additional incentive: a generous reward to any citizen who assists in his capture. Once apprehended—and he would be captured, for no loyal citizen of the empire would assist a madman who would murder the widowed Inca queen of the great Huayna Capac—my generals would impose the same suffering the usurper perpetuated upon his innocent brothers, then burn what's left of his body in the public square, nullifying any chance of entering *hanan pacha.*"

"You may leave us now," Princess Chuqui orders.

"Yes, princess," the emissary says with a dip of his head, "my queen, Princess Cura."

He slowly backs out of the throne room, eyes lowered and mind reeling.

"What will happen now?" Cura asks.

"There's no predicting what Huascar will do," the queen says. She pulls out her gleaming sword, admires its gold and silver handle and razor sharp blade. "We must be prepared for the worst."

It's just after dawn when Huascar arrives by litter in front of the Cuzco palace accompanied by an entourage of guards, most of whom had never seen a day of warrior training, much less a day on the battlefield in their decadent lives; they obtained their highly coveted positions by kidnapping young girls to satisfy the prince's deviant sexual proclivities.

After the carriers set down the litter, Huascar, scowling as usual, steps off it and barges through the palace's gargantuan trapezoidal stone entrance. He intentionally knocks priceless golden and silver artworks off corridor walls and console tables as he stomps down several corridors toward the throne room.

Cura stands in between her sister and the widowed *coya* who impatiently fingers the *quipu* brought to her by Huascar's emissary yesterday morning; the women plan to nullify the prince's ambition to ascend to the Inca throne by whatever means necessary. Though experienced warriors, who walked almost two thousand miles without complaint to accompany the funeral cortege and have proven their undying fealty by fighting alongside the now deceased emperor on the steamy battlefields of the northern empire are prepared to defend the royals to the death, the women are more frightened today than yesterday.

Huascar steps into the room, instantly intimidated by the belligerence on the royal guards's faces, not to mention a similar sentiment on his mother's face.

"My dove, my dearest queen mother," Huascar coos, as he bows before her and lowers his eyes like a common servant, his antagonistic demeanor utterly dissolved, "I'm afraid there's been a big misunderstanding."

"There's no misunderstanding, my son," Queen Rahua Occlo spits. "You murdered your father's high priests and his executors. You also tortured and murdered ten of your brothers; who knows what other atrocities you've committed of which I'm not yet aware."

"Those responsible for those deaths," Huascar lies, "have been punished. You of all people know how easily underlings can misunderstand orders."

"There can be no royal wedding and no coronation." Queen Rahua declares, unmoved by her son's obvious fabrications, "without the blessings of a legitimate queen to marry your full sister. And I will never grant you permission to marry Chuqui and, since you've already assassinated many of your father's *legitimate* executors, you have sealed your own fate. I warn you, Huascar, your barbarous acts do not go unnoticed by the gods and Inca law."

"But it's the gods' wills I'm trying to fulfill, Mother," Huascar whines. "What will happen to Tawantinsuyu without a legitimate emperor of pure royal blood?"

"There are others who are more suited to rule than you are." the queen retorts, "Cusi Atauchi, my sister's son, is much beloved and respected: a great warrior, literate and quite level-headed and of pure royal blood. Paullo is also a reasonable choice, though young and not of pure blood, he's intelligent, level-headed and a born administrator. We must honor traditional Inca law and let your father's remaining executors decide."

Huascar's face reddens at the mention of Cusi and Paullo's names. His sister notes the guilty look on his twisted, miserable face; it can only mean one thing.

"What did you do to our dear Cusi and Paullo?" Chuqui asks, blood draining from her face, barely able to breath.

"Under the circumstances," Huascar declares haughtily, "I was forced to make some difficult decisions,

"Huascar, what are you saying?" the queen mother asks, her voice barely a whisper.

"Paullo was having an affair with one of my beloved concubines," the prince lies, "so I sent him to the dungeon in Calca. After that, we buried Zaramama alive after she refused to confess. I will miss her but, as in all things she attempted, the talented Zaramama died well."

The queen and princess glower at Huascar; not only did they love Paullo but they also knew and loved Zaramama, who charmed the Inca court with her musical prowess and charming dance interpretations. Her life story was well known to all.

Zaramama dances and sings near an open fire, her face and gold-flecked brown eyes aglow, surrounded by adoring family and friends, who whistle, cheer and tap the ground with sticks in acknowledgment of her talent and extraordinary beauty.

"Daughter!" shouts Unque, squatting near the fire, stars

twinkling in the cloudless night, a full moon smiling over them. "Sing another one!"

"Play your flute," shouts her mother, Maywa, a plump jolly woman with the same gold-flecked eyes as her daughter.

She presses a flute to her lips. Her audience smiles and whispers to each other in anticipation. *Which tune will she play next,* they wonder. Before she can blow a single note, two armed Inca warriors step into their village. The girl shrinks back as they approach the campfire.

"Ah, honorable warriors," Unque says casually. He's mayor of the village which has been subjugated for years by the Inca Empire. He points enormous sacks of grain near a small hut, "Lucky for you, we have already prepared our tithes to the Inca."

"We have not come for your grain, old man," the Inca Captain Ahua Panti sneers. He slashes a grain sack and its contents, maize, spills onto the dusty ground.

"Then what?" says Unque, glancing furtively at his wife, "I don't understand."

The captain points at Zaramama.

"We came for the girl," he declares.

"There must be some mistake," says Mayor Unque, trying to maintain a sense of calm. "Our treaty with the Emperor specifically states our children will not be taken from us."

Dozens of Inca warriors step out of the darkness and far more surround the village—archers, ax men, swordsmen, halberd holders, all ready to strike down those foolish enough to refuse to conform to the arbitrary wishes of the Empire; they glare at the unarmed and woefully outnumbered villagers with disdain.

"Do as we say and no one will get hurt," Captain Ahua Panti says.

"She is only twelve," Zaramama's mother sobs, "She belongs here with her people."

A warrior leads the talented maiden to a litter, opens its small wooden gate and guides her into a wooden cage. Zaramama sits cross-legged, tears in her eyes reflecting like gold and diamonds in the moonlight. A carrier locks the gate as the captain waits impatiently.

"The wisdom of the son of the Sun God himself, the Shepherd of the People, his Highness Emperor Huayna Capac," the captain says menacingly, "is beyond reproach."

"Don't worry, Mamáy," Zaramama says, pointing to the full moon, "Mama Quilla will protect me."

Zaramama's mother bows her head, covers her face and sobs.

"Let's go," says the Inca Captain, "We have no time to waste."

"Must you go so soon?" Maywa begs, eyes drooping, voice cracking as she approaches Captain Ahua Panti unsteadily, "Maybe we can feed your soldiers first. Our tribe is known for our good food and hospitality and . . ."

The captain pounds her calves with the blunt side of his sword, knocking her flat on her back. The warriors laugh sadistically. Unque runs to his wife's side, kneels then strokes her hair. Then he turns to address Zaramama.

"One day, my precious daughter, dove of my soul," Unque says to Zaramama, "We will see you in the sacred land of our ancestors. Do not be afraid."

Though not spoken of often, every villager knows once kidnapped, Daughters of the Sun never see their families again, at least not in this worldly realm of *kay pacha.*

"Yes, father," Zaramama says between sobs, her midnight black locks cascading over her shoulders, "I will see you and Mamáy in the glorious realm of *hanan pacha.*"

"Wait!" her father says, holding up a finger, racing back to his family's humble stone hut as the carriers lift the litter. Unque rushes back with a coarse sack filled with flutes and percussion instruments. "You will need this, *urchipáy sonqo,*" he says, stuffing the sack through the wooden bars of the cage. Limping to the cage, her mother reaches out just to touch her daughter one last time.

"You are the dove of my heart, too" Maywa says, "No one can take you away from my heart."

Soldiers drag the girl's parents away, as bewildered villagers look on.

"Go back to your homes!" the captain barks, wielding a bronze sword. "Do it now!"

The villagers scramble to their modest huts, hugging and kissing their children, especially their daughters, thankful the Incas didn't taken them, too. But they know it will be only a matter of time before the dreaded kidnappers return.

Unque escorts his wife to their hut and tucks her into bed as a dozen guinea pigs, which they raise for food in their humble abode, squeak and scatter out of the way.

"Why would Mama Quilla allow me to birth this angel," Maywa whimpers, "only to permit her to be taken away from me?"

"Sleep, my wife," says Unque, gently patting her face with his calloused farmer hands. "Sleep." He scoops *chicha* into a wooden cup and presses it to his wife's lips. She chokes it down, spilling some of the precious homemade brew; guinea pigs lap up as much as they can before absorbed into the wooden floor. Unque scoops *chicha* into a cup for himself, too, glances at his daughter's empty bed, hold his head in his hands and weeps.

The next morning, the sun is sharp and sky clear but village women sit listlessly at their looms unable to focus on their weaving. Men, normally busy tending their fields, sit in a circle in front of Mayor Unque's hut, staring at the dusty ground, shaking their heads. The seeds of rebellion are slow to sprout but they are there.

"Last night was only a test!" Unque's brother-in-law, Rotiqo roars, as villagers nod in agreement, "We should have fought them!"

"The Incas would have slaughtered the entire village." Mayor Unque shouts, "Is that what you want?"

"At least then we could have died with honor." Rotiqo hisses. He points to a llama nursing her newborn, "Our people have become docile as suckling *crias*."

"They will be back soon," a village elder warns, "And the Incas will take what they want."

"My wife will not let the Incas take our children," a young father says, "She would rather slit their throats then hang herself afterward. This she told me, just this morning."

"The Incas will get no more grain from us," Rotiqo spits, "See how they slashed open our fine maize sack, dishonoring Pachamama. They treat us as if we're more useless than fleas."

"If we do not pay tithes," Unque counters, "they will kill us and burn our village to the ground."

"We were already half-dead, like the *kukuchi*, the day we allowed the despised Incas to be our rulers," Rotiqo says, "Let them finish the job. Or let us fight like *runakuna*, like real men of substance for our freedom."

"I will speak to other villages and their leaders," Unque says with finality, "I will leave this morning."

"Other villages?" says Rotiqo skeptically. "They are even more pitiful than our own village."

"We cannot win this fight alone, dear brother," says Unque.

"Then we need to go there," says Rotiqo, pointing at a distant cloud-covered mountain peak.

It is the Chachapoyas region, the domain of the mighty, feared Cloud Warriors. The villagers gawk at the site.

"It is said," croaks an ancient hunchback, knitting his weathered brow, "that Cloud Warriors are sorcerers—half serpent, half demon, with poison fangs and glowing green eyes that can see clearly in the dead of night like the jaguar."

"Have you ever met one?" challenges Rotiqo.

"Well, I . . . " the old man says; he shakes his head.

"Can't you see?" Rotiqo snarls, "The Incas spread these lies to keep the provinces in line, to prevent us from creating alliances with other tribes."

"I care not whether Cloud Warriors are man or demon so long as they fight the Incas," Unque declares, "Now it is time to evacuate the women and children."

"And what of my beloved niece, Zaramama?" Rotiqo asks.

"Because of my foolishness in agreeing to a treaty with the Incas," Unque says, lower lip quivering, "and allowing them to take our weapons, we do not have the resources to save my daughter. But let us now spare who we can."

Inside the hut, Zaramama's mother stares into the semi-darkness, tears streaming down her cheeks.

"Goddess of the Moon," she prays, hand over her heart. "I beseech your protection of my Zaramama."

Prince Huascar had heard about Zaramama's extraordinary talent and beauty through *chasqui* messengers. When she arrived in Cuzco, servants had bathed and dressed her like Inca royalty, though she carries an ordinary brown sack containing her primitive musical instruments.

"Sing!" Huascar orders with a loud clap, "Dance!"

Zaramama gazes at the prince in confusion then looks at the Captain Ahua Panti.

"She does not speak our tongue, my prince," the captain explains, "her village speaks a language unknown to most of the empire."

"What's in the bag she's holding?" the prince asks.

"Her musical instruments," the captain answers, "I will bring it to you."

After snatching the bag out of the possessive hands of its talented owner who protests vociferously, the captain delivers it to Prince Huascar, who opens it, retrieves a small drum and bangs on it haphazardly; Zaramama put her hands over her ears and squints as if in pain. When the prince stops playing, she grabs the drum from his hands, sits cross-legged on the floor and securing the instrument between her legs, plays a hypnotic beat, her gold-flecked eyes sparkling in the early morning light.

After lusting for the talented young artist for a few days, Huascar forces her to be his concubine. And though she continues to perform on occasions when the prince isn't brutally raping her, she looks forward to the day when she can journey to *hanan pacha* and in this glorious upper world, absorb the joyous spirits of her sacred ancestors. Now that she's been murdered by the mad prince, her wish has finally come true.

Tears welling up at the thought of Zaramama's life of woe, the queen mother stares at her son.

"Is Paullo still live at least?" she asks.

Huascar is stone-faced and silent.

Although somewhat reserved, Paullo had always been respectful and eager to serve the empire in any capacity deemed useful, though he seemed to have a special talent for accounting and apprenticed with a well-known Cuzco *quipumayoc* to hone his skills. The young Huascar attempted to learn accounting under the same *quipumayoc*, but quit despite his mother's advice to the contrary. He blamed his half brother for sabotaging his progress claiming Paullo was the *quipumayoc's* favorite.

"How should I know?" Huascar says finally, quite cognizant of that fact that the sincere, defenseless Paullo was beheaded the same day Zaramama was buried alive, "I wasn't the last one to see him."

"And what of our dear brother, Cusi Atauchi?" Chuqui demands, recalling her strong, loyal, smart and funny cousin's handsome face. He was a ray of sunshine, the embodiment of Lord Inti himself, some would say. But, of course, Huascar had always been jealous of Cusi and his military prowess. "He went to Calca to pay homage to you, Huascar. What did you do to him?"

"You and Mother always spent inordinate amounts of time with Father in Quito." Huascar whines. "What can you possibly know of my problems here in Cuzco?"

The queen mother gasps, slowly grappling with the reality of yet even more atrocities committed by her perverse son. The royal women assimilate the unspeakable truth: two more productive royal brothers and an innocent young woman have been falsely accused and punished for crimes extant only in Huascar's warped mind.

"Cusi always treated you well, Huascar!" his mother exclaims, her voice breaking, "What did you do him?"

"Though I'm the only legitimate heir to the fringe," the mad prince spits, tearing clumps of hair from his own scalp then beating his chest, "everyone conspires against me! Cusi only pretended to pay homage to me. I could see right through him!"

The queen's mind is blank, her shock so overwhelming that she feels she could die from grief on the spot. She adored Cusi and thought of him more as her own son than a nephew. She tightens her grip on the royal *quipu*, stands, steps down from the dais, her jaw locked tight with loathing. She flogs her son with the knotted rope; Huascar howls with each stroke. His guards, as soft and spineless as their mad prince, take a halfhearted step forward to protect him but the queen's guards draw their weapons and the cowards hesitate for a moment then skulk away. Huascar covers his face, slumps to the floor with a girlish whimper. The queen mother is spent; she drops the *quipu*, crumbles to her knees and sobs. Chuqui steps down from the royal dais, points at her brother, now curled up in a fetal position.

"Get him out of here!" Chuqui screeches, her face red and dripping with tears as she embraces her mother.

Three of the queen's guards race over to the prince, pull him to his feet and lead him toward the exit. Face a bruised and bloodied mess, he straightens his tunic and turns to face the queen.

"I swear to the gods and goddesses of the Inca empire . . . " he says, pausing between self-pitying sobs, "and upon my dead father's eternal soul, I will do whatever it takes to keep this empire from imploding."

He shakes off the guards, limps into the corridor, followed by his cowardly henchmen. Near the palace's front door, a servant, noticing the royal's lash wounds, attempts to wipe blood from his face; Huascar throws the hapless man to the floor then kicks him in the throat.

CHAPTER FORTY NINE

When the overhead trap door opens, we squint to adjust our eyes to the blinding noon light.

"The animal handler will be back soon." Captain Usna informs us, his giant belly bouncing up and down with each word. "The big cats will greet you by ripping open your necks," he says with a cackle, "then feasting on the tender flesh of your bellies. Any remaining life will be drained out of you by the vipers. Resistance will only serve to extend your agony. Give in to the feeding frenzy and your suffering here in *kay pacha* will end all the more swiftly."

The captain chuckles hoarsely then careful to move his paunch out of the way, bangs the trap door shut, thrusting us into complete darkness again; we're trapped inside the musty recesses of the Dungeon of Horrors.

"Pachamama, Mamaquilla," I pray softly, "*Kaypachiswaychis:* Empower us, protect us, give us strength, vision and wisdom to propel us into the future."

My little black *enqa* wriggles in my pouch; the stone rolls out onto the dungeon floor then transforms into a full-grown condor; the world's largest and most powerful bird perches quietly but heavily on my shoulder. Suddenly, he jumps onto the floor, flaps his gigantic wings and squawks. Chimbo whistles and the bird hops onto his lap. He pets the winged creature, who cuddles up close to his ear and squawks for several minutes; the dwarf nods occasionally then squawks back; they seem to be having a lively conversation complete with laughter, bitter disagreements and finally, nods of agreement.

The captain flings open the trap door again; we gaze at two half-starved caged pumas who screech, revealing yellow fangs buried in black gums; a cold sweat pours down my back. The animal handler stands next to the cage; he's missing his right eye and a purple scar zigzags from his shaved scalp down to his chin on his left temple. Captain Usna holds a loosely woven bag full of writhing vipers.

The needle-thin animal handler, Yauri gazes down upon us; his tunic discolored, with dozens of holes throughout, as if he'd been swimming with a school of hungry piranhas.

"I will bet you a ten year old virgin, Usna," Yauri says with an evil grin, "that the dwarf gets killed first."

"How does a nobody like you," the captain scoffs, "get a hold of ten year old virgins?"

"It's easier than you think," the animal handlers says, "especially in my profession." He licks his lips lasciviously. "On occasion, high priestesses need to rid themselves of rebellious girls, so-called Daughters of the Sun in training. Many are savages who refuse to be indoctrinated in our glorious religious traditions. For a small price, I offer to take care of their problem maidens; my beasts love their tender flesh." he croaks, holding his crotch. "But, first, of course, I have my fun. If you know what I mean." He laughs coarsely then eyes the captain. "Well?"

The captain rubs his protruding belly.

"It's a deal." Usna says. "I say these pumas will attack and eat the mother and her babe in arms first. If I lose, I'll get you a fresh maiden to do with what you please."

"Ha ha!" the animal handler says, "Deal!"

The animal handler opens the cage and the beasts leap into the dungeon. Umiña stands in a corner, her baby strapped to her back. The Cloud Warrior sisters and I stand in front of her, holding our cloaks open and roaring with all our might in an attempt to intimidate the felines. The smaller of the pumas steps back; the bigger cat growls, ears slanted back in attack position. Chimbo waves his hands to attract its attention.

"Come here, little kitty," Chimbo taunts.

The cat springs, smashes into the dwarf's chest, knocking him onto his back; its jaw stretches over his face to the back of his skull; claws dig into the half man's legs and arms.

"What did I tell you!" Yauri, the animal handler shouts gleefully to the scowling captain, who is wondering where in the world he'll be able to get a virgin to satisfy this demented pedophile.

Chimbo's stubby fingers feel around the animal's face; he pushes a thumb deep into the beast's left eye socket; the puma shrieks in agony.

I raise my knife, charge and stab the puma on the back of its wide neck multiple times but the blade barely penetrates its thick skin. I kick its ribs, as the dwarf continues to press into the beast's eye sockets. Finally, the injured animal yowls, loosening its grip on Chimbo's head and pads to the opposite side of the cave, its left eye bloody and sagging.

"Come here!" I shout, as I position myself close to a wall, "Come!"

The injured animal lifts his head, glares at me then leaps. I bound out of the way and the beast bashes its thick skull on the dungeon wall, embedded with protruding razor-sharp shards of glass and obsidian stone. I race to the opposite wall. With blood dripping from its head, the angered puma turns and leaps again, knocking me to the ground; I plunge my knife into its tender underbelly. The animal screeches as I twist my blade, using the beast's ribs as a wedge to obliterating its entrails; blood spurts everywhere. When the animal goes limp, I extract my weapon; blood gushes and pools on the floor. When I realize that I successfully vanquished Lord Puma, a surge of energy flows through me; I push the lifeless creature off me then face the other cat crouching at the opposite wall. I brandish my bloodied knife and stare it down and become Goddess Puma.

"Lord Puma," I growl, "I know you are hungry but this is not the way you don't want to die. Is it?" The bewildered feline, less aggressive than the one just killed, growls but does not bare its teeth. I take two steps forward. "I do not want to kill you. Do you understand?"

The puma tilts its massive head, roars but otherwise remains still.

"What is going on down there?" Captain Usna shouts at the animal handler.

"Throw down the bag of vipers," Yauri screeches. "Now!"

The captain tosses the bag of agitated serpents into the dungeon. In a few moments, a knot of snakes slither and hiss over the floor. Pispis and Solsol's emerald eyes glow; they chant in the incomprehensible tongue of the serpent; the creatures hiss in reply then wind toward them.

Chimbo pulls himself up onto his elbows, shakes his head, his face and body a raw bloody mess.

"Now!" he yells, then passes out.

My condor swoops out of a dark corner of the dungeon,

flapping its enormous wings; it whooshes through the trap door and lands on the animal handler's head, using its powerful beak to peck relentlessly on his only good eye. Yauri wields a large knife and swats at the gigantic flying beast, who evades each stroke, flitting out of reach then flying back and pecking the man's skull, back, thighs and calves again and again. The magnificent creature floats into the perfect blue sky then dives toward Yauri's bloodied face, knocking him onto his back, hopping onto his face then using his enormous beak to scoop out the man's right eye. The bird spreads its wings, flutters to a nearby rooftop and, with a cock of its head, swallows the eyeball whole. When the animal handler regains consciousness, he holds the socket that used to house his eyeball and quickly realizes what's happened.

"My eye," he screeches. "My eye!"

In his hysteria, the now-blind man stumbles and falls through the open trap door, slamming onto the dungeon's hard stone floor, his face a gory eyeless mess, though still alive. The puma gazes at me, its yellow eyes aglow as if asking permission to pounce on the prey that has conveniently landed at its enormous paws.

"Finish him!" I bellow.

The beast springs, rips the flesh off the man's neck. Blood pours from his carotid onto the dungeon floor; the animal handler's legs and arms quiver then become still, life drained out of him.

Captain Usna flees in a panic down a courtyard path; the condor gives chase, pecking and clawing his head, face and eyes and shoulders.

The smell of blood and death permeates the Dungeon of Horrors. The dead puma lies stiffly, fangs still bared, eyes open, belly a gory pulpy mess. The other puma drags Yauri's mangled corpse into a dark corner then proceeds to feast on his entrails. Once sated, the feline purrs, lies on its side, contentedly licking its face and paws.

Solsol and Pispis snatch up one viper after another, smashing them against the studded dungeon walls until their slender spines are exposed and bloody then toss them on the floor along with dozens of other slaughtered snakes.

Chimbo is almost unrecognizable; severe lacerations cover the left side of the his face; dozens of puncture wounds are bubbling blood. He's struggling to breathe; gurgling sounds emanate from deep inside his throat. Umiña, Solsol, Pispis and I kneel around him, our faces dark with worry.

"He's dying," Pispis mutters wistfully, "Isn't he?"

"He needs help," I say, my heart breaking, breath shallow, hands trembling, "of that I'm quite certain."

"What can we do?" Umiña asks.

Solsol points at the surviving puma.

"First, we need to get out of here." she whispers.

The cat's golden eyes glare at me; it bares its fangs, growls and rises onto its haunches. Apparently, gorging on human flesh has revived the beast's natural enmity toward humans. I brandish my knife; the cat's growling subsides and it lowers onto its side.

"Who knows what will set off another attack," Umiña whispers, sweat pouring from her brow.

"I don't want to be puma food," Pispis says, her voice shaking.

"My father used to say," I whisper, in an attempt to allay all anxieties, including my own, "there is little to fear from a creature who has just eaten its fill. Besides, Lord Puma doesn't want to get hurt. And I don't want to hurt it either."

The sisters scrutinize the impossibly high trap door. Umiña nurses little Wawa, but he's restless and whining. I'm terrified a squeaky full blown crying fit will set off the puma's prey instinct.

"Let us pray that help comes soon," Umiña says. "I'm getting really thirsty. Without food or water, I cannot produce adequate milk. And without milk . . ." The young mother tries desperately to stifle little Wawa's cries; the ravenous child whimpers at his mother's all but empty breast.

Accompanied by Queen Mother Rahua Occlo, Princess Chuqui Huipa and a half dozen servants, Princess Cura leads the way down a long palace corridor to an exit that opens to a cobbled path leading to the palace jail where prisoners are normally detained. On the way, they notice Captain Usna's corpulent frame impaled upon a low bronze fence post—mouth ajar, guts seeping onto the ground and stare unsympathetically at the gruesome sight.

"A fitting end," the queen mother says, "for a cruel man. I'm sure he's quite at home now in *ukhu pacha*."

In the perfect blue Andean sky, a dozen condors circle lazily over the dead captain but one bird swoops down from a nearby rooftop, frantically flapping its gigantic wings. They watch in bewilderment as the creature squawks, flies a short distance, circles back, squawks once more then flies off again.

"He's leading us over there," the queen mother says pointing in the opposite direction of the detention facility that most prisoners are put in while awaiting trial for crimes against the state, "to the Dungeon of Horrors."

"Is that where the captain took your friends, Cura?" Princess Chuqui Huipa asks.

Princess Cura gulps, grows pale, her knees buckling at the thought of what must have already happened to her friends. The queen mother faces her then grasps her shoulders

"You don't have to go," Queen Rahua Occlo says, knowing that no one survives once thrown into the Dungeon of Horrors, "The servants, Chuqui and I can handle this."

Cura shakes her head.

"No," she whispers, "I'll go."

The first thing the royals notice when they approach the dungeon's open trap door is the empty wooden puma cage nearby. With a great deal of trepidation, Cura steps closer. Princess Chuqui touches her royal half sister's shoulder lightly.

"There are some things that one should never witness, my dear sister," Chuqui says. "No one will think less of you."

Cura stops and pricks her ears.

"Did you hear that?"

"Help!" I call out in a low calm voice so as not to excite the puma. "We're down here."

Cura peers through the trap door opening; when greeted by a low growl, she springs back instantly.

"Stay back." Solsol says from below, her voice a whisper.

I look overhead and glimpse Cura's ashen face.

"Cura," I explain. "we're all still alive, though Chimbo . . . "

A shaft of light reveals how badly mauled the dwarf is. The royals gape at the bloody sight then avert their eyes.

"T'ica killed the puma that attacked Chimbo," Pispis whispers, her voice trembling.

"That's quite fortunate," the queen mother murmurs evenly as she attempts to suppress her nausea.

"Keep your voices calm and steady," I advise. "We must not excite Lord Puma."

"There's only one safe way to get you out," the queen mother says. She turns to her servants. "Put the cages over the opening, so the puma does not escape." She walks a few feet away then returns to address us. "Wait."

As if we have any choice in the matter, I think with a wry grin.

As royal servants push the cage over the trap door opening, it makes a scraping sound; the puma becomes agitated, screeching and growling. But once in place, the giant cat pads to its corner, stretches down on its side, closes its golden eyes and falls asleep.

The east dungeon wall squeaks and shakes awakening the puma who lifts its head, bares yellow fangs and black gums, stands and screeches. Chest heaving, hands trembling, I clutch my knife.

"Lord Puma," I whisper, "I don't want to hurt you."

The animal's golden eyes glow, scrutinizing me warily but backs away and lies down next to, Yauri's partially eaten corpse.

The dungeon wall squeaks again; a hidden door opens just a crack.

"Quickly!" Cura whispers through the gap, "Umiña and the baby first, then the sisters. T'ica, you'll have to drag Chimbo out by yourself. Can you do that?"

"Yes," I answer. I keep steady eye contact with the puma, "I can do it."

Umiña and baby squeeze through the crack of the up-until-now hidden door, followed by Pispis and Solsol. I grab Chimbo's shoulder with one hand, knife in the other, step back, careful to face Lord Puma to prevent a rear attack as big cats are predisposed to in the wild.

"Hurry!" Cura trills.

Lord Puma growls, ears bent back in attack mode, gigantic rear legs muscles twitching. I wedge myself through the narrow opening then try to drag Chimbo's body through, too, but his tunic gets hung on a piece of obsidian stone jutting out from the door frame.

"He's stuck!" I exclaim in exasperation.

I tug on his tunic, it tears then gives way. Seconds after I drag him through the opening into the corridor and slam the door shut, the big cat screeches, leaps and claws on the opposite side of the doorway. My heart beats out of my chest as I slump to the ground. Cura Occlo quickly secures the barrier with a thick palm wood plank lowered into carved granite.

Four servants gently place the comatose dwarf on a narrow stretcher then stride quickly down the dimly lit corridor; Cura walks alongside her old friend, gazing at him tenderly.

"Don't worry, dearest Chimbo," the princess whispers, "The Qorincancha maintains a staff of the best Inca physicians in the empire."

"We're going to the Temple of the Sun?" Pispis inquires, her face suddenly ashen.

"Many things have changed since you and Solsol left," Princess Cura explains. "Since Prince Huascar has taken over, he has seen fit to terrorize even the *mamaconas*. They are on our side. You will see."

"Don't give into fear, sister." Solsol says. "Not now, not after all we've been through."

"But I just want to go home," Pispis sobs, "back to Mamáy and Tatay. I can barely remember their faces now."

"I want to go home, too and one day, we will go home, Pispis." Solsol says, her hand outstretched, "I promise. But for now we must trust our friends."

Pispis sniffs, wipes away her tears then takes her sister's hand; Solsol leads her younger sibling down the corridor toward the dreaded Temple of the Sun.

The immense wooden door leading to the rear of the Qorincancha squeaks open; we are greeted by Princess Chuqui Huipa and Queen Rahua Occlo.

"Welcome to the Temple of the Sun, my friends," the widowed *coya* says.

Servants carry in Chimbo's mangled body. The queen and daughter Chuqui regard his battered body with alarm then avert their eyes.

"He was my father's favorite adviser," Princess Chuqui says with a sob, "There's no finer man of any stature. Look at what they've done to you, my dear Chimbo!"

"There is no time to cry now, my daughter. Physicians must take quick action to save this man's life." The queen snaps her fingers and two Daughters of the Sun materialize. "Prepare him for surgery," the widowed *coya* says, "and remember to pray for him; he will need all the help he can get."

"Yes, my queen," the girls say in unison. They follow the dwarf's stretcher down the hall to a nearby room.

Another Daughter of the Sun appears, bows.

"Shall I fetch the surgeon now?" the young girl asks.

"Yes," Chuqui Huipa says, "Quickly."

"Chuqui and I can't stay. Prince Huascar's in Calca at the royal estate of *Inti Watana* at the moment." the widowed queen explains, "We must use this time to gather all palace guards in preparation for a critical meeting at the palace here in Cuzco tomorrow."

Princess Huipa gazes sadly at her best friend and half sister, Princess Cura.

"The streets of Cuzco are crawling with Huascar's henchmen. Our brother has caused a great schism, creating many enemies throughout the empire." Chuqui says, voice quavering, "I suspect the start of a civil war very soon. Nobody is safe right now, not *runakuna* and especially not royalty."

Unable to conjure up words of comfort, Cura silently embraces her frightened half-sister, doomed to either marry her mad brother or face a gruesome death. Chuqui clutches her sibling tight, releases then kisses her on both cheeks. The widowed queen taps her on the shoulder; they quickly disappear down an adjacent corridor leading to the front door of the Qorincancha, their servants scurrying behind them.

CHAPTER FIFTY

Servants slip a white tunic threaded with gold filaments over the queen's slender frame, adorn her upper torso with an ornate golden breast plate then place a silky cloak over her shoulders. Her Sun God earring are so large, they rest upon her shoulders and wide golden wrist cuffs shimmer in the morning light.

A servant sets a white feathered headdress upon the queen's long raven hair then slips a Sun God nose ring through her pierced lower nasal septum, which covers her upper lip. When the queen closes her eyes, a servant brushes gold dust powder over her face.

Rahua Occlo, the widowed *coya* of the late Emperor Huayna Capac dresses the part of warrior queen, for today she must stand up to her homicidal son, Huascar, who would be Inca Emperor.

The queen sweeps into the throne room, servants lifting the long train of her resplendent cloak behind her and sits on the throne next her daughter, Chuqui.

The princess is a vision in silver and white, crowned with a headdress adorned with fluffy white feathers stretching skyward, crescent moon earrings resting on her shoulders. A crescent moon hangs from a nose ring and sits over her upper lip, signifying that today she will speak with the wisdom of Mama Quilla as her mother will speak with the wisdom of Inti the Sun God.

"White is purity, innocence, wholeness, completion and new beginnings." the queen whispers in her daughter's ear. "It is also the color of sunlight and moonlight, to honor both our Inti Tatáy and Mama Quilla."

"I'm not so sure Huascar will see it that way." Chuqui whispers back.

"It doesn't matter how he sees it." the queen says, "What matters is the sacredness of Inca law, created and handed down to us by the deities themselves. We will give Huascar an opportunity to defend himself at an official tribunal, an opportunity he certainly did not give his victims."

"Huascar is a snake," Chuqui counters, "Cuzco is crawling with his loyalists. Why not just have our guards kill him here and now and get it over with?"

"We cannot counter tyranny with more tyranny," the queen mother insists, "otherwise, we are no better than any despot who wants to destroy our sacred way of life. And how long after an assassination will Huascar loyalists end up slaughtering us?"

The prince is alone when he walks into the throne room, dressed in a humble brown tunic; he's surprisingly upbeat, though his face is still bruised and swollen from the *quipu* thrashing his mother gave him yesterday.

"Mother!" he says with a crooked smile, holding out his arms in a dramatic show of supplication, "I've come to ask your forgiveness for all my transgressions."

"It is not for me to forgive you," the queen mother replies coolly. Her garments shimmer in the shaft of morning light breaking through an east window. "Forgiveness and adjudication of all legal matters are the provinces of the deities and the imperial council."

"As usual, you are correct, Mother," Huascar says. "Which is why I suggest we consult with the gods directly on the crucial matter of succession to the throne."

Princess Chuqui rolls her eyes and sighs, her silver nose ring glinting in the morning light. The queen mother narrows her eyes and stabs the air with her forefinger.

"Atahualpa fought valiantly by your father's side for years." the queen states, the sun god nose pendant glinting over her lips as she speaks. "He conquered rebellious northern provinces and pacified the Cloud Warriors of Chachapoyas . . ."

"Atahualpa the Bastard?" Huascar cries in dismay. "You're not suggesting that Atahualpa receive the fringe?"

"Though Atahualpa is not of pure Inca blood," the queen says, "he is an Inca of the Heart due to his long years of stellar military service and devotion not only to the empire but to the emperor himself."

"Since when does a bastard," Huascar demands, "have the right to rule the Inca Empire?"

"Atahualpa's mother was the Queen of Quito. Her full name was Paccha Duchicela Shyris XVI." Queen Rahua Occlo says wistfully, recalling the jealousy which overwhelmed her as a young royal when the emperor—who was also her husband and full brother broke with tradition by marrying Paccha Duchicela Shyris XVI, in a lavish public ceremony instead of simply taking her as one of his many concubines, as was and still is the custom.

"Just another one of my father's many whores, dear Mother," Huayna says, pursing his lips impatiently, "without a drop of Inca blood coursing through her veins."

"True, my son. But the savage Caras-Quitus tribe led by the King of Quito, Duchicela Shyris staged a rebellion against your father, Emperor Huayna Capac and his forces, on the banks of a lake. Due to the thousands of mortally wounded bodies dumped there from both sides, the lake turned blood red From that point on, the lake is referred to as Yahuarcocha, Blood Lake." Queen Rahua Occlo explains, "When the King of Quito died a few weeks into that battle, his tribe elected his daughter, Paccha Duchicela Shyris XVI to lead the rebel army. But Huayna Capac grew tired of fighting and offered a peaceful settlement by proposing to marry the beautiful Queen of Quito with the caveat that the first born son of that union be crowned King of Quito upon the Inca emperor's death, incorporating the rest of Ecuador into the Empire."

"Well then," Huascar says, "Atahualpa can rule as governor of Ecuador and Quito."

The queen clenches her fists then takes a long calming breath, gold dust glimmering on her cheeks. Though more than twenty years has passed, the betrayal of the emperor marrying another woman, not of royal blood, still stings. And, she became even more racked with resentment when Atahualpa was born of that unconventional union. When Paccha died shortly afterward his birth, she learned to cherish the motherless child. In fact, she often felt guilty because she grew to love the bright handsome Atahualpa more than her own mercurial son, who she now hated with every fiber of her being.

"Don't you understand, Huascar?" Princess Chuqui interjects firmly, "As part of the agreement of that marital alliance, Atahualpa automatically became King of Quito upon our father's death. Our empire cannot afford another massive northern rebellion because you arbitrarily decide to renege on a treaty that could cause tens of thousands of needless deaths."

Six guards encircle the prince and point spears at his torso.

"Mother!" Huascar cries, "What are you doing?"

"I swear to you, Huascar," the queen states as the guards tie the prince's hands behind his back. "Go peacefully and I will ensure you get a fair tribunal."

"A tribunal?" Huascar shouts hysterically, "For what? For killing those would have killed me first? For being smart enough to save my own skin?"

"You will have a chance to tell your side of the story, brother," the princess states, adjusting her earrings, "soon enough."

"Your sister is correct, my son." the queen affirms. She gazes at the guards. "Take him to the royal dungeon. Don't mistreat him and feed him well."

"Since I am of pure Inca blood and the son of the Sun God like my deceased father, Emperor Huayna Capac, it is my right to demand a consultation with the oracles of the Qorincancha!" he exclaims. "I will abide by their ruling, of course."

The widowed *coya* regards her son, her blood boiling; she knows full well he's lying about abiding by the oracles' rulings; he would stop at nothing to become emperor even if it meant murdering a seer whose reading he disagreed with. The words rejecting her son's desperate plea are on the tip of her tongue, but she hesitates.

Consulting the Qorincancha oracles buys time for our chasquis *to disseminate urgent messages throughout the vast empire and amass troops to squelch the usurper's royal ambitions,* she considers as she drums her right hand fingers upon the wide golden cuffs on her left wrist.

"I have erred my whole life in dealing with you, Huascar." the queen admits, "Whether too strict or too lenient, I do not know but nothing excuses what you've done to fracture our family, not to mention the empire."

"Let the oracles decide my fate!" Huascar pleads.

The widowed *coya* nods at the guards who drag the prince out of the throne room as he kicks and sobs. Once in the corridor, he screeches like a spoiled child; his voice echoes forlornly off stone walls then, in a few moments fades away altogether.

"You're not really considering this," Princess Chuqui asks, "are you mother?" Her high cheekbones burn scarlet with indignation.

"Alas, we do not now enjoy the protection of our vast northern forces, my dove." the queen mother answers. "My plan is simply to placate, for a time, those who would oppose us."

"No, Mother." the princess insists, "This is a mistake."

"We must hold off the hordes of Huascar loyalists in Cuzco. His minions are blood-thirsty perverts, thugs and drunkards who can barely contain themselves as they await your brother's coronation, knowing that they will assume prestigious appointments and all the debauchery afforded by such. What do you think they'll do to us if we murder your brother without honoring his rights afforded by Inca law and without the benefit of our northern allies to enforce the law once a decision is made?"

CHAPTER FIFTY ONE

Her silhouette unimposing, the petite surgeon dons a pristine white robe, an over-sized hood and a mask which covers her mouth and nose. The Cloud Warrior sisters, Princess Cura, Umiña and I regard her hopefully.

"The patient is clean and ready for surgery," a young assistant informs her.

"Your diagnosis?" the surgeon asks curtly. The Daughter of the Sun hesitates, bows her head and lowers her eyes. "Come now, if you want to become a proper diagnostician, you cannot be timid."

The maiden licks her lips then clears her throat.

"Chimbo Sancto suffers from significant blood loss due to a vicious puma attack," she explains, "his condition is critical and blood pressure low. He requires an immediate blood transfusion. I have taken the liberty to make arrangements for such."

The *mamacona* nods then turns to another young medical assistant.

"What remedies have you applied before we begin our surgical procedures?"

"After thoroughly cleaning his wounds," the young herbalist —a *hanpeq* states, "with balsam and saponins, we applied warm boiled pepper tree bark to stem the bleeding then placed activated coca to his lacerations to ameliorate his pain. I also obtained and sanitized bamboo tubes and needles in preparation for the transfusion."

"And where are the blood donors?" the surgeon asks. The young *hanpeq* points at three very pregnant women sitting nearby.

"Excellent."

The *mamacona* pulls off her mask; we stare at the silver-haired matron, slack-jawed with astonishment.

"Is that you?" I exclaim.

"It's Pitu Salla," Solsol says, "the one who helped reunite poor Yma Sumac with her imprisoned mother so many years ago."

"Jap, jap, jap, jap, jap, jap," the Ancient One says with a curtsy.

"What are you doing here?" the wide-eyed Pispis asks.

"No time to explain now, my precious doves," she says, her dark eyes sparkling, "We must put all our attention now on saving our dear Chimbo Sancto."

She sweeps down the corridor toward the designated operating room, her long flowing robe billowing behind her, followed by medical assistants and the blood donors. Inca physicians believe expectant mothers have strong healing properties in their blood and as such are highly esteemed and generously compensated for their life saving contributions. However, even blood transfusions are no guarantee of survival, especially for one that has experienced as much trauma as Chimbo Sancto.

A young Daughter of the Sun leads us to Chimbo's room where he lies on a clean narrow bed after the blood transfusion, his cheeks blooming with color. A medical assistant applies the sap of the *croton lecheri* tree—dragon's blood to disinfect and stem the exsanguination on his worst wounds. Another maiden brings in a small bag of live ants; she loosens the drawstring, then plucks out a large squirming ant with a massive jaw.

"This will sting a little," she says to Chimbo. "Are you ready?"

The dwarf nods, shuts his eyes tight. The girl applies the creature over a gaping wound on his shoulder; it clamps its massive jaws, leaving a neat suture; the apprentice then pinches off its bulbous head.

"Ouch!" the dwarf cries.

"Just a few more, my dove." she says. She repeats the procedure several time over the length of the wound. "All done!" she says cheerfully.

"Thank the gods," Chimbo says wearily. "What other tortures do you people have planned for me?"

The girl giggles then tightens the bag's drawstrings to make sure the insects don't escape.

"We don't have any more torture planned for you right now," she teases. "But we Daughters of the Sun are quite creative. Give us some time and I'm sure we can think of something."

"I'm sure you will," Chimbo says with a wan smile.

The assistant picks up a roll of clean bandages then wraps them around lacerations and punctures on Chimbo's grotesquely swollen face, head and shoulders. Afterward, the only thing showing are his sparkling brown eyes and wide lips. Umiña, Solsol, Pispis and I try our best to maintain a cheerful facade but don't fool our diminutive friend.

"Well, by the expressions on your faces," Chimbo quips, groggily, "I guess this wouldn't be a good time for me to select a mate?"

"No, it isn't, " Pispis blurts out, with the uncensored honesty of a maiden her age.

"We're just glad you're feeling better," Solsol says with a chuckle.

"You risked your life for us, " I say. "You are the dove of our hearts."

"And, you, dear maidens are the doves of my heart, too," Chimbo mumbles with some difficulty, "I couldn't live with myself had I allowed the puma to attack . . . " His eyes dart to the side where Umiña and her baby are standing. "Hello, little Wawa. Your Uncle Chimbo wasn't going to let that puma . . . " His eyes well up with tears; he presses his lips together, trying to control his emotions. "Let's just say, I did what I had to do." Wawa coos and claps excitedly. "You are more than welcome, little Wawa."

Pitu Salla—the Ancient One glides into the room, followed by two medical assistants. The young women take turns scrutinizing Chimbo's injuries and vital signs while Pitu enlightens us on his treatment..

"There are different types of physicians in the empire." Pitu says then points to a petite young assistant. "This is Nayaraq. She is one of my *watukks* whose job is to diagnose and examine the patient's life to determine the origin of the sickness."

"I'm just a *watukk* in training," Nayaraq says with a shy smile.

"She is too modest," Pitu says, "but a very fast learner with a keen eye. She is also in training as a *hanpeq* due to her extensive knowledge of herbs and minerals. And since her grandfather was her village's *pago*, she has inherited his talent for treatment of the soul, because a troubled spirit will not allow the body to heal." She points at another assistant, Kiyari, who appears to be a few years older than Nayaraq.

"Kiyari will soon be certified in a sacred ceremony as a *sancoyoc*," the Ancient One *s*ays. "After more than ten years of extensive training, she is a talented surgeon who uses the hands of the gods to straighten and mend broken limbs, treat open abscesses, perform brain surgery and blood transfusions. In fact, she is the one who performed Chimbo's blood transfusion. She is also a *hampi camayoc*, authorized to preserve remedies and a talented state chemist. Her late father was a *collahuaya*, who supplied the Temple of the Sun with medicinal plants, amulets and lucky charms."

"My father told me that only men are allowed to train in the Inca medical field." I interject.

"Generally medical students are sons of physicians who undergo years of intense medical training in Cuzco with hundreds of hours of practical experience assisting in the battlefield before becoming fully certified. But due to the empire's extensive wars, resulting in innumerable wounded warriors, skilled surgeons are in high demand. Since I am a certified and highly experienced *watukk, hanpeq, pago, sancoyoc, hampi camayoc,* and *collahuaya*, Emperor Huayna Capac himself authorized me to train select Daughters of the Sun years before his death, though I had already been secretly training them anyway."

"So that's what you were doing at the Salkantay Mountain *tampu*." Pispis says. "You were collecting herbal cures."

The old *mamacona* straightens her spine proudly.

"The Qorincancha commissioned me to find a cure for the plague," the Ancient One says. "when the emperor took ill. "

"The herbal concoction you gave me," I say, "cured almost everyone I administered it to."

"I'm pleased to hear that," Pitu says, "but I found it of limited benefit to royals and warriors because, as I mentioned before, 'a troubled spirit will not allow the body to heal.' Many suffer from guilt and will consult neither a *watukk* nor a *pago* to address these impediments to healing. Most hardworking *runakuna* are not burdened by these spiritual travails and as a result are generally able to heal quite rapidly."

After extensive poking and prodding of her patient, Kiyari gazes at her mentor with a smile.

"He seems to be convalescing as expected." Kiyari says, "Do you agree, Nayaraq?"

The assistant nods, beaming like the sun. Taxing medical procedures and invasive examinations have worn poor Chimbo out and before he can excuse himself, his eyes roll back in his head and he dozes off, wheezing and snoring.

"With few exceptions, we're surrounded by murderous Huascar loyalists here in Cuzco," Cura informs us. We are dining in the lavish dining hall, which takes up an entire wing of the Qorincancha. "We need to travel to the safety of the northern provinces."

"We can't leave until Chimbo," I say, "gets well enough to travel."

Cura sighs then shakes her head.

"We can't wait that long, T'ica, " Princess Cura says, "Chimbo is still very sick and will need to stay behind. I hate to leave him but we have no choice. Because he's so small, he'll be easy to hide in the Qorincancha, if there's any trouble so don't worry," she assures me. "We must head north before Huascar decides, in one of his psychotic rages, to murder me, my servants, my guards." She wrings her hands nervously. "And once he discovers that prisoners have escaped the ravages of the Dungeon of Horrors and his favorite sadist, Captain Usna has died, I'm quite positive he will send a search party out for all of us. We must travel to Quito, seek out Atahualpa and explain the terrible interregnum situation here in Cuzco."

"All I want to do is see my Mamáy and Tatáy" Pispis cries, tears streaming down her fair cheeks. "That's really all I want."

"If we take the mountain route," Solsol says, "Chachapoyas is on the way to Quito."

"Very well. We will leave tonight," the princess says, "I've already made all arrangements."

CHAPTER FIFTY TWO

Although the Qorincancha is just a short walk down cobblestone streets from the Palace of Huayna Capac, the queen mother and Princess Chuqui make it a point to ride on an elaborate litter, donning simple tunics and capes of deep scarlet, so as not to compete with the glory of the deities which inhabit, via oracles, the Temple of the Sun.

Huascar trots behind them, wearing the same simple clothes he wore yesterday and surrounded by guards; he was placed in the Kusicancha Palace overnight in a dungeon reserved for wayward royals.

The prince seems uncharacteristically cheerful, though forced to walk the short distance to the Qorincancha, an activity which would ordinarily be considered highly insulting to someone of pure blood since royals almost always ride upon litters even in battle. He looks up entreatingly at the princess sitting on a bench facing the rear of the conveyance.

"Did you know, sister," Huascar chirps, thinking in his own deluded way, that he's won some sort of major victory by being temporarily released from the confines of the royal dungeon, "that the great Inca Viracocha engineered the Qorincancha to function as an enormous calendar?"

"Can you not remain silent for one minute, brother?" the princess bristles.

"Shadows cast by stones placed on the foothills of our sacred mountains can be seen from the temple," the incorrigible prince continues, "marking the solstice and equinoxes, which as you know are faithfully celebrated by our Inca Empire. Later Inca Pachacutiq embellished the Qorincancha enriching it with more gold and silver, not to mention oracles who . . ."

"Why do you torment me with a history lesson that every child already knows?" the princess interrupts, her face pinched into a scowl.

"Just reminding you of all our sacred Inca Empire has accomplished over the years, my dove. Just think of the things we could accomplish when we rule the empire together, sister," Huascar asserts, "as husband and wife."

Princess Chuqui rolls her eyes, lets out a long sigh of exasperation.

"I would rather be thrown into the dungeon of horrors," the princess fumes, "poisoned by snakes and eaten alive by ravenous jaguars. "

"Some day," Huascar chides, "you may very well get your wish, dear sister. Or worse."

The queen mother holds up a hand to silence both daughter and son then twists her body and cranes her neck to look back at Huascar.

"What your sister is trying to say is that we should refrain from making future plans," she says diplomatically, "until we have consulted the appropriate oracles." She turns to face her daughter and eyes her sternly. "Isn't that right, Chuqui?"

"Yes," the princess defers. She reminds herself of the necessity of indulging her mother's scheme to humor the mad prince until they are sufficiently protected by troops loyal to them and not Huascar, "yes, of course. I will obey the commands of the oracles as I'm sure you will, brother."

Huascar shrugs nonchalantly as they near the magnificent Qorincancha.

Viewed from the south, the Temple of the Sun resembles a gold-plated pyramid constructed on a natural hill. Its cyclopean trapezoidal walls incline vertically, typical of the imperial Inca style of architecture. Not even a needle can penetrate the space between each perfectly joined boulder. The rivers Saphy and the canalized Tullumayo flow into the drainage ditch at the edge of the sacred building.

Carriers lower the royal litter; the queen mother and princess step out in front of the temple. Huascar joins them. Grim temple guards, recognizing the royals, allow them through the enormous gold, silver and stone entrance. The queen's guards and litter carriers wait outside.

The royals walk into a gold-plated corridor into a chapel flooded with morning light. Four *acclas*—Daughters of the Sun keep a permanent fire burning adjacent to an immense golden image of the Sun God looming overhead. Seven desiccated Inca rulers, wearing feathered head-dresses, medals, bracelets, scepters of gold, sit side by side, knees to chests upon a long golden bench. Among them is the mummy of the late Inca Huayna Capac, who sits directly underneath the Sun God disc; his fine clothing, along with the other mummies, worn only once, whisked away and burnt daily. Today his raiment is bedecked with rubies, emeralds and sapphires and sun rays flood his heavily made-up face. The queen falls to her knees.

"My husband!" the widow keens, stroking the mummy's leathery cheeks, sightless eyes and carefully combed hair. Though it's only been a few days since she finished traveling with the royal mummy, who she virtually ignored for over a thousand miles in the funeral cortege, her grief returns anew. "Why did you leave me?"

"Where is my father's oracle?" Princess Chuqui demands.

"An oracle has not yet been assigned to the Inca Huayna Capac, since his sacred remains just arrived a few days ago." one of the young *acclas* answers, her eyes lowered. "One of our head priestesses is interviewing eligible candidates as we speak, my princess."

"Take me to the *mamacona,*" the widowed queen says, as she dabs a silky handkerchief onto her tear-stained face. "I would like a say in the matter."

"Yes, my queen," the young *accla* says, "Please follow me."

Before she departs, the widowed *coya* lovingly pats the mummy's desiccated hands, replete with bejeweled rings on each finger.

"I will be back soon, my dove," she peeps to her beloved but thoroughly dead and desiccated husband.

Over two thousand Daughters of the Sun busy themselves inside the gold and silver-plated walls of the Qorincancha. Older *acclas* weave fine cloth and fashion elaborate tunics, capes and head-dresses like the queen and princess wore when they met with Huascar in the palace throne room yesterday.

A group of young *acclas,* dressed in white tunics, sit in a chamber dedicated to Mama Quilla, walls covered in hammered silvery sheets and stunning icons depicting the Moon goddess; they are immersed in a lecture given by an elderly priestess on the precepts of the Inca religion.

Moving past that chamber, the royals stride by Pukamarka, a room dedicated to Illapa, the frightening god of thunder, its onyx walls accented with gold and silver. In this room, young girls snatched from remote provinces are tutored by a priestess on the rudiments of *Runasimi*, the official language of the empire, for which most have little affinity, since they only wish to return to their beloved families. A squirming toddler, no more than three breaks free from her young caregiver, who happens to be her sister and runs out into the hall when she spies Princess Chuqui.

"Mamáy?" the little girls says as she happily leaps into the princess's arms. "Mamáy!"

The princess holds the child tenderly, admiring her rosy skin, plump cheeks and silky raven hair.

"I'm sorry," Chuqui says, "but I'm not your Mamáy."

Her embarrassed sister runs out of Pukamarka to fetch the toddler but the toddler stubbornly refuses to release her grip. Chuqui gently pries her small brown hands off her neck then gives the confused toddler back to her older sister.

"Mamáy!" she wails, her large almond-shaped eyes overflowing with tears as her sister carries her down the vast corridor. "Mamáy!" The siblings disappear into an outer courtyard,

Tears rolls down the princess's cheek for the plight of the young child.

"So," Huascar remarks, "somewhere deep down in the blackness of her soul, my sister appears to have a soft heart for a wretched village child, but not for me, her very own flesh and blood."

Although she would like nothing better than to berate her

brother for the egotistical maniac he is, Chuqui holds her tongue, wipes away her tears and follows their *accla* guide down the vast, lavish silver and golden corridors of the Qorincancha.

CHAPTER FIFTY THREE

"This is way to the Garden of Inti, the Sun God," the *accla* states, with a wave of her hand.

She leads the group through a massive trapezoidal stone exit into a courtyard flush with solid gold masterpieces forged, cast and polished by the most skilled gold and silversmiths in the empire; the garden represents the abundance of the empire in all its glory: life-sized stalks heavy with ripe maize, trees, llamas, tropical fruits, flowers, butterflies, birds, and tools for tilling the land.

When Huascar gazes at the garden of gold, he imagines having unfettered access to these sacred works of art for the purposes of self-aggrandizement not to mention the unlimited ability to utilize the priceless artifacts to bribe friends and foes alike. In contrast, the queen and princess' thoughts are sublimated from the material plane of *kay pacha* to the heavenly world of *hanan pacha,* and, in doing so, they unite with the deities of the cosmos, a spiritual journey in which the debauched prince has no interest.

After walking through the Garden of Inti and into the vast west wing of the Qorincancha, the group strolls past the silver and opal chamber of Ch'aska Quyllur, the Venus star; at that precise moment dozens of *acclas* wend their way through the corridor carrying a variety of artistically arranged fruits, vegetables, grains, meats and fish on silver and golden platters. Huascar eyes the food hungrily as the acolytes scamper past him, their heads bowed, eyes lowered.

"Where are they going?" Huascar asks.

"Food is prepared twice daily for the deceased Inca Emperors," the *accla* guide explains, "who we must honor and nourish even though their spirits reside in *hanan pacha* since we rely on their counsel in the physical realm."

Huascar plucks a banana off one of the large food trays hurtling past him. Though his sister and mother glare at him, the prince shrugs, peels the banana and stuffs it in his mouth. He's still chewing when the group glides into the copper, gold and silver chamber of Cuichu the rainbow god. Precious and semi-precious multi-colored gems form an immense rainbow arch on a far wall. A *mamacona* is speaking quietly to a couple of hooded *acclas* seated in front of her; she stops when she notices the royals.

"Forgive me, *mamacona*, holiest of all high priestesses," the young *accla* says with a deep bow, "The widowed *coya* Rahua Occlo, Princess Chuqui and Prince Huascar request an audience with you to discuss the oracle selection for the departed Shepherd of the Sun, Emperor Huayna Capac."

"The final selection for this vital post will be made," the *mamacona* says, "in a few more days, according to tradition."

"Very well," Prince Huascar says, "it is not my father's oracle I wish to consult at this time. I demand an audience with all the oracles, especially the oracle for the omnipotent Viracocha. Now. Privately. As is my right. "

"As you wish, Prince Huascar," the *mamacona* says with a courteous nod. "Follow me."

Huascar regards his mother and sister, right eyebrow lifted.

"You two stay here." he says.

The high priestess shoots the widowed *coya* and the princess a sideways glance as she exits with the mad prince.

CHAPTER FIFTY FOUR

Understanding the urgency of our mission, Lucanas carriers steal through the dark streets of Cuzco as fast as their muscular bodies can carry our four litters. Thankfully Huascar's minions, who are likely eating drinking or whoring at this late hour, leave us unmolested. We glide past the Sacsayhuayman fortress and finally reach the cobblestone Inca trail leading out Cuzco. Once outside the confines of the southern capital, we head up the steep trail for the relative safety of the sacred mountains. Cura points out the glow of the full moon lighting our way

"Surely," the princess announces, "Mama Quilla blesses our journey."

A dozen Children of the Moon materialize in front of our litters, square teeth gleaming in the moonlight.

"Greetings, Princess, T'ica and friends," they say, their voices deep and melodic, like a song. "Follow us!" They bound off the trail into a tangle of trees and bushes, translucent skin glowing.

"What would you have us do, Princess?" the head Lucanas litter carrier asks.

"Follow the Machukuna," Cura exclaims her light brown eyes sparkling, "Quickly!"

The litter carriers follow the giants' swift, graceful movements weaving through dirt paths, sweeping past trees and bushes, gliding over rocks and around boulders; my fellow passengers and I sway to and fro, hands clenched on the edge of our benches to keep from being thrown off. The giants wait for us at the foot of a sheer rock face reaching into the sky.

"Do you remember this place, T'ica?" a handsome Machukuna

asks.

I scan the surroundings uncertainly then notice a small opening in the rocky formation; my eyes light up in recognition.

"Does this lead," I ask, "to the subterranean tunnels and the home of the Machukuna?

The giant smiles and nods.

Princess Cura's light brown eyes glow in the moonlight; she motions the carriers to lower our litters, gracefully steps off her conveyance, walks toward the mouth of the cave then climbs down steps into the tunnel. We watch intently, frozen in place, our mouths agape at the courage of the petite royal.

"Will this lead us to Mamáy and Tatay?" Pispis asks.

A Child of the Moon steps forward, sapphire eyes glimmering; she holds out her translucent hands to the Cloud Warrior sisters. The girls grab one giant hand each, emerald eyes glistening. The giantess helps them off their litter, through the small opening, down a short stairway until they reach the sprawling subterranean cave and tunnel system. Umiña, her baby and I follow suit. The stunned entourage of four royal servants hesitate for a moment then follow close behind. The litter carriers try to figure out how to pull their conveyances through the tiny mouth of the cave.

"Leave the litters behind," a Machukuna says, "we will not be needing them."

"But it's a long way," a litter carrier says, "to the northern empire."

The giants blue eyes twinkle.

"Not the way," he says, "we'll be going."

* * *

"This seems to be the gateway to an extensive subterranean tunnel system," Cura says, in awe, "which runs underneath the cordillera all the way to the northern empire."

"My father told me about this tunnel as a child," I add, "but I thought it was just a myth."

"*Timpu Pisti* is nigh," a giant says.

"World reversal," another giant agrees with a slow dignified nod.

"The days of the Inca Empire," another says, "are numbered. You must hurry to your destinations before the decimation of the population of royals and *runakuna* alike commences in earnest."

We follow the lithe giantess through the tunnel system until we reach a glistening portal reminiscent of highly polished black opal.

"Think about where you want to go," the gentle Child of the Moon explains, "and the portal, in concert with Pachamama and your guide will lead you there."

CHAPTER FIFTY FIVE

Huascar leads his mother and sister to the Plaza of Rimacpampa—the Place of Those Who Speak. A dozen oracles, each representing an Inca god or goddess sit passively on low wooden stools, dressed in hooded snow white robes.

Huascar approaches an oracle, pulls back its hood; a two-headed snake spirit of Cuichu, the rainbow god pops up, knocking the prince off his feet. The serpent heads stare at each other, flicking red and blacked-tipped forked tongues; the creature hisses, its yellow eyes gleaming then shoots into the sky, creating a glorious rainbow over a nearby mountain.

"See there, Mother and Sister," the prince says with a great deal of satisfaction, "the gods are with us."

Rahua Occlo and her royal daughter are unimpressed since they know that all too often magicians are behind such displays.

"Cuichu, the Rainbow God," Chuqui states dismissively, "is a minor god at best."

"Nevertheless a lovely god," Huascar says lasciviously, "but not so lovely as you, my beloved future wife."

Chuqui glares at her brother, her brown eyes afire.

"So you would subject to us," she says irritably, "to endless demonstrations from each and every oracle?"

A hooded oracle stands tall and lean, holding a gold staff embossed with silver thunderbolts, face covered with a gold mask depicting the image of a benevolent-looking god with a long curly beard.

"I have given *runakuna* and royalty alike many gifts," Viracocha's oracle says, his voice resounding throughout the region, "clothes, language, agriculture, the arts and animals. I have also generously ceded the sun, moon and stars to bring light to the world."

"For which we most humbly thank you," Prince Huascar says with a deep bow.

"And now," the oracle says, "after all your treachery, Prince Huascar, you want more until the universe I so lovingly created vanishes in an unwinnable war."

Huascar's face flushes, obviously unprepared to be scolded.

"My intention is to save the empire." the prince argues, "not to destroy it. But I cannot save the empire unless I become emperor."

"A man unable to control the most base of his emotions," Viracocha says, "cannot control an empire. *Pisti Timpu* is at hand; there is no changing that."

"But I am changed man." Prince Huascar pleads, "Give me the chance to prove myself one more time and I will not let the empire down. I give you my word, Lord of the Universe."

"Queen Mother Rahua Occlo," the oracle says, "according to Inca law, you must bless this union by giving you daughter Chuqui in marriage to her full brother, unless you have good reason not to."

"You must know, Lord Viracocha," the queen mother says, "that my heart is pure in my determination to prohibit this union."

"Then who will rule," the God of the Universe asks, "if not Huascar?"

"Anybody but my murdering brother," Chuqui exclaims. "I beg you, Lord Viracocha."

"We beseech you, my lord," the queen mother says, "to help us find a suitable replacement for my late husband, the much beloved Emperor Huayna Capac."

"The empire's demise," the oracle declares solemnly, "started even before Huayna Capac's merciless reign. And will end, for all intents and purposes, under the barbarous rule of his pure-blooded Inca son, Huascar."

A light breeze blows the oracle's robes; Viracocha disappears in a blinding white light.

Her face ashen, legs buckling, Chuqui tries to wrap her mind around the implications of the oracle's pronouncement; chest heaving, she collapses in a dead heap at the queen's feet. Huascar blithely snaps his fingers and the rest of the oracles rise and walk back to the Qorincancha.

Kneeling next to her inert daughter, Rahua Occlo raises a fist to the heavens; if only she'd taken Chuqui's advice to assassinate her crazed son. But it's much too late for that now.

CHAPTER FIFTY SIX

Pispis and Solsol arrive at the egress of a tunnel situated at the base of the giant Keulap citadel. They duck through a narrow hole, dust off their tunics and regard the familiar cobblestone stairway leading to the gates of their city.

"I can't believe it, Solsol," Pispis says, "We are home. We are really home."

The girls hold hands and race up the wide stone staircase, lined on both side by thick sixty foot stone walls. Upon reaching the top of the steps, they are bewildered by the normally sturdy wooden gate, hanging lopsided from its hinges. When they push through the tattered gate, the aftermath of a heinous battle surrounds them: houses burned and looted, corpses of men, women and children left where they were cut down. They wander the ruined city in utter shock, unable to fathom the carnage. After an all-too-brief happiness to have finally arrived home, the sisters perch upon on a low stone wall and weep bitterly.

A tall bearded man cautiously enters the compound. After morning prayers to the serpent gods, he felt compelled to visit his old hometown though he had more important things to do today than run the risk of bumping into Inca guards who have steadfastly refused to allow his people to properly entomb their dead; Cloud Warrior mummies are believed to have greater powers of sorcery than their living counterparts.

The sisters don't recognize this man. He squints at them from a distance and thinks he must be hallucinating or dreaming. *Yes, that must be it,* he thinks. *It's all a dream.* As he steps closer, his confusion slowly transforms into wide-eyed recognition.

"Solsol!" he cries in a deep baritone the sisters cannot place,

"Pispis!"

He runs toward the frightened maidens then scoops them up in his massive arms. Squirming, kicking and punching, the girls attempt to escape this stranger's embrace. He loosens his grip, sets them down on their feet, pats their blond head and cups their faces in his calloused hands.

"Don't you recognize me, my doves?" the man asks with a friendly chuckle.

"No," Solsol says with a sob.

"It's me," the man says, "your brother, Pullihuaman."

Pispis scrutinizes his red hair and beard skeptically then grunts derisively.

"You're not my brother," Pispis insists, "because Pulli is not yet a man."

"You're just a bad man trying to fool us." Solsol fumes. "You must go away now and let us find our family."

"You don't recognize me," Pulli says with an amused grin, "because in the time you two have been gone, I've grown up."

Attempting to rectify the memory of their lanky freckle-faced brother with the burly adult looming over them, the girls' jaws swing open. Slowly, recognition blooms like a flower in their emerald eyes.

"Is it really you, Pulli?" Pispis asks.

Solsol touches his ruddy cheeks and regards his twinkling cobalt blue eyes.

"Brother," she mutters, "Can it be?"

Silver streaks running through her lush strawberry blond hair, a woman steps into the far side of the compound, along with a middle aged man, leading a llama, his formerly bushy blond hair and beard now white as snow. Sangama watches her son, Pulli having a lively conversation with two young maidens. She squints, rubs her eyes, then squints again.

"No," she murmurs, "it can't be. The serpent gods are playing cruel tricks on my eyes or I am dreaming."

Catequil is busy tying up the llama, so Sangama grabs him by his tunic sleeve and directs his attention to the opposite side of the Keulap ruin. He focuses on the incredible vision, grabs his mate and holds her tight.

"Can it be, wife?" he mutters, unable to speak above a whisper, "Can it be?"

Catequil staggers toward the vision, knowing this must be a dream, so similar to the many he's had about his beloved daughters since that horrible day they were kidnapped. Terrified that he might collapse and awaken from this fantasy before embracing his long lost offspring, he steadies himself by holding his wife's hand.

Pulli directs the girls' attention to the far side of the ruined city. Chests heaving, eyes gleaming, the sisters sprint toward their bewildered parents with the speed and grace of Goddess Puma.

CHAPTER FIFTY SEVEN

The elaborate dual ceremony begins at dawn, when Inti the Sun God radiates his first and most sacred light upon the empire. Prince Huascar and Princess Chuqui are seated on low gilded thrones, heads wreathed with exotic flowers imported by runners from the wilds of the Great Jungle. The princess's silky vicuña gown and cloak are deep purple, bedecked with emeralds; the prince's clothes match his bride's.

The royal nuptials sets the brother and sister apart and above *runakuna,* where incest is strictly forbidden.

The queen mother sits next to the sister-bride, propping her up when she sways drunkenly, too intoxicated to sit up straight.

"I want more *chicha*," Chuqui slurs.

"I know you're upset," the queen mother whispers in her daughter's ear, "but I'm just trying to save our lives. I would have been charged with treason had I not capitulated to the will of Viracocha."

"More *chicha*," the princess insists.

A servant approaches, head bowed and starts to pour more *chicha* into Chuqui's cup but the widowed coya blocks her attempt with a dismissive wave, much to the bride's consternation. She shoots her mother a drunken scowl then hiccups.

Huascar ignores his drunken bride; he sighs, rolls his eyes and taps his foot impatiently as the new high priest and crafty sycophant, Quetzal chants endlessly, invoking the blessings of Pachamama and hundreds of other deities to bless the royal union. Thousands of wedding guests toss flower petals which float down upon the royal couple until they all but disappear under a mound of blooms.

The wedding ceremony officially over, a male servant carries the royal *mascaipacha,* a red woolen fringe that hangs from a woven headband over the forehead; he hands it to the high priest who turns to face the crowd, holding it overhead.

"Each individual red tassel of this *mascaipacha,*" Quetzal cries, "represents the heads of nations brought forcibly under the sovereignty of the Inca Empire."

The priest sets the *mascaipacha* over Huascar's sweat-covered brow; the *chicha* fueled crowd erupts, crying, shouting, singing and dancing. Another servant hands two large white feathers to the high priest.

"Two feathers from the sacred *corequenque* bird," the priest pronounces, "represents the two houses of the Incas—the Hanan and the Hurin."

He inserts the feathers into the front of Huascar's *mascaipacha* then continues the ceremony by pushing huge scowling Sun God earrings into the new sovereign's overstretched earlobes. He hands Huascar a gaudy jewel encrusted chalice, crafted by expert goldsmiths especially for this occasion. Finally, the priest cedes the new emperor a long golden scepter shaped at the end like a pick ax, a symbol of warlike superiority. Huascar lifts the scepter overhead.

"*Aucacunapac!*" Quetzal chants, "For tyrants, traitors, the cruel, the treacherous and the disloyal!"

"*Aucacunapac!*" the crowd repeats, "For tyrants, traitors, the cruel, the treacherous and the disloyal!"

After lining up to greet the new sovereign, before being guided to their sacrificial deaths on mountaintops far and wide over the Inca Empire in commemoration of the glorious coronation, Huascar greets each of the hundreds of Daughters of the Sun with a perfunctory pat on the head and thanks for her allegiance to the Inca Empire. Meanwhile, the ebullient crowd continues to celebrate.

"Drink all you want, wife," the new emperor says scrutinizing his bride with scorn, "but I will bed you tonight and every night, drunk or not."

"I would sooner be tossed off the highest cliff in the empire," the bleary-eyed princess slurs. She extends her large goblet in a tacit demand for more *chicha;* a servant pours her a minuscule amount. "Fill it to the brim!" the new Queen Chuqui commands. The servant gazes at Queen Mother, Rahua Occlo, who pulls back her head and shakes it every so slightly. "I'm the queen now," her daughter hisses, shaking a finger at the confused servant girl, "not her!"

Rahua Occlo takes a deep breath and closes her eyes.

"Chuqui," the widowed *coya* says, "I'm so sorry . . . I . . . ."

Her drunken daughter bangs her empty goblet on the stone floor next to her low throne.

"More *chicha,*" Chuqui screeches. "Where's my *chicha!*"

The servant girl shrugs helplessly, fills the goblet to over-flowing, the queen mother unable to stop her. Queen Chuqui gulps so quickly, the purple liquid streams out of the corners of her contorted mouth. In a drunken stupor, the new Inca queen slides off her throne; servants desperately attempt to lift her sagging body into some semblance of a dignified sitting position but after several unsuccessful attempts, they give up. Not only is the new queen out cold now, she intends to stay that way as long as her despised brother-husband remains alive.

CHAPTER FIFTY EIGHT

"Where was Atahualpa?" Emperor Huascar asks Queen Mother Rahua Occlo from the confines of the palace throne room in Cuzco. "Neither did he attend our father's funeral, the royal wedding nor the coronation. His attendance was mandatory; his treachery will not be disregarded."

"Atahualpa is squelching rebellions," Rahua Occlo explains, "in the northern provinces, as I already told you several times. However, I heard from *chasqui* runners that his emissaries are heading for Calca as we speak."

Huascar paces back and forth, chugging *chicha* from the chalice bestowed upon him at the coronation. He wipes his mouth then pounds on his chest so hard, he loses his breath.

"I am emperor now!" Huascar slurs, "Do you understand? Me! Me! Me! And nobody else."

"You must control your emotions, my son," the queen says, "as you promised Viracocha."

He shoots a bleary-eyed look at the queen mother, smiles salaciously then staggers down the corridor toward the royal bedchamber.

"Where is . . . Ch-ch-chuqui?" Huascar stutters, "Where is my lovely queen? We will go to the royal palace in Calca tonight."

In the throne room of the Calca royal palace, five well-dressed emissaries are accompanied by four llamas burdened with jewelry, pottery, exotic bird feathers and twenty elegant ensembles interwoven with fine gold and silver threads. Quilaco Yupanqui, son of a distinguished council member who died in the plague, takes two steps forward. To demonstrate his everlasting obeisance to the new emperor, he removes his sandals, bows and lowers his eyes.

"Oh, Sun, oh, Day, give light!" he intones, "Oh unique emperor, lover of the poor and son of the Sun God."

"Quilaco!" the queen mother says cheerfully. "So delightful to see you! I trust your long journey from Quito was satisfactory?"

The new reigning Queen of the Inca Empire, Chuqui touches her throbbing head. Determined not to get drunk again today, she chews copious amounts of coca leaves to ameliorate the effects of alcohol poisoning and has no idea whether her incestuous two-day-old marriage has been consummated or not. Since the coca leaves are an impediment to speaking, she removes the wad and places it on a tray a servant is holding. Chuqui is intent on maintaining a semblance of dignity especially today with the arrival of the emissaries; she doesn't want the terrible truth to reach Atahualpa's ears—that since her wedding, she's become a terrible drunk.

"Did you know, Huascar," the new queen says, "that young Quilaco here was reared almost as a son and brother in our Quito household?"

"How delightful," Huascar says sarcastically. He gulps down another large goblet of *chicha*. In contrast to his sister-queen, he's drunk but at this early hour, not enough to slur his words. He also doesn't know whether he consummated his incestuous marriage but from the horrific hangover he's experiencing now, he guesses he did not. "What do you want?"

"Felicitations," Quilaco says, growing uneasy as he was

expecting a much friendlier reception from the new emperor. "we bring you greetings and homage from Atahualpa." He points at the llamas bearing gifts exclusively for the new emperor. "He sends his deepest regrets for being unable to attend the funeral, your wedding and coronation. However, he sends his most sincere regards." He points at two llamas, laden with clothing and jewelry suitable for the widowed *coya* and the new queen. "Atahualpa also pays homage to the new queen and the queen mother."

"Atahualpa's attendance," the new emperor snarls, "to my coronation and marriage were mandatory. I'm sure my messengers made that perfectly clear."

"Yes, my shepherd," Quilaco says respectfully, "unfortunately, several provinces took full advantage of the period of interregnum before your coronation. In Atahualpa's absence, Quito would surely have been sacked. He now requests your formal permission to remain on post in the northern empire."

"I do not accept Atahualpa's feeble excuses!" Emperor Huascar spits. "And do not give him permission to stay in Quito! Not now! Not ever!"

"Huascar," the queen mother scolds, "control yourself."

The madman's face turns beet red; a servant dutifully pours another goblet of *chicha;* he downs it quickly but the alcohol does not calm him. Instead, he points accusingly at his mother.

"I see it all clearly now. You, dear mother, are obviously Atahualpa's prime adviser," Huascar shouts, "and instigator!"

Queen Chuqui, stands, her finger leveled at her brother-husband.

"That allegation is tantamount," the new queen argues, "to an accusation of treason."

Huascar stares a hole through his sister-wife, spits on the floor and wags his hand at the gifts bestowed upon her by Atahualpa.

"Just look at the whore who left her lover in Quito," the new emperor growls, "and now sees her possessions returned to her."

"And who better qualified to judge," Queen Chuqui spits, "than one who regularly keeps the company of whores."

"Atahualpa only wants to please you." the queen mother rages, "but now you goad him to do that which he never intended to do."

Huascar steps off the dais, walks toward a llama carrying gifts meant for the royal women, pulls out a lavish gold and silver threaded tunic and commences to hack it to shreds with a long obsidian knife that he extracts from a leather sheath hanging from his waist. His mother and sister-wife witness this act of barbarity in wide-eyed shock. The emissaries gaze at each other nervously. The mad emperor unfolds another woman's tunic and inspects it with a scowl.

"Strip!" he screams at the emissaries. "All of you."

"I . . . I don't understand," the stunned Quilaco stutters.

"Take off your clothes!" Huascar screeches. "Now!"

The emissaries shoot each other sidelong glance, their faces ashen. The queen mother and her daughter are helpless to intervene in Calca, the new emperor's palace surrounded by his minions who, upon his orders, would strike them all down in an instant.

"Whatever it is you are planning to do here, my son," the queen mother hisses, "don't complain when you experience the full consequences of your actions."

* * *

Atahualpa's emissaries, their heads and faces covered, journey to Quito via litter carriers. Upon arrival at the royal palace, Quilaco bangs on the palace door. After a few moments, the immense portal squeaks open; the ancient doorman stares at the group, mystified by the men's unusual appearance.

"Is Prince Atahualpa here?" Quilaco asks, his brown eyes cast down.

The doorman pauses for a moment then recognizes the emissary's voice.

"Lord Quilaco . . . ? Ah, yes, please come in . . . " he says, "I'll take you . . . to him."

Quilaco and his men follow the doorman down a corridor that leads to the palace throne room where Atahualpa and Princess Cura, who just arrived the night before via the Machukuna's secret tunnel system, are discussing the state of the empire.

"The atrocities committed by Huascar," Princess Cura explains, "against his own people, not to mention his own brothers, will only intensify if ignored. You must consider accepting the fringe for the good of the . . ."

"Forgive me, my prince," the doorman says, interrupting their conversation, "but . . . "

The emissaries step in, dressed head to toe in women's attire that was sent as Atahualpa's homage to the new queen and her mother. Upon Quilaco's signal, they reluctantly uncover the cloths covering their faces.

Prince Atahualpa stares speechlessly at the grisly sight; Cura Occlo gasps then averts her eyes. The men's faces have been mutilated, noses and ears crudely hacked off.

CHAPTER FIFTY NINE

The kind *Machukuna*, light blue eyes gleaming like a beacon, guides me through the underground labyrinth which leads into the eastern empire. After several hours, the giant delivers me at the mouth of a jungle cave. I step into the humid verdant forest, turn to say farewell but not surprisingly my friend has already evaporated into the ether.

"Pachamama and Mamaquilla," I pray, hands lifted to the heavens, "Empower me, your humble daughter, T'ica, protect me, grant me strength, vision and wisdom to propel me into the future. I beseech your aid in summoning the secrets of the past which will guide me to my family."

My hands transform into countless twinkling stars, I become drenched in a river of sweat and cosmic light and my mind floods with lucid images:

1511 A.D.
Piajajalca
Chachapoyas

Taquiri pricks his ears and follows the strange bleating sound; Brilliant Puma—Hankanpuma follows close behind. Twenty feet into the brush, they discover a wailing newborn in a small clearing; next to the infant is its dead Cloud Warrior mother, sprawled on the rocky turf, face down, an Inca arrow protruding from her upper back.

The fair, blue-eyed baby sees the men and stops crying; she coos, gurgles and kicks her tiny feet.

"What do we do now?" Hankanpuma asks.

Taquiri shrugs.

"We have no way to feed this Cloud Warrior child," he says, "We should leave her here for her own people to find."

"Her people are being slaughtered by wave after wave of Inca warriors as we speak," Hankanpuma argues, "After the main battle in Piajajalca is over, soldiers will be combing the mountainside, killing any surviving Cloud Warriors they find, young or old."

They hear rustling in nearby brush; hearts pounding, Hankanpuma pulls an arrow from his quill and sets it in his bowstring; Taquiri lifts his ax. A tan and white llama with a majestic woolly neck and her snow-white, spindly-legged cria *step into the grassy clearing; the dam cocks her head then grazes as her baby suckles from her milk-filled teats.*

With some assistance, Taquiri straps the foundling securely onto his back; Hankanpuma leads the dam with a rope loosely tied around her elegant neck; the cria *follows closely. The deserters and llamas hike down the mountain, looking and listening warily for Inca lookouts.*

The baby llama bleats; its mother stops in her tracks and lets her cria *nurse, then Taquiri milks the obliging dam, squirting her warm milk into a crude wooden cup then carefully filling an army-issue leather flask with the nourishing liquid. Luckily the placid dam doesn't seem to mind at all, standing patiently until he's done pulling her teats. Hankanpuma insists on the honor of dripping the milk into the Cloud Warrior baby's tiny mouth until she falls asleep.*

After successfully evading Inca troops for more than two weeks, the men rest on a boulder near the trail. Hankanpuma lifts the baby from the sling and kisses her rosy cheeks. The infant tries to swat him with her tiny hand; the boy soldier dodges the playful slap and the baby giggles. He lifts a flask of llama milk to her pink lips; the baby drinks deeply.

"Where will you go?" Hankanpuma asks.

"I will travel south to a village near Cuzco," Taquiri says. "My brother lives there. Or, at least he did. I haven't seen him in a long time. I'm sure I can find someone there to take care of the baby."

"Why live so close to the dreaded Inca capitol?" Hankanpuma asks.

"The Incas will never expect me to journey south," Taquiri explains, "Most deserters run north and end up getting caught. I will live right underneath the noses of the Inca dogs. They will never think to look for me so close to their capital city."

"I see," Hankanpuma says pensively.

"And you," Taquiri says, "Where will you go?"

"Home." the young soldier says with a shy smile.

"And where is that?" Taquiri asks.

"Far to the east then to the extreme southern jungle," the boy says.

"And who are your people, my dove?" Taquiri asks.

"The fiercest warriors of the jungle," the boy says, "the Chirihuanas."

"Do you mean the Chirihuana cannibals?" Taquiri asks. He stops, the whites of his eyes glowing like a silvery moon; he digs into his pouch and stuffs coca leaves into his suddenly dry mouth.

"Don't worry, Tatáy" Brilliant Puma teases, "you are too thin and sinewy to be tasty enough for my people."

"Thank the gods," Taquiri murmurs in between chews.

"We would just tie you onto an ant hill," the boy teases, "where you would be consumed in days or eaten by a jaguar." Taquiri's eyes move side to side uncertainly. "I'm kidding mountain dweller! My people are peaceful, except when it comes to the Incas; we are forced to treat them harshly and yes, we consume their flesh because it serves as a warning to the empire. Most warriors would rather desert than risk being captured and eaten piece by piece by Chirihuana cannibals. However, honored friend, if you are ever in trouble, you can always seek refuge with my tribe."

"How would I find you?" Taquiri asks.

The boy picks up a stick and draws a map in the dirt.

"Look. Go south on the Great River," the young deserter says, as he taps the dusty ground, "in the direction of the Gran Chaku where the tributaries of the river Madeira take their rise. Then ask to see the prince of the Chirihuanas."

"The prince's name?" Taquiri asks.

"Hankanpuma," the boy says, eyes brilliant in the afternoon sun, "Brilliant Puma."

Taquiri and Hankanpuma's shoulders are slumped from hunger, thirst and weariness. They sit in a clearing, squirting llama milk into the foundling's little pink mouth; she swallows the sweet liquid in large gulps then falls back to sleep; Taquiri keeps her cradled in his arms. Despite the dire circumstances, the baby has grown considerably in the last few weeks and rarely cries, except when hungry. The men drink some of the warm milk themselves as they note the deteriorating condition of their army issue sandals, which are so frayed and worn after nearly a month of continuous walking that they're barely usable. If still in the army, they would be eligible for new footwear because the empire has an enormous surplus of clothes, weapons and footwear for their warriors; of course under the circumstances, they have to be content with what they have and make repairs as necessary.

"I will come visit you, my dove, as soon as the gods allow," Taquiri promises. "Journey well to your jungle home of Gran Chaku, Prince Hankanpuma."

The boy embraces his friend.

"Don't forget me, Tatáy," the young prince says, eyes wet with tears, "because I will never forget you. If not for you, I would never be able to see my family again."

The boy faces east but takes one last look back at his friends— an odd aggregation of army deserter, llama, cria and human foundling then disappears down a leafy path leading deep into the Great Jungle.

Taquiri intends to keep his promise to visit his young friend, in case he needs a reliable refuge if threatened with arrest for desertion—a catastrophic but common occurrence.

Exhausted from endless weeks of hiking up and down steep

mountain trails without adequate nourishment, except for the occasional native Andean fruit such as mountain papayas and sachotomate *and whatever llama milk is leftover after the* cria *and the thriving rosy-cheeked Cloud Warrior infant drink their fill, the emaciated and bedraggled Taquiri staggers into his brother's village.*

The foundling begins to wail; a couple of wrinkled brown-skinned matrons look up from their looms, stand and approach the gaunt, filthy stranger then scrutinize the fair-skinned infant strapped to his back.

"That baby is hungry!" one of the women says, waving her finger. Her dark brown eyes squint at the exhausted man. "As a grandmother many times over, I know hunger cries when I hear them."

"Where is the infant's mother?" the other weaver woman asks. She is half the size of her companion with big teeth set in a wide jaw.

"She's an orphan," Taquiri says listlessly, "surviving only with the blessings of Pachamama and milk from my llama."

"Oh, poor baby," the first matron says with a frown, "Give her to me. I know just what to do."

With the help of the women, Taquiri loosens the frayed cloth binding the foundling to his back; they pull her out and take turns nuzzling and lightly pinching her pink cheeks. The taller woman pats the baby's back. The infant lets out a long, sonorous burp; the ladies laugh with delight, cooing over the beautiful child and chattering nonstop.

"No more llama milk for you, my little dove," one of the

*grandmothers coos, "*Runakuna *needs milk from* runakuna. *Yes, that's nature's way. Isn't it?"*

The baby responds with a tiny grunt and chortle; the women smother her with loving kisses, admiring her tiny hands, feet and toes and contrasting her ivory skin to their dark brown color. They stroll around the tiny village, showing her off to neighbors as if they'd given birth to the child themselves. Taquiri stumbles along behind them.

"Wait!" Taquiri rasps. "Do you know a man by the name of Tupakusi?"

The weaver women stop, turn, and gaze at him.

"Why yes," the smaller matron says, clutching the baby possessively, "He lives over there with his wife."

The women point at a stone hut no farther than a hundred feet away.

Taquiri slumps to his knees, raises his hands in gratitude to the gods, tears glinting in his dark eyes.

Inside her tiny but neat stone hut, Asiri busies herself preparing an enormous meal in honor of Taquiri, the long lost brother-in-law she just met. Her husband, Tupakusi sets a large platter of food in front of his emaciated sibling, who guzzles chicha *from a wooden cup.*

"Enough chicha, *my dear brother," Tupakusi says, "You need to eat, too."*

Taquiri picks up a skewered and grilled guinea pig from the platter, sinks his teeth into it, closes his eyes and swoons with delight.

"I wonder how the baby and my sister are getting along?" Asiri asks. "And I also wonder why she didn't join us for a meal?"

"Her husband wouldn't let her," Tupakusi spits, "That's why."

"I'm going to check on the baby as soon as I finish here," Taquiri says, as he peels a banana.

Asiri wrings her hands and bites her lower lip.

"You should go now, Taquiri," she says. "I will keep your food warm."

At the entrance of Zoila's hut, his body scrubbed clean in a nearby stream, Taquiri dons fresh clothes borrowed from his brother and an Inca army ax, which hangs from his belt.

"May I enter your blessed household?" he asks politely.

"Come in!" a cheerful voice chirps.

Taquiri slowly opens the old creaky door and steps into the hut. Sitting cross-legged next to a stove Zoila, a teenager, caresses the foundling. The baby cranes her chubby neck to look at Taquiri, her blue eyes twinkling; she coos and kicks her feet excitedly when she sees him.

"How is she doing?" he asks.

"At first," the girl explains, "she didn't know how to latch on to the breast but, with encouragement of the village women, we kept on trying until we met with great success." She looks at the

baby, *"Didn't we, my little dove?"*

When Taquiri draws closer, he notices a black eye and several bruises on her neck.

"What happened to you?" Taquiri asks.

"Oh," the girls says, pressing her full lips together, "It's nothing."

"Your husband beats you, doesn't he?" Taquiri asks. "You cover the bruises so no one can see them. But I can see them clearly now."

The cowed young woman pulls a frayed woolen scarf over her head and stares at the floor.

"It's only when he drinks," she whispers.

"What happened to your own baby?" Taquiri inquires.

A grizzled man who looks old enough to be Zoila's grandfather plods into the hut, glowers at Taquiri. The teenager's face reddens to a deep scarlet.

"You can leave now," the old man says to Taquiri with a scowl.

"I was invited into your home by your . . . wife," Taquiri says. "And I intend to stay until she asks me to leave. After all, tradition deems that the home is the woman's domain."

"Tell him to leave, Zoila," the old man croaks. He points at the foundling. "And tell him to take that cursed Cloud Warrior bastard with him."

Zoila clutches the infant.

"No, Llacsa." she says, her voice trembling, "I will not ask him to leave and I will not give up this baby."

Llacsa works his jaw, grabs a crude wooden cup off a nearby shelf, steps over to a wide mouth clay jar of chicha, *plunges the cup into it, pulls it out and presses it to his sagging mouth. He guzzles the potent brew in one breath, wipes his lips with his sleeve, tosses the cup onto the floor, turns and stares at his young wife. Head bowed, Zoila braces herself for the worst.*

Llacsa lunges, hands balled into tight fists. Before he can reach her, Taquiri grabs the old man's right arm, twists it behind his back then with a quick move learned in the Inca army, snaps the wife-beater's forearm in two; the broken limb dangles limply by his side.

Llacsa moans so loudly, he startles the baby who pouts as Zoila tries to comfort her.

"Now, now, now," Taquiri scolds, "you're upsetting the cursed Cloud Warrior bastard. And we just can't have that, can we?"

He shoves the hoary old man outside then pushes him to his knees. Llacsa touches his broken arm and winces.

"I will kill you for this," he yells hoarsely, "As Inti is my witness, I'll kill you!"

Curious villagers, including Taquiri's brother and sister-in-law timidly poke their heads outside their huts then, emboldened by the site of the despised old villager kneeling in the dirt, gather to form a semi-circle around the two men.

"Llacsa is çupay—*a bad spirit," the ancient village mayor says the corner of his lips pulled down in disgust, "We grew up together and I will tell you; even as a young boy he had evil in his*

heart. Zoila is his fourth wife. He beat his other wives, too, until, one day, they disappeared under suspicious circumstances. Left to his own devices, he will make Zoila vanish, too. The gods and his deceased wives are watching us from the heavenly realm of hanan pacha; *they know the truth."*

Zoila steps out of the hut without her head scarf, lovingly cradling the foundling, her blackened eye and neck bruises especially conspicuous in the stark midday sun. The villagers gasp at the appalling sight. Formerly afraid of Llacsa, because of his penchant for lashing out at his spouses and at them, too, the villagers now gawk menacingly at the vile old drunk. Zoila flutters her thick dark lashes at Taquiri; he acknowledges her with a bow. She turns, steps back into the hut and closes the door behind her. Llacsa notices the tacit communication between the two, a look of terror on his ashen face.

"Zoila, my dove!" the old man begs, his left hand raised in supplication, sweat cascading from his brow onto his misshapen nose and furrowed face. "I never meant to hurt you . . . or our baby . . . you must believe me . . . Zoila!"

"You could put an end to my sister's life of misery right now, dear brother-in-law." Asiri informs Taquiri as she glances at his ax. "You're the only one in the village who could."

The Inca army deserter and expert ax man strokes the weapon hanging from his belt. For the first and probably last time in his life, he's glad to be a trained warrior.

"No!" Llacsa croaks, "I'll be good from now on! I promise."

Taquiri pulls the ax from his belt; the thought of this monster harming a young girl and her newborn baby stirs something inside him that breaks his heart and brings his blood to a boiling point.

In all the years of warrior training, he never possessed the desire to kill or hurt anybody; that is, until now. With a determined groan, he swings the blade, decapitating the decrepit old drunk in one fell swoop.

Llacsa's head rolls onto the dusty ground, lips moving, silently mouthing: Zoila, Zoila, Zoila. *His jaw grows slack revealing a smattering of spindly yellow and black teeth. Blood-splattered, stony-faced villagers gaze at each other then at Taquiri; he muses that he probably should have waited for a proper tribunal before taking such drastic action but it's too late now. He closes his eyes and hangs his head in shame.* What has become of me? *he thinks. The villagers race back to their huts, chattering merrily. The mayor grabs Llacsa's decapitated head by its matted shock of gray hair then spits on it.*

"I told you, didn't I, Llacsa," the mayor says, "that one day you would be punished for your crimes but you didn't believe me, did you? And the worst is yet to come. Yes, Llacsa. We're going to burn your body till there's nothing left but ash. Then you will journey to the gruesome lower world of ukhu pacha, *barred from the heavenly realm of* hanan pacha *for all eternity."*

With a wave of his hand, the old mayor signals a group of young men. They dart through the village politely soliciting donations of kindling and firewood.

"Yes, of course!" each villagers chirps, "whatever our mayor needs, my dove."

The mayor's helpers create a pyre in front of Zoila's hut, set Llacsa's blood and dust covered head and body upon it then light it with a couple of flint strokes. The kindling ignites quickly; the sulphury stench of burning hair and flesh fill the air.

Villagers toting homemade drums and flutes encircle the funeral pyre. Others bring firewood, which they merrily add to the the blaze, which pops, crackles; black clouds of smoke billow into the heavens.

Musicians commence pounding drums and blowing into crude flutes carved from bone or wood; singers raise their voices in a raucous tune; dancers of all ages spin in wild abandon, grabbing Taquiri's calloused hands, who, though reluctant at first, finally relents and joins in the festivities. Other grateful villagers kiss his cheeks, ply him with chicha and shower him with crimson trumpet-shaped blooms called qantu.

Caressing the foundling, Zoila steps out of the hut and taps her foot to the rhythm of the lively music. A toothless old woman reaches her wrinkled hands out to the baby; Zoila hands her the child. Another old lady takes Zoila's hand and, with cheers and whistles from revelers, unites it with Taquiri's. The music soars. Taquiri enjoins Zoila in a lively native dance; he pulls her close, then pushes her away, guiding her into a graceful spin.

"What is the baby's name?" Zoila asks.

"Name?" Taquiri asks with a shrug, his rugged face flush with embarrassment, "I didn't think to give her name. I just call her Wawa. She is yet too young for a name."

He swings his partner then pulls her close again.

"Ah! Then I will call our baby, T'ica," Zoila states steadfastly, "T'ica—our white flower."

Fin

BIBLIOGRAPHY

Allen, Catherine J. *The Hold Life Has—Coca and Cultural Identity in an Andean Community* Smithsonian Institution, 2002

Betanzos, Juan d. Roland Hamilton (trans.) *Narrative of the Incas*, Austin: University of Texas Press 1996

Brundage, Burr Cartwright *Empire of the Inca*, Norman: University of Oklahoma Press, 1963

MacQuarrie, Kim *The Last Days of the Incas*, New York: Simon & Schuster 2007

Buck, Charles William *Under the Sun* Nabu Press, 1922

Childress, David Hatcher *Lost Cities & Ancient Mysteries of South America* Kempton, Illinois, Adventures Unlimited Press

Cobo, Father Bernabe Roland Hamilton (trans) *Inca Religion & Customs,* Austin: University of Texas Press, 1990

Garlisco de la Vega, El Inca, Harold Livermore (trans.) *Royal Commentaries of the Incas,* Parts 1 and 2, Austrin: Univeristy of Texas Press 1966

Giffhorn, Hans *Wurde Amerika in der Antike entdeckt? Karthager, Kelten und der Ratsel der Chachapoya* Bech. C. H. 2013

Gordon, Oakley E. *The Andean Cosmovision*, Oakley E. Gordon, 2014

Sarmiento de Gamboa, Pedro Sir Clements Markham (trans.) *History of the Incas*, Mineola, Dover 1999

Markham, Sir Clements R Apu Ollantay: *A Drama Of The Time Of The Incas Sovereigns Of Peru* Whitefish, Montana Kessinger

Publishing, 2010

_____ *The Incas of Peru* New York: E.P. Dutton and Company. 1910

Yupanqui, Titu Cusi Ralph Bauer (trans.) *An Inca Account of the Conquest of Peru* Boulder, Colorado: University Press of Colorado, 2002

Polich, Judith Bluestone *Return of the Children of the Light—Inca and Mayan Prophesies for a New World* Rochester, Vermont: Bear and Company

Websites:

https://www.chimuadventures.com/blog/2017/02/cloud-people-peru/

http://www.ancient-origins.net/ancient-places-americas/cloud-warriors-mysterious-power-lost-chachapoya-culture-004628

http://www.ancient-origins.net/ancient-places-americas/kuelap-peru-ancient-fortress-cloud-warriors-002915

https://news.nationalgeographic.com/news/2007/01/070119-peru-inca.html

https://www.forensicmag.com/news/2017/12/dna-analysis-finds-descendants-warriors-clouds-peru

https://owlcation.com/humanities/The-Habsburg-Jaw-And-Other-Royal-Inbreeding-Deformities-and-Disorders

http://www.academia.edu/21558766/Chachapoya_Was_America

_discovered_in_ancient_times

ARTE: Karthagos vergessene Krieger– Chachapoya:

https://www.youtube.com/watch?v=npwi_aG3x98

A 2000-year history of disturbance and recovery at a sacred site in
  Peru's northeastern cloud forest:
http://journals.sagepub.com/doi/10.1177/095968sacrifices3617702
232

Inca tax man collected child sacrifices:
http://www.abc.net.au/science/articles/2005/05/30/1379822.htm

El Enigma de las Momias: Momia Juanita:
https://www.youtube.com/watch?v=iOte8C7G998

AUTHOR'S NOTES

At the beginning of my research for this book, I was appalled to discover documented historical accounts of the Incas unrelenting penchant for war and brutality; I told my mother that I didn't want to write a book about my insanely cruel ancestors. But she, along with my four sons, insisted I continue, despite dark times where I felt thoroughly ashamed of my heritage. My sister said it all too concisely, "The Incas were not nice." What an understatement! My sibling's succinct remark, oddly enough, encouraged me to persist.

The Inca Empire's 3D Writing System

The people of the Inca Empire had a system of writing via the use of the *quipu*—a set of colored strings frequently used by highly educated *quipumayoc*—accountants and scribes. There is compelling evidence that this device was originally developed by the Cloud Warriors. The Incas were fanatic record keepers as it was the only way to prevent wide-spread corruption in their vast 2,000 mile empire. *Quipus* were carefully knotted and used for inventory control and recording historical events; from all accounts, it was a very efficient, descriptive third dimensional writing system. Unfortunately, when the Conquistadors conquered the Inca Empire, Catholic clerics deemed the *quipu* to be the work of the devil; sadly, the Inca's vast stores of *quipus* (kept neatly organized in clay pots) were summarily destroyed. However, even after that dictum, indigenous converts still brought homemade *quipus* to Catholic masses, furiously tying knots to record priests' sermons, in order to share the tenets of the new religion with friends and families.

Though a smattering of intact *quipus* still exist and a partially preserved *quipu* key has been recently discovered in a remote Andean village, it's estimated that decoders will need at least twenty more years to completely decipher the sophisticated, intricately tied knots regularly used in the Inca Empire.

My challenge was to attempt to sort out contradictory historical chronicles without the information that could have been derived from *quipus*. After a few frustrating years, I decided to base my writing on a most unscientific principal: I would use those accounts which seemed to be the most interesting and best served my story while attempting to stay true to confirmed events.

Capacocha—Human Child Sacrifice

A couple of years into my research, I ran into a friend who insisted that the whole concept of widespread child human sacrifice in Central and South America was a fiction, dreamed up by the Spaniards to justify their mistreatment of indigenous populations. So, somewhat crestfallen, (as the existence of widespread *capacocha* was the premise on which my novel was predicated) on my next trip to Lima, Peru, I harbored a triple purpose: to visit my elderly mother, unearth the truth of child human sacrifice in the Inca Empire and separate fact from fiction regarding the mysterious Cloud Warriors.

When I checked into my usual hostel in Mira Flores, just a couple of blocks away from my mother's nursing home, I shared my mission with the friendly, helpful desk clerk. His eyes shot wide open with excitement as he directed me to a brand new, massive archaeological site called Huaca Pucllana, located in Mira Flores less than a mile away. I was so excited, I tossed my bags in my room and sprinted down the bustling city sidewalks, occasionally colliding with pedestrians and impatiently waiting at crosswalks.

When I finally reached Huaca Pucllana, I gladly paid the nominal entry fee then stepped through the gates; I gazed in horror and fascination at the thousands of swaddled newborns that had been recently excavated, all victims of *capacocha*, human child sacrifice. A Huaca Pucllana archaeologist told me that *capacocha*, especially of infants and small children was a common practice at that time, though the people responsible for this huge ceremonial and administrative center were called Limas, not Incas. However, he went on to inform me that archaeologists were uncovering more conclusive evidence of this barbaric ritual and that I should go with my original assumption of its ubiquitousness in the Inca Empire.

The Cloud Warriors

The existence of a fair-skinned, blond or red-haired race of people, the Cloud Warriors, living in the Chachapoyas region of northern Peru is even more hotly contested than the frequency of *capacocha* in the Inca empire. Contradictions abound in historical Spanish and English chronicles, most of which were written decades after the fall of the Inca Empire.

Separating fact from fiction regarding this enigmatic tribe of northern Peru turned out to be a daunting task, especially since they'd been virtually wiped out by a combination of the plague (small pox) which decimated the Inca Empire as well as their unrelenting resistance to Inca rule. Unfortunately, due to familial and work commitments, I was unable to travel to Chachapoyas, so I had to content myself with internet research. I studied countless videos (in German, Spanish and English—luckily not an issue for a polyglot like myself) and websites but, like most of my research into the ancient Inca civilization ran into a myriad of contradictory assertions.

Chiara Barbieri, a geneticist at the Max Planck Institute for the Science of Human History in Jena, Germany recently concluded that despite Inca conquest, the population of Chachapoyas (Cloud Warriors) *remained genetically distinct* and not assimilated with the Inca Empire. German researchers such as Hans Gifforn contend that Cloud Warriors were descendants of Celtic and Celtic Iberian tribes who escaped by boat from war-plagued Europe around 800 A.D.

Men, women and children with blond or red hair, fair skin or freckled skin with blue, gray or green eyes living in Chachapoyas have been recently genetically tested in European labs; those findings show their DNA contains the genetic markings of ancient Celtic tribes, corroborating Herr Gifforn's frequently disputed theories.

Chachapoyas chronicler Pedro Cieza de Leon wrote of the Cloud Warriors: "They are the whitest and most handsome of all the people that I have seen, and their wives were so beautiful that because of their gentleness, many of them deserved to be the Incas' wives and to also be taken to the Sun Temple."

Mysticism and Inca Religion

Deities, legends, religious rituals and supernatural myths have been an integral part of South American culture for millennia. Though the Inca Empire had its own state religion (worship of the Sun God, Inti) conquered provinces were not expressly prohibited from engaging in their own religious practices. Instead royals encouraged subjugated peoples to incorporate Inca deities into the own religions; Inca emperors claimed to be the son of Inti the Sun God and therefore deities themselves. There is also historical proof, that the notion that Inca emperors were themselves son of the Son God was primarily fostered to enlist citizens' blind allegiance to the Holy Inca Empire. Starting with Pachacuti, Inca emperors employed the "sacrament" of *capacocha*—human child sacrifice as a political tool; if a conquered province could hand over their young children to Inca priests and priestesses without reservation, royals felt confident that these people had been thoroughly subjugated. Apparently, this was a bone of contention for the Cloud Warriors (and other subjugated tribes) who worshiped serpent gods and wanted nothing to do with the Inca religion or their sacraments.

My primary intention was to be the voice of indigenous tribes so cruelly subjugated by the Inca. What I found is that most *runakuna* (the common man or woman of substance) were and still are overtly spiritual, embracing legends, deities and rituals as an integral part of every day life; contemporary Peruvians who didn't convert to Christianity are every bit as spiritual and connected to their deities as they were five centuries ago.

Inca Incest

Throughout history, royals from all over the globe have searched for ways to consolidate wealth and power, especially through the practice of incestuous marriages. Offspring from these unions often suffered early deaths, severe deformities or the effects of incurable genetic disorders like hemophilia. Though there's little evidence of physical deformities in inbred Inca royals, who, like Egyptian royalty customarily married their full sisters, each succeeding generation seemed to exhibit some degree of psychopathy which undoubtedly hastened the fall of the Inca empire.

The Dwarf, Chimbo Sancto

In early fall of 2017, my manuscript for *Daughters of the Sun* was all but finished, however, I had the nagging feeling that something was missing. A big admirer of William Shakespeare, I was disheartened to confront the fact that there was absolutely no comic relief or comic characters in the entire novel, something that I believed was desperately needed in a tale rife with human child sacrifice, pedophilia and warfare. Even in The Bard's darkest tales there were almost always moments of levity. I was stuck.

I pushed myself back into research mode, rereading many of the books I had used as a reference and I eventually found what I was looking for in Juan de Betanzos' meticulously researched, "Narrative of the Incas."

Chimbo Sancto was a highly esteemed leader of a rebel confederation, captured by the Emperor Huayna Capac who was so enamored by the dwarf's intelligence and insouciance that he pardoned him, made him his honorary eldest son and bestowed upon him the title "Inca of the Heart," one of the highest honors in the Inca Empire.

ABOUT THE AUTHOR

Theresa Vivanco grew up on the east coast of the US, the offspring of a Peruvian mother and American father. At eleven, her mother took her and her two siblings to Lima, Peru where she attended school in Mira Flores and became fascinated with Peruvian culture and the Incas. After returning to the US, she studied French and Latin and continued her study of Spanish. As a voice major in college, she also learned Italian and German, then worked as a proofreader and editor at a now defunct vanity publishing company in New York City.

In 1995, she moved to Frankfurt and after intense private study, became fluent in German, translating primarily business, technical and legal documents. In 2012, she became a a freelance literary translator for Amazon Crossing. Since then she's translated more than fifteen titles under her maiden name Terry Laster, some of which became Amazon bestsellers, including the historical novel, "The Secret Healer" by Ellin Carsta.

The product of over seven years of intense research, where Spanish and German fluency came in very handy, *Daughters of the Sun* is Theresa's first solo novel. She is currently working on the second novel of the Inca series dealing with the brutal seven year Inca Civil War between royal brothers, Atahualpa and Huascar; many of the same characters from the first novel will reappear in this and in the third novel about resistance against barbaric Spanish rulers by the indigenous tribes of the Inca Empire.

Please feel free to visit her web page:

www.thedaughtersofthesun.com

GLOSSARY

- abaguña, purple potatoes
- accla: chosen women, virgin of the sun or daughters of the sun
- aha: powerful brew made from chicha and various medicinal herbs
- altumisayuq: coca leaf diviner of the highest order
- Amaru: inter-dimensional son of Goddess Mountain with llama head, serpent body and fish tail
- añaychay: thank you
- apoya: Inca bear dancer
- apu: god, goddess or spirit
- Apu Salkantay: Goddess Salkantay Mountain
- aulanchis: ancient ancestor
- aucacunapac: used at Inca coronations: "for tyrants, traitors, the cruel, the treacherous and the disloyal!"
- awaq machas: weaver goddesses
- ayllu: a village or group of affiliated villages
- ayrampu: tasty and medicinal cactus
- collahuaya: official supplier of medicinal plants, amulets and lucky charms
- chacu: the hunt
- chicha: corn beer
- Cocalmayo: location of sacred hot springs
- copoasu: wild Andean fruit with a hard outer shell that tastes lie pineapple
- coya: an Inca queen married to her full brother, the emperor
- Chachapoyas: mountainous area in northern Inca Empire, home of the Cloud Warriors
- ch'aska: star
- chasqui: official Inca runner/messenger
- Ch'illca is a green leafy plant with white flowers, which when boiled with collpa—a mineral compound, produces a bright shade of green;

- cuy: guinea pig
- cria: baby llama
- curaca: a member of the Inca provincial nobility often acting as administrator or ruler over an ayllu or group of.
- cacique: a native chief
- capacocha—Inca sacrament of child sacrifice
- ch'uño: freeze-dried potatoes, a staple food of the Andean indigenous culture
- çupay: a bad spirit
- cochineal, an insect that produces bright red dye.
- enqa: a stone that takes the shape of an animal, a gift from the gods
- Epunaman: God of War
- guacacue: diviners who walk naked through nature and stare at the sun to gain knowledge.
- haampu: Come in!
- hallpaykusunchis: Let us chew coca together.
- hamusayki?: May I come in?
- hampi camayoc: authorized to preserve remedies and a talented state chemist
- hampiq: person knowledgeable about medicinal herbs
- hanan pacha: the glorious upper world; heaven
- hanpeq: Inca herbalist
- hatun apu: Inca general
- hila nayra huahua—first born son
- hinallatapas: you're welcome
- huarachicho: puberty ceremony/athletic contest for young males
- huacha-utek: dangerous desperate men
- hucha: chaotic energy
- Incasimi: language spoken by Inca royalty
- Inti Patáy: Father Sun
- kamayuk: Inca officer
- kay pacha: earthly realm
- Kaypachiswaychis: Empower us, give us strength and vision.

- k'eperina: a sturdy woven cloth tied onto back and shoulders to carry babies or provisions
- Kimat: queen of the underwater world
- Kollahuayas: the magician/healers from Acamani
- kukuchi: zombie
- Lake Yahuarcocha: Blood lake
- layqa: sorcerer
- llipt'a: black substance which activates ingredients in coca leaves
- machu: great, giant
- Machukuna: giant Children of the Moon
- machula aulanchis: dream spirits
- makiy kiwah: let me weave with your hands
- mascaipacha: red fringe worn by the emperor
- mamacona: Inca high priestess
- Mamaoello, the goddess who taught runakuna how to spin and weave.
- Mama Quilla: goddess of the moon
- Mama Tuta: goddess of the dark, the void, the stars and the night.
- Mamáy: mother, mommy
- munay warmikuna: a women of substance.
- ñawin: a golden coin used as a third eye by sorcerers
- nishu luku: extremely crazy; insane.
- pago, a religious specialist ; shaman
- pachakuti: the time of great upheaval
- Pachamama: Mother Earth
- pacha kuyuy: an earthquake
- Pisti Timpu: time of pestilence and great upheaval
- Plaza of Rimacpampa: the Place of Those Who Speak in Cuzco town square
- puna: a high mountain grassy field.
- pututu: conch shell used to alert community or signal retreat
- q'olle: flowers from a small, low lying tree to make yellow dye
- Qorincancha: the Temple of the Sun

- quero: a large clay pitcher
- quilla hunt'asqa: full moon
- quipu: three dimensional writing and record keeping system made of knotted strings
- quipumayocs: Inca tax collector
- Quitoloma: rebel fortress near Quito
- rayu: lightning
- Rumi Maki: Inca fighting technique; Stone Hand
- rumi sonqo: a heart of stone
- runakuna: common man
- runa kurku k'anchay: luminous body
- Runasimi: common language of ancient Inca empire; known today as Quechua
- runa uturunca: shapeshifter
- sachotomate: wild Andean tomato
- saiwachay: energy connecting the three worlds of hanan pacha, kay pacha and ukhu pacha
- samca hausi: the Dungeon of Horrors filled with pumas and vipers
- salqa wind: a wild wind driven by a spiritual force
- samiyug: owner of liveliness and power a genius, an ebullient spirit
- soroche: high altitude sickness
- tampu: a one room stone inn built by and used exclusively for Inca royals or warriors
- Tatáy: father,
- Tawantinsuyu: Inca Empire, country of the inextricably linked four corners (suyus)
- Tirakuna: sacred places
- Tumibamba: birthplace of Emperor Huayna Capac
- ullucus: a root vegetable
- ukhu pacha: the underworld
- ukyakunsunchis: Let us drink together.
- unkhuña: a finely woven cloth
- urpicháy: dove,

- urpicháy sonqoy: dove of my heart
- ususi: formal name for daughter
- uvilla: golden berry found in high mountains of Peru
- vicuña: a wild animal hunted but not killed for its fine fur
- watukk: an Inca doctor who addresses spiritual ills
- Wawa: a generic name for all babies under two years old
- yusul payki: thank you

75045771R00217

Made in the USA
San Bernardino, CA
25 April 2018